A Heritage to Honor, A Future to Fulfill

BY RALPH K. BEEBE

CENTENNIAL
1891 - 1991

NEWBERG, OREGON

*Produced by George Fox College
in celebration of its first one hundred years.*

A HERITAGE TO HONOR,
A FUTURE TO FULFILL

George Fox College, 1891-1991

International Standard Book Number: 0-913342-71-8

Library of Congress Catalog Card Number: 91-73704

Design by Judi Timmons
Composition and lithography by The Barclay Press

THE BARCLAY PRESS
600 East Third Street • Newberg, Oregon 97132-3106 U.S.A.
503/538-7345 • 800/962-4014

Contents

Acknowledgments

THE AUTHOR expresses appreciation to the many persons who made this book possible. Foremost is my wife, Wanda, who provided encouragement and assistance. She also skillfully selected most of the pictures from the many thousands available.

Several students helped immeasurably. History majors John Hurty, Jerry Miley, and Tim Hagen spent numerous hours in the archives, searching, verifying, correcting. I needed their help and appreciated their patience. Writing and literature major Laura Engle read, edited, and reread, always with helpful suggestions. Vincent Wilhite, a history major at Whitman College, contributed while doing a summer historical method field experience with me. Student assistants Stacy Wright, Karen Schuck, Tiffany Thompson, and Jenny Bozeman added to the process. Our divisional secretary, Jo Sivley, willingly put up with the extra work and helped out cheerfully.

I also appreciate Margaret Lemmons, Arthur Roberts, and Lon Fendall. At my request, they read the manuscript and recommended improvements. Time and again, college archivist Frank Cole provided congenial service; he never seemed to tire of the endless requests. Genevieve Cole added her expertise, as did Anita Cirulis, the College's director of Public Information and Publications. The administrators willingly opened all except confidential personnel files and interpreted when necessary. Registrar Hector Munn and assistants Janelle Claassen and Janet Lyda also helped when asked. Director of Library Services Merrill Johnson also assisted. Ivan Adams, who served a record 42 years on the Board of Trustees, compiled for the Appendix the list of board members.

The Centennial Committee, chaired by Barry Hubbell and Lon Fendall, provided encouragement and general supervision. The Barclay Press manager Dan McCracken gave friendly, patient advice and service, along with Dennis Headrick and Dick Eichenberger. I also thank Judi Timmons for her excellent design work. All this praise does not mean everyone relished my demands on their time. Some dreaded to see me almost as much as I dreaded to see them seeing me.

At the Centennial Committee's request, I departed from the normal historian's procedure and included no source citations. However, I depended on standard historical materials such as board and faculty minutes, *Newberg Graphic*, *The Crescent* and *L'Ami*, statistical records maintained by the various campus offices or stored in the archives, and some personal correspondence.

Several helpful research papers exist, including works by Amos Stanbrough, Steven Perisho, Allison (Kingsley) Scott, Scott Ball, and Mike Royer. The College published a 1941 booklet entitled *The First Fifty Years*, and several special city and college memorial booklets exist.

Daisy Newhouse Read's lively booklet *My College: Memories of Long Ago* added a personal touch. Milo Ross left a scintillating, as yet unpublished account of his GFC years entitled "A Mid-Century History of George Fox College."

The GFC archives contain many boxes of Levi Pennington's personal papers and some from other college luminaries. Among them are some of Emmett Gulley's papers, thanks to a recent donation by his son, Ross.

A 100-year institutional history requires checking a myriad of details. I know some errors have intruded; I just don't as yet know where they are. I will undoubtedly be told! However, please don't. Instead, tell whoever revises this for the bicentennial.

There also may be errors in judgment. Some readers will believe I gave too much space to unimportant characters and too little to important ones—notably themselves and the people they knew back in college days.

Nevertheless, I have emphasized what seems important to me, given the limitations of available data and time to search. I apologize to those who may disagree, but assert that were I to write it again, it probably would come out about the same.

—Ralph K. Beebe

DEDICATED

to my grandchildren and great-grandchildren,
and to many other grandchildren and great-grandchildren,
whose lives may someday be enriched by the vision
and sacrifice of those who loved the
"good old Quaker college."

Introduction

WILLIAM HOBSON, an Iowan, sought a Northwest site for a Quaker community. After studying the area of Newberg, Oregon, in "the grubby end of the Chehalem Valley," he recorded on May 26, 1876:

"I have been impressed...that some settlements of Friends ought to [be] formed in these parts.... In the Providences of God...this selection is made.... I hope now Our dear friends...will...form a settlement here and make it a garden of the Lord."

Many adventurous Friends (Quakers) answered the call. They soon initiated home meetings for worship and the next year established "Chehalem Monthly Meeting of Friends" (later renamed Newberg Friends Church). Concern for their children soon led to "first day Sabbath school" and public elementary education. They launched Friends Pacific Academy in 1885 and added Pacific College (renamed George Fox College in 1949) six years later. In 1929 they decided to discontinue the Academy.

Today approximately 8,000 of the 300,000 Quakers worldwide comprise Northwest Yearly Meeting of Friends Church, George Fox College's sponsoring body. By 1991, nearly 3,400 men and women had graduated from the College founded by Quakers in 1891.

Strong religious convictions led to the Friends movement in England three centuries ago. (See Appendix.) They still influence the College. Today the school represents historic Quakerism as modified by American frontier revivalism, twentieth-century religious fundamentalism, and the post-World War II North American neo-evangelical movement.

Today about half the faculty and over 80 percent of the students extend beyond the Quaker nucleus, representing Wesleyans, Baptists, and at least a score of other evangelical Christian persuasions.

George Fox College's central characteristic remains its spirituality. The school emulates Jesus Christ, with all trustees, all administrators, all faculty, all staff, and most students—however disparate in individual heritage and political persuasion—sharing a common personal commitment to His lordship.

The Quaker conscience leavens the College, providing depth in devotion and breadth in human concern. The variety of other evangelical constituents promotes healthy diversity. Its unique blending of spiritual integrity and academic viability makes the Newberg institution attractive and distinctive.

With recent upgrading of faculty, library, curriculum, and equipment, the school has become an effective academic institution, an excellent learning environment. National recognition as one of "America's Best Colleges" and as one of the nation's foremost "character building colleges" suggests that the reputation matches the reality.

George Fox College has always been small, its enrollment never having exceeded 1,000 until 1990. The institution's influence, however, clearly exceeds its numbers. For the students, for Northwest Yearly Meeting of Friends Church, for evangelicalism generally, and for the Kingdom of God, the College has been highly significant.

A century and a half ago, in arguing before the Supreme Court the case of his alma mater, Dartmouth College, Daniel Webster asserted: "It is...a small college and yet there are those who love it."

There are those who love George Fox College, too. A century of successes and failures have prepared it for second century challenges. At age 100, GFC stands ready for extended ministry.

Chapter One

Southeast Newberg in 1887, looking from near the center of current Newberg. Partially visible at the extreme right is one of the Friends Pacific Academy buildings (later renamed Hoover Hall), where the Newberg Friends Church now stands. To its left is the Jesse Edwards house, still standing. At the extreme left is the home of Academy principal H. J. Minthorn. Herbert Hoover lived there at the time.

"LIVE LOW AND SPARINGLY till my debts be paid; but let the learning of the children be liberal; spare no cost, for by such parsimony all is lost that is saved."

Early advertisements of Friends Pacific Academy, the forerunner of George Fox College, quoted this advice Pennsylvania's Quaker founder William Penn offered his wife.

Oregon Friends' commitment to education came early. They opened what may have been the first continuous school near Newberg in 1877, at the home of David J.

Wood, about one mile northwest of Main and Illinois Streets. As the elementary students began to graduate, the settlers discussed further education.

Chehalem Monthly Meeting (renamed Newberg Friends Church in 1886) appointed Mary Edwards, David J. Wood, Ezra Woodward, and Elias Jessup to study the issue in 1883.

A favorable report soon prompted the Monthly Meeting to authorize the same committee to seek funding for a new academy; within several months they raised $1,865 in pledges. Elias Jessup and Mary Edwards visited Friends in eastern United States and obtained additional funds.

Chehalem Monthly Meeting decided to locate its new academy at the Friends Meetinghouse (north of the Friends Cemetery) or, if that wasn't feasible, within one mile of it.

After a study of possible locations, the church members purchased for $200 "a beautiful lot of 4 acres" from the farm of Jesse Edwards between Third and Fourth streets in south Newberg (site of Newberg Friends Church in 1991).

They described the school as "situated in the suberbs [sic] of the town of Newberg about ½ mile S.W. of the

Fall Regular Student Enrollment, 1891-1910

1891—15	1898—52	1905—42
1892—29	1899—48	1906—46
1893—25	1900—45	1907—22
1894—48	1901—45	1908—29
1895—43	1902—57	1909—28
1896—50	1903—54	1910—33
1897—41	1904—50	

Meeting House." They advertised it as "...on the Portland and Willamette Valley railroad, twenty-two miles from Portland, and one mile from the Rogers' Landing on the Willamette River."

The group soon erected "a fine substantial two story building 36 x 48 feet upon the ground..." (first called "Academy Building" and many years later "Hoover Hall"). Nineteen students and three teachers began classes in September 1885. The next year 26 enrolled, then 51, and by 1889 the academy had grown to over 100 full-time students.

The first faculty included Henry J. Minthorn as principal, with W. R. Starbuck and Laura E. Minthorn the only other teachers. School officials added a boarding hall for ten young women and four small cottages for other girls the next year. They erected a 40- by 60-foot, two-story structure in 1886-87 (later named Kanyon, now Minthorn Hall). The upper floor housed 24 boys; the lower served as a gymnasium and provided worship space for Chehalem Monthly Meeting of Friends. The school furnished a stove for each room, but the students had to procure their own

---

"Live low and sparingly till my debts be paid; but let the learning of the children be liberal; spare no cost, for by such parsimony all is lost that is saved."
—William Penn
Quaker founder of Pennsylvania

---

wood and kerosene for heat and lights. Officials charged $29 tuition, with board and room bringing the total cost to $110 a year.

Friends Pacific Academy offered a five-year course (later expanded to a six-year course), the first two years at an elementary level. Students who passed the grammar school examinations advanced to the third-year (freshman) class. The school reflected traditional Quaker, Christian values. The first catalog outlined the required standards of conduct:

"Since immoral and sinful practices are incompatible with the highest mental or physical development, no one is desired as a student who is not willing to abstain therefrom, and since some amusements (while they are not considered sinful by some) are calculated to distract the minds of pupils from their studies, they also are strictly excluded from the pastimes or recreations of pupils while attending the Academy. The attendance of the pupil then is taken as assurance of a ready and willing cooperation with the teachers in those measures thought necessary for the best

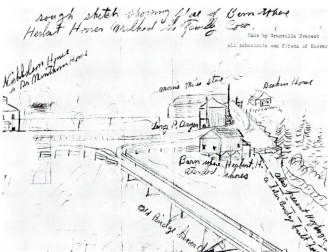

A sketch by Granville Everest showing Minthorn-Hoover House and the original bridge that angled into River Street one-half block south of the present stoplight. Minthorn's barn was on the edge of the canyon.

interests of the school, and it will be the aim of the instructors to so fill the time with profitable and interesting employment that there will be no room left for evil."

"We make no pretensions of a 'reform' school for students who cannot be managed at home," an 1889 *Newberg Graphic* advertisement reiterated. "Our school is designed for those who are desirous of a good education, and those who are willing to cheerfully submit to what few rules and regulations may be made by the faculty and Board of Trustees."

2

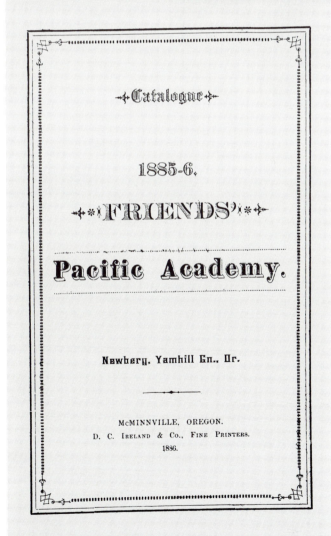

The new school's motto stated: "The whole of your life must be spent in your own company, and only the educated man is good company for himself." A *Newberg Graphic* advertisement stated that "the large number of students who have fitted themselves for business or for teaching is our best recommendation." The grammar school course included "all the common branches," while the Academy offered work in history, higher mathematics, science, Greek, and Latin.

The same 1889 advertisement emphasized: "Two dormitories and a Boarding Hall have been erected for the accommodation of students. These are under the strict discipline of a Governor and Matron."

This satisfied most constituents. One visitor noted that "there is congregated there 68 young ladies and gentlemen from different parts of the state and of some of the best families in Oregon." In 1888, the local newspaper editor expressed community pride. He wrote that "the grounds are beautiful and the buildings have been erected with an eye to architecture so that the attention of the stranger on his arrival at Newberg is at once called to our commodious school facilities . . . ." The article continued:

"The school has been founded and carried thus far by the united efforts and the expenditure of time and money at great sacrifice to those interested, but Friends Church can point today with pride to 'Friends Pacific Academy' the reputation of which, as an institution of learning, is equal to that of any in the Pacific Northwest, and it is not saying to [sic] much to add that it is the pride of Chehalem Valley."

The author noted further that the school provided the town a population of the most desirable people and kept out undesirable influences. "This will continue as long as our academy is properly sustained and properly appreciated."

Board chairman Ezra Woodward reported in 1888, however, that the school had expelled one young man for disciplinary reasons. The school's reputation would be maintained anyway, he asserted. The following year the Friends Pacific Academy Advisory Committee, which sometimes visited weekly, regretted unspecified outside influences that it considered a hindrance to some pupils' best interests.

The committee usually submitted positive reports, however. Newberg Monthly Meeting minutes also included glowing reports. For example: "All the students who were . . . not already Christians experienced a change of heart . . . ."

Chehalem Monthly Meeting of Friends briefly managed the Academy through a body known as "Trustees of Friends Pacific Academy," but soon changed the name to "Board of Managers of Friends Pacific Academy" to prevent

Friends Pacific Academy faculty and student body. In front at left is Principal Henry J. Minthorn. Herbert "Bertie" Hoover is the small boy second from the left in the first row.

confusion with the Monthly Meeting trustees. The name became "Trustees of Pacific College" in 1891.

Fourteen patrons agreed to the following pledge during the Academy's first year:

"We whose names are subscribed below pledge ourselves to back the trustees of F.P.A. in the support of said school. Will use our influence for the building up and sustaining the school. And should there be a deficiency in fitting up and defraying running expenses of said school, we agree to pay the percent subscribed below prorata of such amount as may be necessary to defray expenses for one year."

The subscribers included Jesse Edwards, five percent; Geo. W. Mitchel, six percent; Samuel Hobson, two percent; John Brown, two percent; J. Hobson, four percent; J. T.

Smith, three percent; B. S. Cook, five percent; D. J. Wood, three percent; L. M. Haworth, one percent; N. C. Maris, two percent; N. L. Wiley, one percent; Wm. Hobson, two percent; E. S. Craven, one-half of one percent; and J. L. Hoskins, one percent.

One of the first academy students signed his name "Bert Hoover." Orphaned in Iowa, the future president came at age 11 to live with his uncle, academy principal Henry J. Minthorn. Young Hoover earned his keep by watering horses, grubbing stumps, weeding onions, and doing other chores. He paid his tuition by tending furnace, sweeping floors, and cleaning blackboards.

President Hoover later wrote: "As a young student there for three years I received whatever set I may have had toward good purposes in life." A century after the

4

1891-92.

GRAPHIC PRINT, NEWBERG, OREGON.

thirty-first president's enrollment at the Newberg school, one George Fox College professor averred: "I cannot afford to underestimate the potential of *any* student. The steady gaze of young Bert in those old photos won't let me!"

About 70 percent of the early academy students resided in Newberg. Most others lived close by, some walking to campus from Springbrook across the Hess Creek canyon railroad trestle. A scattering from Portland, Sheridan, Willamina, Silverton, LaGrande, and other Oregon towns boarded on campus. A few came from other states; for example, in 1888-89 the Academy enrolled one Alaskan and two Kansans.

By 1890 one student had graduated. Within a few years many others followed. Most wanted further education. Opportunities included McMinnville (Linfield) College, and Pacific and Willamette universities, all less than a day's buggy ride away. Albany (Lewis and Clark) College the University of Oregon, Oregon State Agricultural College (Oregon State University), Oregon Normal School (Western Oregon State College), and Mt. Angel College were not much farther away.

However, almost as a matter of course, the Quakers in the Chehalem Valley added higher education to their offerings because no other Quaker college existed closer than William Penn in Iowa. (California's Whittier College, about 900 miles distant, also opened in 1891.) Determined to perpetuate their unique religious heritage, Friends hardly considered allowing outsiders to educate their youth.

The Friends Pacific Academy managers announced the founding of Pacific College on June 6, 1891. They selected the name with no apparent concern for potential confusion with the already existing Pacific University, less than 25 miles away.

THE NEW COLLEGE opened for the first of three annual terms at 2:00 p.m. on September 9, 1891. Inaugural exercises began with choir music and a prayer by Mary Edwards. Board member Jesse Edwards reviewed the Academy's success. Now, he pointed out, the circumstances demanded another step forward.

The board introduced Thomas Newlin as president of Pacific College. According to the *Newberg Graphic* (which had been purchased by Quaker Ezra Woodward), the crowd greeted the new president with a standing ovation, hearty cheers, and waving of handkerchiefs. The reaction to Newlin's address certified that "had a vote of confidence been taken the unanimous verdict would have been that no mistake was made when Professor Newlin was elected to the position of President of Pacific College."

Thirty-five-year-old Thomas Newlin had a long Quaker heritage and followed the tradition himself. He spent most of his life serving Friends across the United States, and was recorded by Oregon Yearly Meeting as a Friends minister. Born in Indiana, he attended Earlham College, then transferred to Haverford in Pennsylvania, completing a bachelor's degree in 1886. Five years as principal of Spiceland Academy prepared him for his nine-year Pacific presidency.

In later years Newlin served at three other Quaker colleges—as vice president at Wilmington (Ohio), dean at Guilford (North Carolina), and president at both Whittier and Guilford. He spent his final eleven working years as sociology professor at Fullerton Junior College in California. In 1905 Newlin earned an M.A. from Chicago University; later, Whittier and the University of Southern California honored him with conferred doctorates.

The Memorials section of the 1939 Oregon Yearly Meeting minutes includes these comments about Pacific's first president:

"His vision and liberality sometimes brought criticism from the older and more conservative. But they were the qualities that made him a stimulating force to youth. The tolerance and the vigorous progressivism of his life and teaching awakened students and sent them facing forward into the unknown with the explorer's curiosity and the seer's faith."

Pacific College opened with two juniors, four sophomores, two freshmen, and seven listed as college students but deficient in preparatory work for full freshman standing. (The Academy enrolled 136 that year.) Seven faculty members served the 151 students, including President Newlin (philosophy, political economy), G. N. Hartley (Latin, Greek, mathematics), J. J. Jessup (natural science, mathematics), L. Ella Hartley (English, drawing, painting), C. E. Vance (Latin, Greek, mathematics), Rebecca (Hinchman) Smith (English), and Ada M. Howard (English, music).

President Newlin invited students interested in the "regular College course" (review work, the practical business course, vocal or instrumental music, art) and the "Normal Course" (for current or prospective teachers). "If your wants lie along any of these lines Pacific College is able to satisfy them. We desire to stand for that which is permanent and useful, being opposed to shams and pretensions in education," the president announced in the *Newberg Graphic*.

Students could purchase all this for $8.00 to $12.00 per term for tuition, and $2.50 per week in the College Boarding Hall or $3.00 with private families. They could rent rooms and prepare their own meals at some savings.

The College stated its purpose in the first catalog:

"The object of this college shall be to give a thorough training in the Arts, and Sciences, and to teach those subjects ordinarily coming in a course of college training. It shall strive in every possible manner to spread Christian culture.

"The whole of your life must be spent in your own company, and only the educated man is good company for himself."
—early Friends Pacific Academy and Pacific College motto

"The Aim of the College: The purpose of the college is to offer to young men and young women the benefits of a liberal Christian education. The courses of study are arranged to give that broad culture which should be the possession of every intelligent man and woman. The founders recognized the great importance of religious training, and the work of the classroom is not merely con-

sistent with Christianity, but decidedly Christian in its tendencies. It is the fond hope of the management that Pacific College shall send forth many Christian teachers, ministers, and missionaries, and that it shall be a strong support not only to the Friends Church, but to Christianity wherever its influence may reach."

Newberg Friends Church controlled Friends Pacific Academy. Upon adding the College, however, the church's trustees sought incorporation under the laws of the state of Oregon, with the local congregation turning the school's management to Newberg Quarterly Meeting, which included all the area's Friends churches.

Soon after, Newberg Quarterly Meeting named a nine-person board, including E. H. Woodward as president, Moses Votaw as treasurer, and G. W. Mitchell, Vannie Martin, Jesse Edwards, B. G. Miles, Paul Macey, Maryelle Hoskins, and Jesse Hobson. President Newlin served in an ex-officio capacity.

The board met four times each year, after each quarterly meeting of the church. It conducted much work through the following committees: faculty and officers, buildings and grounds, laboratory, and museums and

**Early course of study.
Bottom: Pacific College's
first dining room, 1891,
Miss Macy, matron.**

CONSPECTUS OF THE COURSE OF STUDY.

All students recite one hour per week in Scripture, and each student will appear at least once each Term with a public literary exercise.

PREPARATORY DEPARTMENT				COLLEGE DEPARTMENT													
SUB-PREPARATORY	FALL	WINTER	SPRING	FRESHMAN YEAR	FALL	WINTER	SPRING	JUNIOR YEAR	FALL	WINTER	SPRING						
Arithmetic	5	5	5	Geometry	5	5	5	Latin									
English Grammar	5	5	5	Higher Algebra		5		Greek		4	4						
Geography	5	5	5	Latin	5	5	4	History		4							
Reading	4	4	4	General History	4	4	4	English									
Scripture	1	1	1	English History		4		English Literature	5	5							
				English	1	1	1	Mathematics	5	5							
JUNIOR PREPARATORY				Botany		4		Physics		5	5						
Arithmetic	5	5	5	Scripture	1	1	1	German									
English Grammar	5	5						Zoology		2							
English Composition	5			SOPHOMORE YEAR				General Biology	2	2							
Physiology		5		Trigonometry	4		4	Scripture	1	1	1						
U. S. History				Analytic Geometry		5											
Civil Government				Surveying			5	SENIOR YEAR									
Scripture	1	1	1	Latin		4	5	Greek		4	4						
				Greek	5	5	5	Psychology	4								
SENIOR PREPARATORY				German				History			5						
Algebra	5	5	5	Chemistry	5	5		Economics			5						
Latin	5	5	5	Rhetoric	3	3	3	Christian Evidences		5							
Elementary Physics	5			Philology			5	Ethics			5						
Book Keeping or Zoology	5			History				Astronomy									
Physical Geography	5			Scripture	1	1	1	Geology	5								
Scripture	1	1	1					Logic									
								Chemistry									
								Scripture	1	1	1						

Yearly Meeting held some of the stock and had five votes. A 12-member board, including at least nine Quakers, had management responsibilities.

However, the stock feature inhibited donations, especially from eastern Friends. In 1908, therefore, college personnel formed a new corporation with a Board of Trustees composed of 12 corporation members and the college president, each having one vote. Oregon Yearly Meeting elected half the stockholders. This management method continued until the 1950s, when the Yearly Meeting disbanded the corporation.

THE FOUR ACRES purchased in 1885 had provided adequate space for the academy. However, adding the College made relocation necessary. Newberg Monthly Meeting appointed Miles Reece and Evangeline Martin to investigate options.

The church first considered four sites: (1) 25 acres belonging to the Edwards family just south of Ninth and west of College streets, (2) 20 acres offered by J. L. Hoskins and others, (3) 18 acres east of Meridian and north of Ezra Woodward's residence (the Woodward house still stands on the northeast corner of River and Hancock streets), and (4) another 18-acre plot owned by Jesse and Mary Edwards.

In January of 1892, Newberg Monthly Meeting decided to accept the fourth offer. However, for unknown reasons, the college board overruled the Meeting and decided on the site lying north of Ezra Woodward's residence. Then on May 7, the Monthly Meeting disregarded all four options and chose another site, a 23½-acre plot located north of property owned by a Dr. Clark and Ezra Woodward. (Monthly Meeting and College Board minutes seem to suggest that this was a fifth option, but it may have been only a 5½-acre addition to option three.)

Soon afterward, the trustees awarded a $1,359 contract to R. A. Clark of Portland for moving the two existing buildings (those later named Hoover and Minthorn halls) and putting in basement walls. (His offer of $738 for moving and $621 for constructing the basement walls was the lowest of several bids.) Clark completed the work before September, when school opened.

The *Newberg Graphic* described the move:

"Mr. Clark, the Portland house mover, came on the first of the week, bringing his outfit for moving the college buildings, up the river on the old Jefferson street ferry boat which he bought a short time ago. He has had everything on the move during the week with men and teams hauling sand and brick and others getting the buildings loaded ready to move. It is evident that he understands his business . . . .

library. (In late 1892 the board switched museums to the laboratory committee, leaving library separate.) An executive committee controlled finances, advertising, and printing and had the power to act on "matters that do not materially affect the financial or educational interests of the college."

Iowa Yearly Meeting established Oregon Yearly Meeting of Friends Church (consisting of Oregon, Idaho, and Washington Friends) in 1893. Newberg Quarterly Meeting then turned the College and Academy ownership to the new Yearly Meeting.

Two years later the college board decided to enlarge its constituency and recommended a reorganization that would transfer management to a corporation composed of stockholders. As a result, the new corporation sold $40,000 in capital stock—800 shares at $50 each. Oregon

Pacific College in 1893, one year after these buildings were moved to present campus. On the left is Kanyon (Minthorn) Hall. At right is the "College Building," later renamed Hoover Hall. The wing without a bell tower was constructed after the move.

"The buildings were placed on the new foundations without the slightest injury. The foundations are better than the old ones and since the buildings have been leveled up, they are in much better condition than they were before being moved."

School officials remodeled both buildings. They enlarged the "college building proper" (later named Hoover Hall, razed in 1954) with a 36- by 58-foot addition and elevated it enough to provide a basement furnace. The first floor became a chapel or general assembly room, while the second provided classroom space. However, the *Newberg Graphic* noted on July 22, 1892, that the upper room of the new part would not be finished immediately, "but a floor will be laid and this will give the young ladies a room in which they can swing Indian clubs to their hearts content on rainy days during the winter." The basement served as an exercise area for the young men in bad weather.

Workmen also raised the other building (later Kanyon, then Minthorn Hall) four feet and provided a basement

furnace, kitchen, dining room, cook's bedroom, and storeroom. The first floor they "divided up into rooms and fitted up in first-class style for young ladies who desire good accommodations." The upper floor they "fitted up in a like manner for the boys."

Thus, well ahead of its time, the building became a coeducational dorm, with men's and women's areas strictly segregated (as with similar dorms a century later).

Each floor contained ten furnished and carpeted residence rooms, heated and ventilated from a furnace so students did not have to tend their own fires.

Officials touted this as one of the most complete boarding halls in Oregon, "under such careful management that parents may feel perfectly safe in placing their children there for a home while in attendance at college."

Meanwhile, in 1893 Newberg Monthly Meeting moved to the newly vacated four-acre site, and the Monthly Meeting donated all its additional property to the College. The sanctuary building at Third and College streets still stands.

8

The 36- by 48-foot gymnasium, constructed by moving two barns together in 1895.

Bottom: The gymnasium and "College Building" in the late 1890s.

1893 photo of Newberg Friends Church pastor Herbert Cash, standing, left, and college personnel Rose Hampton Dixon, Charles Jessup, L. Ella Hartley, and Cecil E. Vance; sitting, Rebecca (Hinchman) Smith, Jane H. Blair, and Julius Hodson; on floor, Edgar Ballard and Ada Howard.

In 1895 college students constructed a 36- by 48-foot gymnasium by bringing together two barns. The school supplied boarders with hot and cold water in 1899, and students raised money to provide electric lights three years later. Beginning in 1904, the school assessed a 25-cent-per-term user's fee for library improvements.

NEAR THE END of his first year in office, President Newlin reported the College's major need: a faculty large enough to teach about 33 classes each day (with no one teacher to have more than seven). The College lacked a business instructor to teach bookkeeping, penmanship, and arithmetic; an English teacher for English, elocution, reading, essays, and declamations; a lady "who will be companionable to the girls, who can lead them in physical exercises as well as in their intellectual and spiritual lives"; a

science teacher; and a Latin and mathematics instructor. Newlin also requested at least five recitation rooms, a financial agent for full-time fund raising, better-equipped dormitories, a girls' gymnasium, and increases in the college library.

Although most of Newlin's recommendations could not be accomplished, the school prospered. By 1895 enrollment had grown to 43 students, academic standards were rising, and the College had implemented a course of study for ministers and Christian workers. Two years later a gift from Mary Edwards added 300 volumes to the library.

The faculty and trustees extended to the College its conduct requirements for academy students. They issued the following statement: "We, the Board of Trustees of Pacific College, do endorse the rules for the government of students, as adopted by the faculty, and we pledge our entire support in executing them, as they deem proper."

The prohibitions included habitual profanity, intoxicants, tobacco in all its forms, card playing, carrying concealed weapons, and attending dancing parties. The regulations required even students living in their own homes to observe all restrictions regarding study hours and general deportment. This included a general ban on week-day evening parties and leaving town without the faculty's permission.

The College also guarded the students' spiritual lives, requiring attendance at weekly prayer meetings and

9

The entire campus from 1895 to 1911. To the left is the "Dormitory Building" (Minthorn Hall), with the gymnasium and the "College Building" (Hoover Hall).

Sabbath afternoon devotional meetings. The board mandated that "great care be taken about mingling of the sexes and the whereabouts of the students at all hours.... Students who cannot cheerfully accept the conditions here outlined are requested not to apply for admission."

The College thus saw itself, through its faculty, acting in *locus parentis*. Yet little evidence exists that those who chose to attend the school failed to "cheerfully accept the conditions." Phrases such as "good spiritual life," "deeper

> *"Students fail each year because they will not submit to the conditions of success. Isolation is more difficult situated as we are than it would be if we were more remote from the community interests."*
>
> —President Thomas Newlin, 1900

experiences," and "waves of revival" occasionally punctuate the board minutes. The minutes also report, to cite one example, that students preached more than 100 sermons during the 1896-97 school year.

School officials also required faculty to uphold rather rigid Christian standards in their classes and personal lives. President Newlin emphasized: "It is our intention to make all our exercises tend directly toward Christian Culture. We strive to avoid sectarian teaching, and to inculcate the principles of vital Christianity."

In addition, the stockholders unanimously adopted this resolution:

"Be it resolved . . . that no teaching either by teacher or text book should be permitted in Pacific College that in any

way discredits the authenticity of any portion of the Bible. It is further expressly declared to be the sense of this meeting, that in all Bible teaching, its truth is to be admitted without question. The Board of Trustees is required in the selection of the Faculty and in arranging the course of study to carry this resolution into effect."

PRESIDENT NEWLIN sought to impress upon the Yearly Meeting its financial obligation. He told the board in 1897 that after several years of gradually increasing indebtedness, the previous year proved triumphant—the faculty's patience and self-denial kept the College from closing its doors. Then he added: "Could every member of Oregon

Pacific College faculty in 1903-04. Top: Mabel H. Douglas, Acting President C. E. Lewis, F. K. Jones. Middle: R. W. Jones, President H. Edwin McGrew, O. C. Albertson. Bottom: Mrs. Albertson, Miss Britt, Miss Macy.

Yearly Meeting share equally with the faculty in the blessing of sacrifice, there would be no question as to the triumphant results."

Expressing faith that the life and healthy development of Oregon Yearly Meeting depended on the College, the president noted: "No one can lightly speak of Pacific College without weakening the church to the same extent. We therefore ask the hearty moral as well as financial support of all who are interested in building up the Master's Kingdom."

After nine years as president, Thomas Newlin resigned in 1900. The board expressed its appreciation for his services:

"And it is the sense of this board that in accepting the resignation, we do so with the greatest regret; and that we owe to Thomas Newlin a debt of gratitude for his noble efforts to upbuild and sustain Pacific College through these years of struggle for a place among the Christian colleges of this country; and so long as this institution shall stand, his name will ever be remembered as a chief factor in its incipient development."

Newlin verbalized his regret at leaving, but optimism for the College's future:

"It gives me great satisfaction to know that in all my connections with the College, there has been no unpleasant feeling existing among members of the faculty, nor has there been any note of discord sounded in the internal management. I greatly appreciate the privilege which I have enjoyed of working under your management, and with a noble band of devoted, self-sacrificing teachers."

IN MAY 1900, the board considered a replacement. After lengthy discussion, it offered the position to H. Edwin McGrew, a Quaker from Iowa with two degrees from William Penn College and experience as principal of its preparatory department. In 1904, while on a one-year leave, McGrew earned a master's in philosophy and ethics from Haverford College. He came to Pacific at $800 for the year, $200 less than Newlin had received.

Pacific experienced difficulty paying the bills, making it continually necessary to secure outside funds. During the College's initial year, the trustees, observing that every successful college had a financial agent, temporarily released Professor G. N. Hartley to solicit funds from Friends east of the Rocky Mountains.

At the same time, the managers hired Elias Jessup to do financial work in the West. A limited enrollment paying low tuition rates failed to supply expenses, even though the College paid faculty members less than $1,000. When Newlin left in 1900, the College faced a $12,000 indebtedness.

The new president and the board met the problem squarely. Noting "the very friendly feeling toward us in Salem Quarterly meeting," they decided to appeal for $6,000 within Oregon Yearly Meeting and another $6,000 from Friends in eastern United States:

"It is the sense of this board, that heroic efforts shall be made to raise funds to meet the entire indebtedness of this institution; that six thousand dollars be raised in Oregon, and that President McGrew be sent East to solicit for this cause. Pledges shall be made conditioned on the entire amount being raised."

Then they thoroughly solicited the College's patrons and friends in Oregon. "Great pains should be taken in this canvass, and it should be made plain to all that the college cannot continue unless this amount is made up," the board announced in advance. "We need to show to our friends in the East that the college has the support of friends at home."

After one year of intensive activity, the board reached its goal. Pledges came from throughout the constituency, including Friends on the East Coast. In January 1902, Pacific College students and patrons sang this song:

Ring the good old college bell,
And ring it extra long,
Ring it with a spirit,
That will make a joyous song.
Ring it as 'twas never rung
In days that now are gone
While we've been marching through college.

Chorus:
Hurrah, hurrah, we'll sing the jubilee.
Hurrah, hurrah, for from the debt we're free.
And so we'll burn the mortgage
That has hung o'er old PC,
While we're marching through college.

While the board of managers
Were shaking in their shoes.
As they faced the mortgage
And collected little dues.
Now they have forgotten
That they ever had the blues,
While we've been marching through college.

While our President we greet,
Who brought the news to town.
The bell will ring so clear and sweet
With music all around.
We'll sing a song to celebrate
His honor and renown.
While we're marching through college.

An enthusiastic assembly rang the bell, sang the song, and burned the mortgage. Jesse Edwards gleefully put the note into the bonfire and held it high as the flames consumed the paper.

NEVERTHELESS, monthly obligations continued to out-distance income and soon diminished the euphoria. Pacific College faced another major deficit unless it could raise an endowment to yield a continuing income. Board chairman B. C. Miles' 1904 report requested increased yearly meeting support. He specifically recommended "a thorough awakening among the members of Oregon Yearly Meeting along the lines of a thorough Christian education, which will not only store the mind with knowledge, but will prepare the heart for useful Christian work."

Meanwhile, the board and administration faced pressures to increase expenditures. The board minutes of November 10, 1902, record some faculty dissatisfaction with salaries. Two months later the salary committee reported satisfactory adjustment, however, merely by raising Professor Francis K. Jones' salary $100 for the year.

The board did not resolve all problems so easily, however. For example, for the 1905-06 school year, the trustees accepted a $2,000 deficit. One year later the stockholders agreed to ask the Yearly Meeting for $1,500 to meet the next year's anticipated deficit. The August 7, 1908, college board minutes record an expected budget shortfall of over $4,200.

The managers reiterated the need for an endowment. In 1902 a Newberg Friend, Henry Mills, deeded his $1,200 home to the College in order to initiate such a fund. Three years later the board devised plans for a major campaign to raise $50,000. A committee composed of B. C. Miles, A. R. Mills, and E. H. Woodward sent President McGrew throughout Oregon and to the East Coast to begin the effort. While the president was away, the trustees chose Professor Francis K. Jones as temporary acting president.

Constituents soon pledged $12,000, but McGrew resigned the presidency due to poor health. His successor,

Evangeline Martin and
Amanda Woodward, with
"Faithful Old Kit," July 4,
1910.

Bottom left: Wood-Mar
Hall nearly completed.
Gymnasium and corner of
Hoover Hall in
background. Right:
Chemistry class, 1905-06.

W. Irving Kelsey (1907-1910), a graduate of Earlham and former head of the Friends' missionary work in Mexico, tried valiantly but unsuccessfully to complete the campaign. Meanwhile, the board secured short-term loans to pay teachers' salaries.

THE SCHOOL soon enjoyed another major financial success, however. Eight years after the flames from the mortgage died in 1902, the board launched a drive to raise $30,000 for a much-needed building. At a mass town meeting on February 10, 1910, city mayor N. C. Christenson presented the concern. Newberg patrons immediately subscribed $16,335. After that, Amanda Woodward and Evangeline Martin, long-time Quakers and friends of the College, canvassed Newberg businesses and individuals in a buggy drawn by "faithful Old Kit," spending several months successfully appealing to more than 600 donors.

The city celebrated the fund drive's completion July 10, 1910. Again, Woodward and Martin drove their buggy through the city streets, this time triumphantly decorated with a sign that read:

> new Building for
> Pacific College
> $30,000 subscription completed

Within a year, the builders completed their work. Honoring the two ladies' heroic efforts, the board named the new Willamina brick building "Wood-Mar Hall."

DURING ITS FIRST years, Pacific College taught two courses of study: classical and scientific. Students chose between bachelor of arts and bachelor of science degrees. However, the College required many of the same classes in both areas. For example, the school mandated philosophy, elocution, classical history, and natural theology for both majors.

Sometimes commencement lasted a full week. Before construction of Wood-Mar Hall, Newberg Friends Church hosted all events. The typical graduation week included a Friday program by the music department, Saturday Junior-Senior banquet, Sunday morning baccalaureate sermon for both College and Academy, Sunday afternoon Academy graduation, Monday night senior "Class Day Program," and Tuesday alumni program. The eagerly awaited College commencement occurred Wednesday morning. Typically, the Oregon Yearly Meeting sessions immediately followed these celebrations.

COCURRICULAR activities included football, basketball, baseball, track, soccer, Christian associations for both

The class of 1897 was Will G. Allen, Harley S. Britt, Sarah L. (Bond) Cash, S. Lewis Hanson, Oliver J. Hobson, Drew P. Price, Ore L. Price, George T. Tolson, and Charles Wilson. The order of the graduates in the picture is unknown.

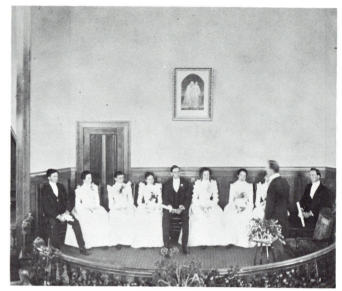

The class of 1899 in graduation ceremonies at the Newberg Friends Church. Left to right: Walter Parker, Clara Vaughn, Anna (Hoskins) Jones, Gertrude (Lamb) Whiteis, Hervey Hoskins, Edna Newlin, Jessie Britt, May Lamb, and Fred Jackson, with President Thomas Newlin in front.

men and women, drama performances, the Ladies' Glee Club, and for brief periods, the Agoreton, Helianthus, Euphemian, and Junta literary societies. The College organized a tennis association and constructed two new courts in 1910.

The Whittier Literary Society published the *Academician*, which in 1891 became *The Crescent*. The school reduced this highly acclaimed journal, devoted to literary as well as college matters, from 20 to four pages in 1914.

During the early years, Pacific distinguished itself with the best oratorical record of all the state's colleges. Its first 15 years in the State Oratorical Association, Pacific won first place four times, second three. Winners included Amos C. Stanbrough (1893), Elwood S. Minchin (1901), Walter R. Miles (1905), and Katherine (Romig) Otis (1907). Gertrude (Lamb) Whiteis (1894), Lucy (Gause) Newby (1903), and Paul V. Maris (1906) won second-place honors.

After each victory all Newberg celebrated. The *Newberg Graphic* described the 1901 festivities:

"The next day about noon when the victorious delegation (about 60) was expected in on the train, the main business houses closed their doors and all Newberg gathered at the depot.... A carriage had been appropriately decorated with bunting, a streamer inscribed with 'victory' stretched across the top, and above all waved a new broom, eloquently expressive of a clean sweep. Snatched from the train to the shoulders of his admirers, young (Elwood) Minchin was borne triumphantly to the carriage, and thrust

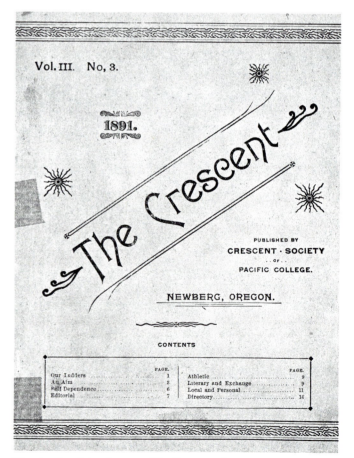

Vol. III. No, 3.

1891.

The Crescent

PUBLISHED BY
CRESCENT · SOCIETY
..OF..
PACIFIC COLLEGE.

NEWBERG, OREGON.

CONTENTS

	PAGE.		PAGE.
Our Ladders	1	Athletic	9
Au Aim	3	Literary and Exchange	9
Self Dependence	6	Local and Personal	11
Editorial	7	Directory	14

The *Academician* became *The Crescent* in 1891.

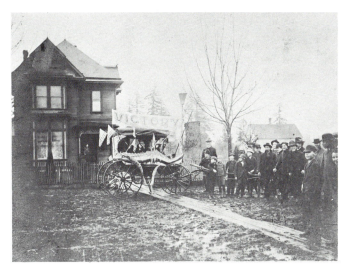

Celebrating Pacific College's victory in the state oratorical contest, 1901, in front of E. H. Woodward's house. Champion Elwood Minchin (in the carriage) spoke on "Wendall Phillips—the Agitator," closing his speech with: "And this thy epitaph while time shall be, He found his country chained, He left her free." Newberg's entire business district closed for the celebration.

PACIFIC COLLEGE.

into the seat of honor. With him were placed his sister Miss Julia Minchin and Professor and Mrs. Kelsey. Eager hands caught the rope that had been attached to the vehicle, and a triumphal procession was started through the streets, accompanied by the blowing of whistles, the ringing of bells, and yes (we can't afford to lose the expression) by 'a fanfare of trumpets'—of the tin horn variety. The carriage was pulled over to E. H. Woodward's where the ubiquitous camera was brought into service."

The state championship speech of freshman Katherine (Romig) Otis in 1907 severely criticized sweatshop child labor in the United States. The *Newberg Graphic* reported that the six judges—who included the president of Stanford University and the managing editor of the *Oregonian*—gave Romig five firsts and one third. The story continued:

"...there seemed to be a general feeling that the 'little girl' was in too fast company to show up well, and even some of her loyal supporters feared that in comparison to the sonorous, rich toned voices of the men she would suffer in the consideration of the judges.

"But from the first she had the big audience at perfect command. Her subject itself challenged attention, and as she pictured in burning words the conditions of child labor in America and the dangers with which it threatens our country, as she plead for the overburdened little toilers of the silent, infant army, she carried her hearers with her in sympathy. Her striking climaxes were marked by the

thrilling hush which is the tribute to real oratory. She was ease personified, her gestures faultless—in short she outdid herself and the judges as well as the audience capitulated.

"Newberg had a delegation of two hundred people present to cheer and yell their orator on to success. The Newberg excursion train rolled in over a half an hour before the hour of the contest, giving the Quakers a chance to get located early and start up the preliminary fireworks. Having the largest delegation present, the followers of the Old Gold and Navy Blue made the house ring with college songs and yells, led by Clarence Brown and Paul Maris...."

Many years later Daisy (Newhouse) Read, at that time an academy student, recalled the drama of Katherine Romig's victory:

"As there were only 88 of us in the student body, both Academy and College, we all knew each other very well and knew a lot of what each one was doing.

15

Left: In front row is the first Pacific College band, 1905, outfitted by the Woodmen of the World for the Lewis and Clark centennial in Portland.

Bottom: The 1910 championship debate team; members included Claude Newlin, Kathryn Bryan, and leader Roy Fitch.

1906 graduating class. Front row: Ruth (Romig) Hull, Walter Miles, Alverda (Crozier) Rice, Ray Pemberton, Mary (Minthorn) Strench, Ernest Bales. Back row: Marie Alice Hanson, Wilfred Pemberton, unidentified, Lenora (Parker) Pemberton, Lillian Nicholson, unidentified, Lewis Saunders. The other three class members were Myrtle (Gause) Bell, Mabel (Newby) Huff, and Bernice (Woodward) King.

"As March approached in 1907, the excitement grew, as we had been told her oration was excellent. This was the fifteenth oratorical contest, and Pacific College had won three. The citizens of Newberg chartered a steam train, and a big crowd went to McMinnville for the contest. Katherine's oration was 'The Goblin Army' and when the crowd from Newberg arrived at the hall they greeted the crowd with such yells as

Cha-lunk! Cha-lunk—Cha-lunk—Cha-lack
P.C. will take the medal back
That's what we're all up here about!
And the goblins'll git you,
If you don't watch out.

"All the other orators were large men and farther along in college. Katherine looked so tiny against all the other orators, but when her time came she had such poise and graciousness and such a timely subject she won the oratorical contest . . . .

"I will let you imagine the rousing cheer that went up from the Newberg crowd. When the train arrived in Newberg after the contest, someone had a six-horse team drive Katherine down First Street to the College. The contest was on a Friday night. The following Sunday she gave her oration at the Friends Church, and the church was packed. There were no fire ordinances then, so there was standing room only."

At least one orator succeeded nationally, when in 1904 Walter Miles won the national contest of the Prohibition Association of Colleges. E. S. Craven provided a colorful version of this achievement in the November, 1904, *The Crescent*:

"The greatest oratorical contest between college students that has ever taken place in the United States was held in Indianapolis on June 28, 1904, before an audience of from 2500 to 4000 people. In the contest twenty states were represented [from such schools as the University of California, University of Michigan, Wheaton College, Cornell College, and Pacific College].

"All the orations . . . were masterful productions and delivered with telling effect. When the . . . last orator stepped to the front, paused a moment and with flashing eyes surveyed the audience, a hush fell over the vast assemblage. It was then that Walter R. Miles, in a clear and steady voice, began his winning oration. Soon the audience caught the 'Victory Spirit,' and Mr. Miles himself seemed electrified by something supernatural. At one time he leaned forward almost on tiptoe and lifted his hand as though it was now or never to save the lives of his fellow-

16

men and shouted, 'Shall we surrender?' The audience involuntarily shouted back, 'No, no!'

"Miles seemed no longer our Sophomore as we knew him, but appeared almost transformed, and with a voice not his own forced to speak from a great heart filled with

---

"Our boys played a good game and hotly contested every inch of ground but they were lacking in the necessary avoirdupois to win the game."

—Story of first football game in 1894 *The Crescent*

---

a greater spirit. Once again he interrogated his auditors: 'Is there yet heroic blood?' Probably a thousand men answered in the affirmative, while the whole audience went wild in applause. One man shouted out, 'Another Patrick Henry.'"

During these years the Pacific College debate team also enjoyed success. In 1907 Paul Maris, Ralph W. Rees and Clarence M. Brown took the league championship, arguing the affirmative to "Resolved, that the Government Should Own and Operate the Railroads." Three years later Pacific College again won the championship, represented by debaters Claude Newlin, Kathryn Bryan, and Roy Fitch.

THE Willamette University football team came by steamboat in 1894 to play in Newberg's first intercollegiate football game. One hour before the contest, the players marched from the west part of Newberg along First Street and then to the college campus. Pacific College's first drive went to the one-foot line before being halted, but Willamette eventually won, 16-0. *The Crescent* story concludes:

"Our boys played a good game and hotly contested every inch of ground but they were lacking in the necessary avoirdupois to win the game. It would be interesting

17

to see them matched with a team from Willamette of the same weight.

"The best of feeling prevailed throughout the game and the boys all seemed in the best of spirits when the game was ended. No accidents worth mentioning occurred. Lunch was served for the visitors at the hall where all went merry as a marriage occasion.

"Enough interest has been aroused to insure a good crowd next Saturday to see the game between our boys and the Portland High School team. If you think the game worth seeing put an extra fifteen cents in your pocket and help the boys out. They work hard for the amusement of the public and deserve some recompense."

Intercollegiate football caught on and, except for five years during the late 1920s and part of World War II, the sport continued through 1969.

At 5:00 a.m. on June 6, 1896, about 100 Newberg residents boarded the steamer *Grey Eagle* for a seven-hour upstream trip to Salem. The destination was Willamette University for Pacific College's first track meet, against the University of Oregon, Portland University, Oregon Agricultural College (Oregon State University), Monmouth Normal (Western Oregon State College) and Willamette University. Pacific took fourth place. *The Crescent* reported:

"At the gate a general kick was made by the public at the charge of fifty cents gate fee and many Salem people refused to go, saying they did not care so much for the particular fifty cents but they did not want to encourage the management in such extravagant charges...."

"No charge was made this year for seats in the grand stand but not a single program could be had short of ten cents...."

A long delay for a competitive military drill between the Oregon Agricultural College cadets and the Salem state militia caused further problems. The meet ran overtime, and, according to *The Crescent*:

"The captain of the *Grey Eagle* got nervous and pulled out before the time announced for leaving Salem and left something more than thirty of the excursionists in the city. Most of the 'crowd went to the Armory where they were well provided with militia blankets for the night and the boys had a jolly time. They came down on the *Ramona* Sunday morning."

Competition included bicycle races and baseball batting and throwing. Pacific's Fred Scott gained special commendation for his victorious pole vault of nine feet, three inches. T. W. Heater eclipsed the record two years later with a nine-feet, six-inch vault. Roy Heater almost single-handedly won the 1902 league championship with victories in the dashes, hurdles, and jumping events.

1905 basketball team. Standing, guards Worth Coulson and Perry Macy, center Chester Hodson, and forwards Marvin Blair and Wilfred Pemberton. Seated is manager Ray Pemberton.

Thomas W. Hester saw a basketball game played in 1898 at the Portland YMCA. He secured a ball and brought it to campus. Since its 36- by 48-foot gymnasium was unequipped for the sport, the College played its first basketball game on the third floor of the old Commercial Hotel on Newberg's North Main Street.

Recognizing that inadequate facilities prevented college teams from coming to Newberg, the student body acted in 1904 to improve the gymnasium. Professor Francis Jones suggested a campus fund-raising drive; Marvin Blair chaired the student committee. They raised the entire amount (nearly $150) by subscription. Students contributed $39.50 and the faculty $22.50.

The funds provided the gymnasium (originally two barns joined together) with a 14- by 42-foot lean-to addition. Headlined "A Long-felt Need Supplied," *The Crescent* noted that "at long last we have a satisfactory place to play public games of basket ball and to give other indoor athletic exercises."

From the beginning, the faculty placed stringent controls on athletics. For example, the 1894 Faculty Minutes record that students without passing grades and satisfactory deportment could not play baseball. The faculty also prohibited games and team travel on Sundays.

Pacific College's first twenty years brought the predictable triumphs and failures of a small educational undertaking. During the two decades, the college student

body grew from 15 to 35 (after peaking in 1902 at 57), the faculty from 7 to 12, and the annual operating budget from $4,784 to $11,258. (Faculty and budget figures include the Academy.)

Not surprisingly, lack of money plagued the College through its first 20 years. Board minutes regularly lamented that "the financial standing of the college is not very encouraging" and "we face a cloud of debt." On the other hand, the staff and administration expressed faith and optimism: "Our efforts for Pacific College are for the Master; this work is His," and "God reigns and Pacific College still lives." The constituency firmly believed, as recorded in the June 23, 1898, board minutes, that the school had been conceived by the spirit of God and nurtured by prayer. "Self-sacrifice will lead to certain victory."

Before leaving office in 1900, President Newlin reiterated the school's objectives:

"The true end of college life is hard study, and whatever defeats this is a drawback to the college.... Home duties, social ties, athletics, immoral habits or even church work, any one of these may kill the college spirit in the student. None of these should be so exacting or so absorbing as to defeat the true end of the college. No student can keep up with his studies and play a full part in any other sphere in life. College work means isolation. Students fail each year because they will not submit to the conditions of success. Isolation is more difficult situated as we are than it would be if we were more remote from the community interests.

"Our record is the best of any institution in the state for Christian work, and our work in athletics and oratory is praiseworthy."

Through its first 20 years, Pacific College's commonly understood sense of mission overcame many problems. The presidents—Thomas Newlin (1891-1900), Henry Edwin McGrew (1900-1907), W. Irving Kelsey (1907-1910)—all entered enthusiastically into the College's goals. Constituents shared a concern to see that the institution continued, obstacles notwithstanding.

Very early the board had set high standards: "The friends of Pacific College, and they are legion, are determined that the college shall come to the front and stand second to none in the country."

Pacific College's first two decades ended as they had begun. A small school, insignificant by many standards, continued an important ministry, with the strong support of its central constituency. The hopes and dreams of the faithful flourished; happily, the next era brought a measure of stability unattained in the founding years.

Professor William J. Reagan replaced retiring President W. Irving Kelsey in 1910 and served one year as acting president. Meanwhile, the trustees sought a permanent replacement. Their search succeeded beyond anything they could have dared to hope.

19

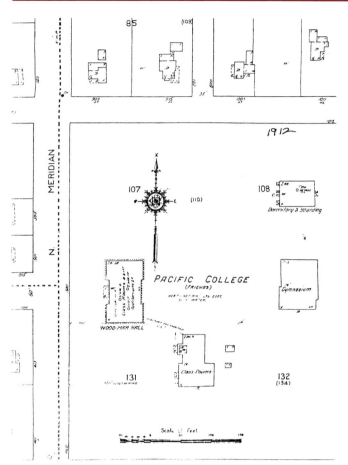

Campus plat, 1912. "Dormitory & Boarding" is currently Minthorn Hall; Gymnasium was constructed by moving and joining two barns in 1895; "Class Rooms" was Hoover Hall, where Carillon Bell Tower now stands; Wood-Mar was constructed in 1910-1911.

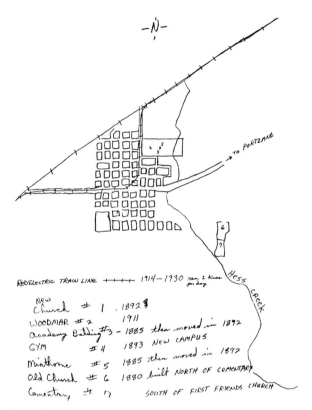

Drawing of early Newberg, done in the 1930s, including some misspelled words and Minthorn Hall misdated (1887). The Red Electric Train left the Southern Pacific line and proceeded south on Meridian, stopped in front of Wood-Mar Hall's west, main door, and continued south to First Street, where it continued west to rejoin the main line.

The campus from the roof of Wood-Mar Hall, with Rex Hill in the background.

Chapter Two

A snowy day on campus.

Students and faculty putting in new Wood-Mar Hall lawn, 1911.

LEVI T. PENNINGTON served as Pacific College president from 1911 to 1941—the school's entire third, fourth, and fifth decades. Today's observer must give the witty, personable Pennington much credit for the College's continued existence.

Levi's Quaker parents migrated from the East Coast to Indiana, where he was born in a log cabin in 1875. His father served as a country store proprietor, farmer, and Friends pastor in Indiana and southern Michigan.

Young Pennington's early life centered around the Quaker Meeting. As he grew up, he became Sunday school superintendent, president of the local and congressional district Christian Endeavor Union, and a fill-in pastor. The Society of Friends had recorded his father, uncle, great-uncle, and great-grandmother as ministers. Levi felt led in the same direction.

Teaching also interested him. He received his first certificate at two days past age 16½—which made him legally 17 and therefore eligible to teach. After teaching in five rural schools and serving as principal in one, he embarked upon a brief career in another interest, newspaper work.

Fall Regular Student Enrollment, 1911-1925		
1911—41	1916—51	1921—55
1912—35	1917—54	1922—68
1913—40	1918—27	1923—65
1914—40	1919—40	1924—73
1915—47	1920—37	1925—75

Levi married Bertha May Waters in 1898. She died five years later, leaving two small children. After remarriage in 1905 to Florence Rebecca Kidd, he pastored several Indiana Friends meetings.

For two years Pennington worked concurrently as pastor and college student at sites 40 miles apart. Early each Monday morning he commuted by train to Earlham College and returned Friday afternoon to lead the church's prayer meeting. The congregation changed its "mid-week" meeting time from the traditional Wednesday evening to accommodate the pastor's schedule. During Christmas vacations he conducted special evangelistic meetings.

While Levi attended school, Rebecca Pennington cared for the two children and fulfilled the pastoral duties of calling on the sick, the bereaved, and the otherwise needy. "It was said that she did everything but marry 'em and bury 'em," Pennington remarked later. "My best friends did not hesitate to assure me that she was a better pastor than I was. She used to say that she practiced during the week what I preached on Sunday."

Earlham gave Pennington its highest honor, the prestigious Haverford Scholarship for graduate study. He declined the enticing opportunity, however, feeling morally obliged to give a full, undistracted year to the church he pastored.

On June 17, 1910, Levi Pennington wrote in his diary: "Got my A. B. from Earlham." Four days later he casually penned: "Most of day working at home. Got offer of presidency of Pacific College." He soon received a similar invitation from William Penn College in Iowa.

Pennington refused both offers for the reason he had declined the Haverford scholarship. One year later, having fulfilled his commitment, the 35-year-old pastor/teacher accepted a second invitation to the Pacific College presidency.

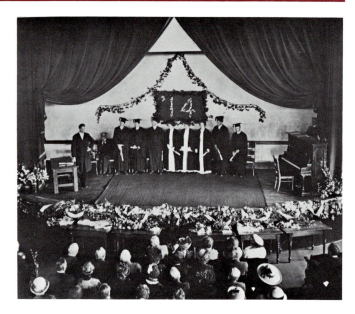

Letters written to Pennington by Acting President William Reagan are hopeful and optimistic, but provide some forewarning that the job would not always be easy. Reagan noted that raising money for the recently completed Wood-Mar Hall "took all the extra, so it has been unusually hard to make ends meet. We are about 3 months behind on salaries here." In another letter Reagan announced: "You will be head janitor of the institution as President. The head janitor gets to do the extras."

Pennington's qualifications did not include graduate work, administrative experience, or even acquaintance with West Coast people and problems. Still, his zest for life, sharp wit, and exceptional oral and written communication skills made him an engaging leader. Coupled with a

---

"You will be head janitor of the institution as President. The head janitor gets to do the extras."
—Letter from Acting President William Reagan
to new President Levi Pennington

---

healthy tenacity and strong ego, he possessed the most essential ingredients for the presidency: He brought deep faith in God and a sense of mission that coincided with the College and Academy constituency.

Noting that the new president faced a "staggering load" that became "a crucible of administrative experience," Pennington's biographer, Donald McNichols, added:

"He held to the conviction that a Quaker college holding to the principles of Friends could and must make a badly needed and unique contribution to the nation, to society, and to the church. He perceived that such a college could assist young people develop in such a way that

their contribution would add a significant moral, spiritual, and intellectual ingredient to national life.... It was this concern, this call to service that prompted him to sacrifice and ask for sacrifice of others to make such training possible for future leaders in all phases of society."

Within a year, Pennington accurately analyzed the school's problems. His first annual report to Oregon Yearly Meeting identified continued constituent allegiance as the greatest need. It advocated similar sacrificial loyalty from "many who have not yet felt as fully as they should their responsibility for the college and its need for their help." Secondly, progress required financial stability. That necessitated a secure income beyond available tuition and donor gifts.

THE NATIONAL Educational Association, in cooperation with the United States Bureau of Educational Standards, had established standards for all colleges, including a $100,000 minimum endowment. Only months into his presidency, Pennington urged the board to attempt a $100,000 endowment campaign. The ensuing drive consumed much of the new president's energy for nearly three years.

Pennington faced several major obstacles. As William Reagan had warned, the campaign for Wood-Mar Hall had nearly exhausted potential sources; in addition, two $50,000 endowment attempts had already failed. Nevertheless, the challenge envigorated the new president.

The 2,500 Northwest Quakers could not bear the entire burden. Pennington therefore turned his attention to Midwest and East Coast Friends as potential contributors.

22

Young Women's Christian Association cabinet, 1912-13.
Front row: Daisy (Newhouse) Read, Elma (Paulsen) Hadley,
Myrtle (Mills) Franzen, Mildred Benson. Back row: Florence
(Kaufman) Harris, Esther (Miles) Haworth, Vera York, Mary
(Jones) DesBrisay, Violet (Craw) Jones.

However, in spending much of his first two presidential years on the railroad, he gained only modest positive results. By 1913, he had raised less than half the goal.

Oregon Yearly Meeting then decided as a vote of confidence that when the College raised $50,000, it would pay the interest on an additional $50,000 until the total of $100,000 had been secured. As a result, the Yearly Meeting as a body (beyond individual gifts) contributed $2,129 to the school's general fund the following year.

College personnel redoubled their efforts during 1914. With Yearly Meeting consituents leading the way, the effort exceeded the $100,000 goal by New Year's Eve. One-half century later, Levi Pennington recalled the heroism:

"The struggle for that first $119,000 of endowment is a story that will never be told adequately, though it deserves to be. It has its bright side, and some not so bright. I think of one family living in an unfinished house and without so much as a mat on the floor that pledged hundreds of dollars; of students who were fighting their way through college 'on their own' who pledged gifts in three figures east of the dollar sign and west of the decimal point; of one young school teacher who had been saving for a long time to buy herself a muff, and gave the money to the college—she could wear mittens. On the other hand there were those who refused to pay pledges that were to become effective when the total reached $100,000, because J. J. Hill had refused to pay his pledge of tens of thousands because our $100,000 was not all in cash.

"One man who pledged $400 fell on evil times, lost his farm, was on relief for some years, lived with his son after his wife's death, but saved up money a little at a time, and one day, years after his note had been outlawed, he came to me and paid that $400. I said to him, 'It used to be said that a Quaker's word was as good as his note. Here is a Quaker whose word is better than his note. Your note is

not legally worth anything, but your promise to give to the College is worth fully the sum you named.' (There was more than my usual fervor in my handshake with this man.)"

Levi Pennington remembered the ensuing celebration, which reminded old-timers of the debt liquidation festivities in 1902:

"The old Victory Bell in the tower of the original building of Friends Pacific Academy rang with a note that seemed more impressive than any that had been heard after the most impressive athletic victory that ever came to the college. (At the big bonfire celebration that followed, Mrs. L. M. Parker . . . carried out her promise that if the college raised that $100,000 she would celebrate by burning her hat. There was a real cheer when she tossed that hat into that bonfire.)"

Pacific's academic program failed to meet several Bureau of Educational Standards specifications. For example, the College required only three years of high school, the library lacked the specified 5,000 volumes, and the biology and physics laboratories remained deficient. The College attempted to correct these inadequacies while seeking the $100,000 endowment. During the ensuing 15 years, for example, library volumes increased from about 2,000 to nearly 9,000.

Much to the disappointment of College officials, however, the Bureau of Educational Standards in 1912 raised the required minimum endowment to $200,000. Undaunted, President Pennington and the trustees attempted to meet the new criterion, only to be delayed by the outbreak of World War I.

THE COLLEGE struggled to meet annual budgets. Pennington set his first budget at $11,602.19, but reduced it by $3,000 the next year. The budget gradually grew to

$24,435.64 in 1917, before being cut in half during 1918, the war year. It then climbed to about $37,000 by 1926.

Through all the difficulties, Pacific College maintained its mission. Levi Pennington put it well in his 1913 report to the Yearly Meeting:

"It should go without saying that a school of the character of Pacific College should have as its definite end the advancement of the Kingdom of God among men. It should not be forgotten that a general education, without which our children, whatever their calling in life, will be handicapped, can be secured to them under more favorable moral and spiritual environment than other institutions provide. This alone would be worth a tremendous sacrifice on the part of all who are interested in the coming generation. But this is not all that is desirable, and this is not enough for Oregon Yearly Meeting to seek for Pacific College and to expect of the college. The institution ought definitely to advance the cause of the Kingdom. It should not only send out men and women competent to enter business or fit themselves for the professions or take their places on the farm or behind the accounting desk, but it should send them out as Christians to take up these lines of activity in the world's work. In the motto of the college, Christianity and Culture, Christianity is rightfully put first. Nor is even this enough. From Pacific College should go, in ever increasing numbers, those who are to take their places in the special work of the Kingdom, as Ministers, Christian Association workers, Home and Foreign Missionaries and others who shall give their lives in this peculiar way to the definite work of the Kingdom."

But to carry out this mission—indeed, merely to pay the bills—required an ever enlarging student community. Exuding optimism in 1918, the administration and trustees of the 27-student institution projected an eventual 500 student "efficient college."

Realism forced concentration, however, on the difficult present. Without standardization, the school faced difficulty attracting students. Even a few Quakers from Oregon Yearly Meeting went elsewhere. Some upperclassmen transferred to colleges offering accredited degrees.

The College enrollment numbered 33 the year before Pennington came and immediately jumped to 41. It fluctuated for several years before reaching 54 in 1917, only to be cut in half by World War I. In 1912-13, the Academy enrollment peaked at 80, but declined through the rest of the decade.

Board chairman Ezra Woodward told the Yearly Meeting in 1914 that the College's teaching force could accommodate 80 students. "The college needs this added number of students and there are those in the territory that we cover who need what the college has to offer young people."

WORLD WAR I brought the decade's most severe blows. Not only did enrollment decline, but the Quaker school's nonviolent constituents suffered from the militant patriotism that flooded the country.

President Pennington agreed with President Woodrow Wilson, who lamented the horror of war, at home as well as on the battlefield. Wilson believed that a nation at war loses its basic morality, its ability to judge right from wrong, its ability to criticize itself.

"Once lead this people into war," a friend quoted Wilson, "and they'll forget there ever was such a thing as tolerance. To fight you must be brutal and ruthless, and the spirit of ruthless brutality will enter into the very fibre of

24

Class of 1915 in front of Springbrook Friends Church
parsonage, where Walter Wilson was pastor. Walter Wilson,
Harry Haworth, Lisle Hubbard, Eva (Campbell) Knight, Ellis
Pickett, Thomas Arthur Benson, Florence (Kaufman) Harris,
Gladys Hannon.

1916 freshman class. Front row: Margaret Hodson, Marie
Hall, Lestia Newlin, Frances Elliott, Gladys Terrell, Mildred
Ferguson, Olive Johnson, Gladys Paulson, Eva Parrett,
Marjorie Hazelton. Second row: Lionel Kramien, Elmo
Shannahan, Ralph Knight, Myrth McNay, Pearl Grieve, Hazel
Bear, Blanche Mellinger, Paul Elliott, Willard Wiley, Howard
Elliott. Third row: Benjamin Darling, Dave Marr, Frank
Colcord, Clinton Baron, Earl Pinney, Alfred Haworth.

our national life, infecting Congress, the courts, the police-
man on the beat, the man in the street . . . ."

Yet from its beginning, most Pacific College constituents reflected Oregon Yearly Meeting's official opposition
to Christian involvement in war. According to Levi Pennington, Pacific was the only college in Oregon that continued to teach the German language during the war. It
also declined to institute the Reserve Army Officer Training Corps on campus.

The president argued that the Quaker school's refusal
not only correlated with Jesus' teachings and Quaker tradition, but was wise on practical grounds. "We have not
been running a college, but a military training institution,"
Pennington quoted another college president as complain-

ing. The Pacific College president added that some Christian colleges substituted military for moral standards.

Some Pacific College students entered military service,
but many could not because of conscience. Twenty-five
Pacific students performed war relief service in France,
Belgium, and Germany, most with the newly formed
American Friends Service Committee. They participated
in food production and conservation work "not that war be
carried on, but that the hungry world may be fed."

President Pennington asserted that Pacific College was
better represented, proportionately, in war relief service
than any other college in the world. Following the war,

1916 baseball team. Front row: Paul Elliott, Delbert Replogle, Harold Hinshaw, Sewel Newhouse. Back row: Alfred Haworth, Vern Harrington, Emmett Gulley, Frank Colcord, (unknown first name) Pearson.

Paul Elliott, Virgil Hinshaw, and other Pacific College students played a major role in Newberg's successful effort to send a carload of flour to starving people in the war- and revolution-wracked Soviet Union.

Although Oregon Yearly Meeting officially opposed military service, most members displayed a tolerant atti-

"The world, gone astray, must be led back to the right way, and the problem of leadership is the problem of the present and early future. The world must have broad leadership, a capable leadership, a trained leadership, a Christian leadership."
—President Levi Pennington during World War I

tude toward those who disagreed. One student enlistee wrote apologetically to President Pennington, explaining his decision to join the military. Pennington expressed a Quakerly attitude:

"I honor a man for doing what seems to him the right thing to do. I have felt, as you know, that a college-bred young man could find a larger service for the country he loves than the one you have chosen. But I have tried to make it clear that I feel the deepest sense of loyalty to America, and feel that it is the duty of every one of us to serve our country to the very limit of our ability.

"Feeling as you did that your enlistment was the duty you owed your country and your flag, there was nothing else for you to do but to enlist....

"But oh! I am praying for the early coming of the day such sacrifices as are being required today may no longer be necessary. That God may hasten the coming of a just and permanent peace, and the reign of love and righteousness is my daily prayer.

"May he keep you true to your highest ideals, save you from the dangers that you may have to meet, whether they be on the earth, in the air, or on the battlefield of your own spirit. And may you come back to us—I wish that it may be soon—strong and safe and clean in body and spirit, is the wish of your sincere friend, Levi T. Pennington."

As THE WAR neared an end, the Pacific president related the College's mission to the world's needs in a way that clearly expressed Pacific College's deepest purposes. For these reasons, he submitted, the institution existed:

"The present world situation calls for every man and woman to consider seriously and earnestly the personal

Footbridge across canyon
near Kanyon (Minthorn)
Hall.

My College: Memories of Long Ago

by
Daisy Newhouse Read

By 1990, Daisy (Newhouse) Read had been the College's only living pre-World War I graduate for 27 years. Building in background is Kanyon (Minthorn) Hall.

question of personal duty. Great problems are facing the world today. Every man should make whatever contribution he can to their solution. But the greater problems still will confront the world when the present war is over and the race faces the problem of rebuilding a devastated world—a world laid waste industrially, financially, socially, morally, spiritually.

"The world, gone astray, must be led back to the right way, and the problem of leadership is the problem in the present and early future. The world must have broad leadership, a capable leadership, a trained leadership, a Christian leadership."

SUCH LEADERSHIP required an education that promoted Christlike morality and high scholarly standards. While the school proved adept at imparting lasting morality, it constantly sought to improve its academic program.

Pacific switched in 1912 from a schedule based on three terms to two semesters. In 1914 the College switched from offering two majors—classical and scientific—to three, each requiring 40 semester hours: (1) philosophy, Bible, history, public speaking; (2) sciences; and (3) foreign languages, including Grek, Latin, German and French, with Spanish added in 1921. All students took 87-97 hours of "prescribed work," including Bible (7), science (10), mathematics (6), foreign language (20), philosophy (8), history (10), public speaking (6). All took 20-30 hours of English (depending on the major) and completed the required 135 hours with electives.

27

GEORGE FOX COLLEGE AUXILIARY

A group of Newberg women interested in Christian higher education initiated the Pacific College Women's Auxiliary in 1910. The organization still actively served the College 80 years later.

The women answered two initial challenges: Wood-Mar Hall was being built and the dormitory building needed assistance. The Auxiliary declared its purpose as "primarily to enlist a larger constituency in the promotion of the interests of the college socially and to aid in its better equipment for work, along such lines as may be found to be effective."

The first committees included Care of Sick Students, Membership, Buildings, Ways and Means, Social, and House, to coordinate with corresponding committees of the Board of Managers. Near its inception, the Membership Committee launched a contest between two sides, resulting in 225 members. Through the years, membership has varied from 52 to 425. The Auxiliary maintained three branches for many years: the Seattle area, Salem, and Portland.

The Auxiliary has provided furnishings for dormitories and Wood-Mar Hall—including the president's office, the auditorium, offices, classrooms, and hallway. The women took great interest in the grounds, purchasing shrubs, flowers, lawn seed, sidewalks, lighting, driveways, and trees. Members helped students find work and canned hundreds of jars of vegetables, fruit, jams, jellies, and pickles for the dining hall. They also engaged in various money-raising projects.

Members served dozens of banquets for college-related events and community groups. They sold aluminum cookware, Silica paste, cookbooks, fancy work, foods, rummage, and paper. They sponsored benefit lectures, musical and dramatic events, and other entertainments, sometimes selling snacks during intermissions. The Auxiliary pledged $3,000 toward the first endowment campaign and participated effectively in later fund drives. Members helped set up the college domestic science (later named home economics) and commercial departments.

The Auxiliary opens every meeting with prayer. The 1912 minutes record that "Evangeline Martin prayed earnestly, expressing deep gratitude to our Father for His blessings upon us . . . and His very evident blessing upon our efforts to assist the college both in finance and enlisting people's interest . . . and His continued blessing invoked upon the college and all its interests, especially upon the faculty. A hush of solemnity came upon the meeting as we realized that we are co-laborers with Him in the effort to make the lives of our young people broader, better and more fruitful of good to the world."

In 1914 the group prayed that the "cause of righteousness might prevail in the countries at war with each other and in our own state for the abolishment of the liquor traffic." In 1921 the Auxiliary purchased five barrels of flour to assist the American Friends Service Committee in Russian relief.

Newberg community members often presented programs of general interest, sharing their professional or travel experiences. Since the 1970s, many college faculty have presented their work.

The *Newberg Graphic* commented in 1924: "Who could tell the thousand and one things that the Auxiliary is forever doing for the college? They have done so many things that no one can remember them all, but they are such fine splendid things that nobody could possibly forget them all and everybody is grateful."

For ten years, the Auxiliary sponsored a Fine Arts Festival each spring. The art and music departments were featured, along with Oregon artists showing their work in several fields. Poetry readings and drama productions were also featured.

In recent years, an annual Christmas season bazaar has been the main money-raising event. Held in the Cap & Gown Room of Heacock Commons, thousands of dollars have been raised. In consultation with the administration, the Auxiliary selects a major financial project. Through the years, every building and department has benefited from this substantial assistance.

The name became "The George Fox College Auxiliary" in 1978 in order to encourage additional male participation.

Presidents of the Pacific/George Fox College Auxiliary:

1910-1913	Ella Macy	1966-1967	Mildred Colcord
1913-1919	Rebecca Pennington	1967-1968	Elva Gregory
1919-1921	Berta K. Terrell	1968-1971	Mildred Colcord
1922-1940	Rebecca Pennington	1971-1972	Alice Ross
1941-1942	Tracie Tate	1972-1974	Helen Street
1943-1947	Louisa Hoskins	1974-1976	Verna Munn
1947-1948	Esther Thornburg	1976-1978	Elizabeth Edwards
1948-1952	Wilma Mills	1978-1979	Ruthanna Hampton
1952-1953	Elenita Bales	1979-1981	Virginia Millage
1953-1955	Fern Roberts	1981-1982	Becky LeShana
1955-1959	Mary Sutton	1982-1985	Shari Bowman
1959-1962	Arlene Moore	1985-1987	Linda Stevens
1962-1963	Rachel Gettman	1987-1988	Bonnie Hollinshead
1963-1965	Genette McNichols	1988—	Beth Bagley
1965-1966	Pauline Kent		

1911-12 basketball team. From left, seated: Ross Newby, Professor William Johnson, coach. Standing: Claude Lewis, Richard Williams, Harry Haworth, Christian Smith, Victor Rees, Howard George, Russell Parker.

1915-16 basketball team. Clockwise beginning front and center: Emmett Gulley, Frank Colcord, Walter Guyer, Coach Russell Lewis, Harold Hinshaw, Delbert Replogle.

AMOS STANBROUGH'S death in 1963 left Daisy (Newhouse) Read, Class of 1914, the only living pre-World War I graduate. (One alumnus, E. Locke Silva, was two years older, but did not graduate until 1922.) Sixty-four years later, Daisy Read wrote a booklet entitled *My College: Memories of Long Ago*. In it she recalled a day's reprieve from classes in the spring of 1911 to carry books into the "library," which occupied the southwest corner of the new Wood-Mar Hall (the president's office before 1991). The students also swept the Wood-Mar auditorium, "the biggest room I had ever seen," its floor covered with sawdust and lumber scraps.

Daisy Read remembered a day the administration canceled chapel because a prankster had left some hydrochloric acid [perhaps with iron sulfide producing hydrogen sulfide—"rotten egg gas"] in Wood-Mar auditorium "and it sure was generating! It took several days to get the smell out." She also mentioned the compulsory daily chapels, and one speaker who warned that cigarette paper soaked in water would kill a mouse. "Some of the young men caught some mice and had them drink the water the paper had been soaked in, and it didn't even make them sick. Some of these young men, when they found out that the mice didn't die, started smoking cigarettes, and one that I know of smoked as long as he lived."

The early administrations valued athletics, but assigned no one specific coaching duties until 1910, when the school appointed science teacher William Johnson as athletic director and coach. In 1916 athletes Frank Colcord and Harold Hinshaw directed a gymnasium repair crew. The building had been drafty when constructed from two barns 21 years earlier, and age had not improved it. According to *The Crescent*, the repair work succeeded:

"The seats have been boarded up so that the spectators will no longer suffer from the cold wind from below. The water pipes have been packed in sawdust to prevent freezing, the foundations have been repaired, chimneys rebuilt and electric lights changed."

Pacific College produced some noteworthy basketball teams. The 1915-16 squad won 11 games and lost only two,

Delbert Replogle scores 40 points as Pacific College downs Philomath College 72-21 on January 29, 1916. The next day he scored 22 in a 56-9 win over Albany (Lewis and Clark) College.

scoring 673 points against only 249 for the opponents. Delbert Replogle, one of the outstanding scorers in the College's history, starred. Friday, January 29, 1916, he scored 40 points against Philomath College; the next day he added 22 against Albany (Lewis and Clark) College.

The following season Coach Russel Lewis's quintet won the Willamette Valley League championship and defeated Oregon State Agricultural College (renamed Oregon State College three years later) 34-25. Replogle had graduated, but several stars remained. The team included Walter Guyer, Lester Wright, Lloyd Edwards, Harold Hinshaw, Frank Colcord, Howard Elliott, and Captain Emmett Gulley.

The Crescent reported the final game of the 1916-17 season, a 19-14 win over McMinnville (Linfield) College:

"...A hundred Newbergers, and supporters of the P.C. team from Springbrook, Dundee and near-by towns, went down on a special [electric train] Friday evening to see the P.C. boys finish the task of winning the pennant for this year. They were not disappointed...."

1916-17 championship basketball team. Front row: Walter Guyer, Lester Wright, Emmett Gulley, Lloyd Edwards, Harold Hinshaw. Back row: Frank Colcord, Coach Russell Lewis, Howard Elliott.

March 2, 1917.

REMEMBER THE GLEE CLUB, MONDAY, MARCH 12

THE CRESCENT

PACIFIC COLLEGE OREGON · CHRISTIANITY AND · 1891

VOLUME XXVIII | NEWBERG, OREGON, FRIDAY, MARCH 2, 1917 | NUMBER 10

PACIFIC WINS CHAMPIONSHIP

LEAGUE ALL-STARS PICKED BY LEWIS

Gulley, Colcord and Elliot, of Pacific College, Chosen by Coach.

The task of picking the All-Star team of the league is especially difficult this year on account of the scarcity of real merit among the forwards. Otherwise one can pick a team of distinguished ability. Gulley of P. C. is center. Colcord of P. C. would play one guard, and Irle of P. U. the other. Irle's experience in the game and his good generalship make him captain. We shall ask Fenenga of P. U. to change from center, where he has played this year, to forward. He has been one of the best men in the league at scoring, and plays consistently. For the other forward, one looks in vain. Of three candidates, Champion of McMinnville, Hinshaw of P. C., and Elliot of P. C., Elliot impresses me as being the best man to work with the rest of the team I have chosen. This judgment is based not alone upon points scored, but on aggressiveness and team work as well, on his natural adaptability to the game, in short.

R. W. Lewis, Coach.

THE PERCENTAGES

	Won	Lost	Perc.
Pacific College	5	1	833 1-3
Pacific University	4	2	666 2-3
McMinnville College	3	3	500
Philomath College	0	6	000

LYCEUM NUMBER BY DR. HERBSMAN PLEASES

The lecture entitled "Life's Balance Sheet" delivered by Dr. J. C. Herbsman Saturday evening in Wood-Mar Hall, was one of the best Lyceum numbers that have been given yet this year.

The lecture was a discussion of the characteristics of the fresh-

Continued on page 4

LAST TWO GAMES WON BY QUAKERS VARSITY PLAYS FAST BALL

Special Train Helps Team to Defeat McMinnville College 19 to 14.

Accompanied by three carloads of enthusiastic rooters, 100 in all, Pacific Varsity invaded McMinnville and carried off the game by a score of 19 to 14. This was the final game of the season and gives P. C. the championship of the non-conference colleges in Oregon.

The large floor, which is used for dancing, had been scrubbed and was still wet, making it extremely slick resulting in several hard falls. In spite of this they outplayed the Mac team, who were not so seriously hindered. At the end of the first half the score stood 12 to 11 for Pacific.

Between halves Mac tried to instill confidence in her team by a demonstration in which P. C. was characterized as a baby which was in need of a spanking

Continued on page 4

Pacific Avenges Defeat at Pacific University With a Score of 37 to 19.

The Quakers evened up old scores in their last home appearance by defeating Pacific University 37 to 19. The game was slow in the first half but hotly contested throughout. But once, near the end of the first half, were the men from Forest Grove in the lead and that lasted but for a few minutes.

The score was 15 to 14 for the Quakers at the end of the first period. None of the varsity seemed able to hit the basket and the fouls were numerous. Robinson of P. U. put in their only two field baskets in this half and 11 points were made on free shots by Fenanga.

Things were much different the second half. The Quakers seemed to hit their stride and nothing could stop them. Paci-

Continued on page 3

DAVID STARR JORDAN GIVES TWO ADDRESSES

Pacific is Fortunate in Hearing Great Pacifist. Chapel Talk Given.

David Starr Jordan, chancellor of Stanford University and known the wide world over for his interest in peace, honored Pacific College and Newberg by giving two lectures on Peace, last Wednesday and Thursday. He held two large audiences for an hour and one half with his stories of the horrors of war, and ever present wit. He also spoke at length on Herbert C. Hoover, once a student in Pacific Academy and now world famous for his work in Belgian relief.

Dr. Jordan spoke with such personal familiarity of great people and great events all over the world that no one could help but know he lives in a world of big things. He is a man who firmly believes in peace, but not at any price, because "when we get to haggling over the price we don't have any peace." Dr. Jordan believes that a compulsory system of military training would be the worst calamity which could befall the United States.

He does not blame either the kaiser or the German people for the atrocities practiced in the present war, but the military system which has control of the government, ruling both ruler

Continued on page 3

MEN ARE SHOWN MORE INTELLIGENT

That women, who received the best grades last semester, do not have so general a knowledge of affairs as the men was shown in the results of the President's investigations. In response to a cry from the men protesting that they really knew more than did

Continued on page 2

THE TEAM THAT DID IT

Irene Hodgin

31

1914 baseball team. Front row: Vestel, DeMag, Jr., S. Newhouse. Second row: Hinshaw, D. Butt, Frank Colcord, E. George, Delbert Replogle. Back row: R. Langworthy, Emmett Gulley, M. Elliott.

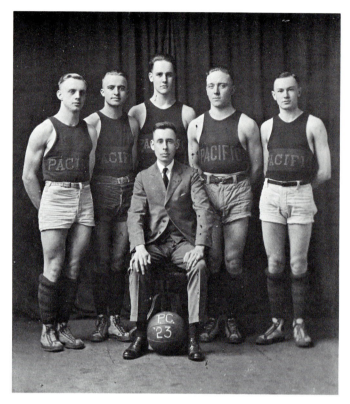

"Gulley, who was playing his last game of basket ball for P.C., as he graduates this year, was a tower of strength both on offense and defense. He held the strong McMinnville center scoreless while he himself made four points, broke up McMinnville plays constantly and was a contributing factor to many of the scores made by his team mates.

"Elliott played a star game at forward, with a total score of 11, the highest number of points made by any player, part of which resulted from his foul goal throwing.

"*The Oregonian* asked Coach Lewis to name a league all-star team. His selections included Emmett Gulley, center, Frank Colcord, guard, and Howard Elliott, forward, along with two Pacific University players."

The 1917 baseball team went undefeated behind Emmett Gulley's pitching and Howard Elliott's hitting. Each made the league's all-star team.

The 1924 baseball nine again won the league championship. Team captain Hubert Armstrong, center fielder Dick Everest, and pitchers Wendall Woodward and Gus Hanke also excelled.

Other intercollegiate sports during this period included men's track, football, and tennis. An intramural basketball program also generated considerable campus enthusiasm. In 1916 the College formed a "Gold Q Club" for men athletes, but later changed it to the "Gold P Club." (In 1934 the women athletes formed a new "Gold Q Club.")

During these years, Pacific women began to develop a program in intercollegiate athletics. For a time, Gladys (Hannon) Keyes and Lucille Davis headed the tennis association, which had been reorganized in 1912. In 1917, the College formed a Women's Athletic Association and built tennis courts in front of Kanyon Hall for women's use. On

1912 baseball team. Seated: Delbert Replogle, Langworthy, Elliott. Standing: O. Hadley, Wiley, R. Butt, Coach Ronk, C. Smith, Vincent, Craven, E. George.

May 17, 1918, Pacific College beat McMinnville (Linfield) College 7-2, 2-6, 7-5 in the Newberg school's first intercollegiate women's tennis match. *The Crescent* told the story:

"President Pennington was given a new and uncommon pleasure on Monday, June 3, when he awarded gold Q's to the two victorious lady tennis players—Pearl Grieve and Mary Pennington [Pearson]. In the two matches with McMinnville Pacific's representatives won both single and double tournaments . . . .

32

1921 baseball team. Coach Floyd Perisho, Harlan Rinard,
Paul Elliott, Lester Wright, Zenas Perisho, Wendell
Woodward, Brooks Terrill, Eldon (Dick) Everest, Hermon
Elliott, Cassius Carter, Chi Sung Pil.

"For the past two years especially interest has been
growing in gym work and tennis, but not until this year
have the Pacific College girls ever participated in intercollegiate athletics. The results have been exceedingly gratify-
ing and certainly give encouragement for future and more
extended activity."

The Women's Athletic Association decided to award letter sweaters in 1922. Females could win the gold "Q"
through success in tennis or hiking—the latter requiring
300 miles of activity.

THE LYCEUM COURSE and Forensics team remained
active, providing nonathletic cocurricular activities. The
College especially emphasized speaking and public debate.
Royal Gettman won the state oratorical contest in 1924,
speaking on "The Ku Klux Klan and National Unity."

President Pennington, himself a superb speaker and
writer, filled Lyceum and Chautauqua lecterns for many
years and won several state and regional adult oratorical

33

1924 football team. Seated: Glen Rinard, Charles Beals, Harold Rinard, Arthur Everest, Eldon (Dick) Everest, Marion Winslow. Middle: Wendell Hutchens, Wilbur Elliott, Floyd Lienard, Ivor Jones, Glen (Tub) Brown, Alfred (Spud) Everest, Edgar Street, Homer Nordyke. Back: Assistant Coach Frank Roberts, Ralph Hester, Milton (Spike) Wells, Harry Schmeltzer, Ernest Knapp, Robert Whitlock, Hubert Armstrong, Coach Dwight Michener.

The first pulpit used in Newberg, and inspiration for the Old Pulpit Extemporaneous Speaking Contest, later named the Extemporaneous Sermonette Contest.

contests. He continually emphasized both oral and written discourse.

A few years earlier, Evangeline Martin and Amanda Woodward found the pulpit built by David J. Wood and used in the original Friends Meeting in Newberg. They could not bear to see it destroyed.

"As we gazed upon it we could visualize dear old William Hobson delivering his earnest messages from behind it; Dr. Elias Jessup holding the people spellbound by his powerful sermons; Dr. H. J. Minthorn, Jesse and Mary Edwards, Martin Cook, and many others...."

They put the pulpit in the college museum; in 1917 Professor Mark Mills used it to initiate the Old Pulpit Extemporaneous Speaking Contest. That year Lloyd W. Edwards won. In 1918, Irene Hodgin defeated eight other contestants. She spoke on "What a Pacific College Girl Expects of a Pacific College Boy." According to *The Crescent*:

"She said that a P.C. girl wished a P.C. boy first of all to be a gentleman, one who is living up to his ideals, full of initiative, vim and pep, a good student, neat and clean in appearance and courteous. In the second place she expects him to be a good friend. She does not want a foolish friendship, rather a true comradeship. Last and most important, she expects him to be a Christian, for only Christians can hope to have the distinctive characteristics of a noble personality."

A preliminary contest preceded the championship competition. In the finals, the top five contestants each received three topics and had two class periods to prepare to give a chapel address without notes. The College discontinued the contest in 1963.

Pacific College women seeking increased literary appreciation and fellowship formed the Trefian Literary Society in 1914. The Agoreton Literary Society continued to serve similar needs for men. During this period, the College performed from two to four dramatic events each year, including such titles as *Prudence Says No* (1919), *MacBeth* (1921), *The Sisterhood of Bridget* (1925), and *The Goose Hangs High* (1926).

Beginning in 1919, President Pennington took a leave for two years to lead the "Friends Forward Movement." This program aimed to develop unified goals among American Friends and to promote evangelism, intercession, and stewardship of property. It served Friends nationally by reemphasizing direct personal relationship with God and direct personal service to humanity.

Professor John Mills served as acting president during Pennington's absence. A graduate of William Penn College, Mills had pastored several Friends churches and served as Nebraska Yearly Meeting clerk. He discontinued seminary to move to Newberg. Like Pennington, Mills emphasized that the College's success depended upon the Yearly Meeting's spiritual power and active support.

Acting President Mills reported in 1920 that "an epidemic of la grippe, or influenza, unprecedented in the history of the College," cost 60 percent of the student body

Queen Anna (Mills) Moore and her May Day float, 1922. Bottom: All-school picnic, 1923.

Right: May Day court, 1924, Florence (Lee) Lienard, Mary (Elliott) Edmondson, Eva Miles (queen), Delight Carter, Flora Campbell.

Queen Anna (Mills) Moore and her May Day float, 1922. Bottom: All-school picnic, 1923.

Right: May Day court, 1924, Florence (Lee) Lienard, Mary (Elliott) Edmondson, Eva Miles (queen), Delight Carter, Flora Campbell.

from one to three weeks' schooling. In addition, *The Crescent* reported that the terrible, nationwide epidemic caused a ban on public gatherings that closed the school more than eight weeks. Students and faculty replaced the missed time with Saturday and holiday classes.

FRIENDS COMPRISED 70 percent of the 1918-19 student body; the next year that percentage rose to 73 (103 of the 141 college and academy students). An increasing enrollment necessitated some improvements, including new furnaces for the science building and dormitories.

Mills sounded a familiar note: His major problem was finances. The $119,000 endowment helped, but proved inadequate. In 1920 the managers launched a campaign for an additional $175,000 endowment. The income, they projected, would supplement meager operating funds, provide essential salary increases, and lead to standardization.

Mills' 1920 report to the Yearly Meeting emphasizes: "Professors who were already giving as much as one-half their possible salaries to the College could not be asked to continue when the high cost of living reduced even that meagre pittance by one-half." Further, the College found it increasingly difficult to retain students without standardization.

The campaign began in December 1920 at the Newberg Friends Church, where the 200 in attendance—including many college students—pledged $25,000. First Friends Church in Portland soon added $10,000. Salem Quarterly Meeting and Newberg businessmen contributed an additional $12,000. Levi Pennington and William V. Coffin, endowment secretary for the Friends Forward Movement, visited Eastern Quakers and they donated $51,000.

Then the drive slowed. Some officials in the Bureau of Educational Standards advised Pennington, who had returned to the presidency in 1921, to make Pacific a two-year school because of the competition for students and funds in Willamette Valley. They also cited the narrowness of the College's constituent base: "On account of the extremely small but very faithful body of Friends in the state, it is doubtful if the institution should aspire to do more than Junior College . . . ."

Nevertheless, a final effort in 1925 put the drive over the top. Several times that year, Pennington traveled to Washington and exchanged nearly 100 pages of correspondence with a Mr. Zook, higher education specialist with the U.S. Bureau of Education, attempting to prove that the College merited standardization. Finally, on December 12, 1925, the Bureau representative sent Pennington the following telegram:

"I am glad to inform you that after careful investigation by our specialist of higher education of the situation at Pacific College, I feel that the Bureau of Education is justified in recognizing Pacific College as meeting the present requirements for standard colleges in Oregon."

The next day Levi Pennington, who was in the East at the time, telegraphed the College: "On Zook's recommendation U.S. Bureau of Education recognizes Pacific as standard college." *The Crescent* described the ensuing cerebration:

"Monday morning when announcement was made to the students and the day was declared a holiday, students rushed about collecting noise machines and whetting their pep. All the while the old bell in the Academy building was

---

*"On Zook's recommendation
U.S. Bureau of Education recognizes Pacific
as standard college."*

—Telegram from President Pennington

---

clanging out the good news. As soon as everyone was on hand with his instrument of clamor, a grand procession led by the seniors enthroned in a trustworthy Ford upon which they had lavished much Old Gold and Navy Blue crepe paper, set out from the college campus to parade the town.

"First street was bombarded with songs and yells and noises undescribable, and the high school suffered alike. Mrs. Martin, who has done so much for the college, was not forgotten and the procession stopped in front of her house that she might see and enjoy their enthusiasm.

When the crowd had again assembled in the chapel, Mrs. Woodward reviewed some of the history of the institution and told how they raised money for the building fund in the old days. The rest of the celebration was postponed until President Pennington's return."

The next January 4, Newberg rejoiced again. The 7:30 p.m. event included a major parade of 20 cars through the town, a bonfire at the College, and music by the Newberg Berrian Band. Then the crowd transferred to the Wood-Mar auditorium, where S. M. Calkins gave the city's congratulations and appreciation, Chairman Thomas Hester represented the trustees, and President Pennington expressed the College's indebtedness to its supporters.

THE FIRST HALF of Levi Pennington's 30-year presidency brought hard work, frustration, and considerable success. The president deserves honor for the College's endowment and standardization—indeed, for its survival.

The board recorded this resolution in 1926: "Resolved, that the Board of Managers extend to President Pennington an expression of the gratitude and appreciation it feels for his untiring efforts during the past months and years in helping to secure standardization of Pacific College."

The hard times had not ended, however. Financial and theological problems made Pennington's second 15 years even more difficult than the first.

Chapter Three

PACIFIC COLLEGE grew from 15 to 76 students and from seven to 22 faculty during its first 35 years. (The faculty served both the Academy and College.) During the same period, the annual operating budget increased from just under $5,000 to slightly over $37,000, and the United States Bureau of Educational Standards recognized the College as a standard institution. By 1926, some might have felt confident the newly accredited school had turned the corner to prosperity.

That would have been too optimistic an assessment, however. Although the College had attained a sizeable endowment and standardization, many problems remained. During Pennington's final 15 years as president, an unstable financial picture continued. Divisions in American Protestantism and Quakerism eroded the College's support base and eventually threatened its very existence.

Not long after standardization in 1925, the school faced its worst financial crisis to that time. Although the increased endowment provided some new income, it did not fully meet month-to-month operating expenses. At that time, College assets totaled approximately $500,000. Tuition, endowment earnings, and gifts each produced about equal income. The administration tried numerous methods to increase each revenue source.

Sometimes the entire Pacific College community cooperated in small-scale money raising. For example, in 1929 Newberg resident W. W. Silver offered the College all the prunes the students and faculty could pick in one day. The administration declared a holiday and the student body and faculty labored together in the prune orchard.

The Crescent reported that "work was begun with a will, and the spirit of 'all we can do for the College' never lessened throughout the entire day." Students and faculty picked 1,822 boxes, worth $872.50, which the College and student body shared equally. (For a brief time thereafter, Pacific College athletic teams bore the nickname "Prunepickers.")

Class of 1927. Front row: Hilma (Hendrickson) Winslow, Esther (Haworth) Woodward, Fleeta (Leland) DeGraff, Edna (Doree) Hartin, June Whitlock. Back row: Walter Cook, Ralph Hester, Therman Evans, Marion Winslow.

Winding the Maypole, 1928.

Such cooperative hard work and generosity helped, but barely dented the deficiency. The year after accreditation, the board borrowed to cover part of a $13,000 deficit. In November 1928, it offered the faculty "deepest regrets" that it could not pay that month's salaries.

IRONICALLY, that very week nearly all college personnel probably cast their presidential ballots for their own alumnus, Herbert Hoover, and for his campaign theme of national prosperity. "Two chickens in every pot and a car in every garage" seemed a reasonable expectation. The

Fall Regular Student Enrollment, 1926-1940		
1926—81	1931—84	1936—95
1927—73	1932—75	1937—98
1928—59	1933—105	1938—97
1929—75	1934—126	1939—87
1930—86	1935—119	1940—86

OLD BRUIN

Speech given by a member of Pacific College's first graduating class, Amos Stanbrough, 1893, at the alumni banquet, June 1, 1931. Stanbrough's memory erred on a few points, but for the most part, this is probably an accurate accounting. See Page 101 for the rest of the Bruin story.

Students in late 1920s with 40-plus-year-old Bruin hide. Front row: Rachel (Lundquist) Huntington Winslow, Gwen (Hanson) Winters, Rosa (Aebischer) Hester, Velda (Livingston) Sweet, Bruin. Back row: Sandy Brown, Bill Sweet, Everett Gettman, Arthur Winters, Glen Rinard, Stanley Kendall, Charles Beals, Glen Everest.

When Pacific Academy opened its doors to students for the first time on September 28, 1885, there were enrolled three members of the Frank family, Reuben, John, and Lenora.

The father of the Frank children, besides being a farmer, was also a music teacher. His specialty was the old fashioned "singing school," practically a chorus class, that met once a week in some convenient place. Since many of Mr. Frank's pupils were Academy students, it was quite logical that some of the meetings were held in the Academy building, though having no connection with the school.

In the autumn of 1887, Mr. Frank and his son, Reuben, were hunting in the mountains west of Carlton when they found a large black bear with a small cub. Mr. Frank shot the adult bear and Reuben caught the cub. They brought the baby bear home with them and Reuben gave it to Lenora for a pet. The cub soon learned that Lenora was the one who fed him and would follow her around like a dog and enjoyed wrestling with her. During the next summer Bruin grew so much that the wrestling games had to be discontinued. Also, it was no longer possible to allow him to run at large. As winter approached, the question of better protection than a chain fastened to a post or a tree in the yard presented a problem.

Professor George Hartley and his wife, both teaching in Friends Pacific Academy at that time, had built a large log house east of the Wynooski creek canyon and a few hundred feet north of what we called the Portland road (now highway 99W), or east Main Street. Lenora Frank offered to give Bruin to Professor Hartley and he gladly accepted the gift. The Hartleys had built a foot-bridge across a ravine that was between their house and the Portland road. The floor of this bridge was probably about 12 or 15 feet above the bottom of the ravine. Professor Hartley constructed a bear pit in the ravine just at the side of the bridge so we could stand on the bridge and throw peanuts and apples to the bear. Bruin became quite adept at catching with either his mouth our his paws.

Bruin had good quarters and excellent care. He became fat, but he missed the races he had enjoyed with Lenora Frank. He became restless and managed to escape

from his pen two or three times. Since he knew nothing of life away from people he was easily found and led back to his home. However, the last time he escaped he got into a neighbor's chicken house and did considerable damage. As Professor Hartley was not to be with the Academy the next year, he thought this was a good time to get rid of Bruin. The Portland Zoo had all the bears it could care for and Professor Hartley would not allow Bruin to fall into the hands of someone who might mistreat him, so the problem of what to do with him became a serious one.

Finally, Nate Stanley, who had a meat market on First Street, suggested a solution. Many people of Newberg had heard pioneer talk about how good bear steaks were, but had never had an opportunity to try them. Mr. Stanley promised that Bruin's demise would be painlessly accomplished, the meat market would take care of the edible portions, and Professor Hartley could have the skin. He proposed that he and Amos Stanbrough would preserve the skin, stuff and mount it as an addition to the very meager museum that had been started. Mrs. Hartley had not been very enthusiastic about the rug idea, so the new plan was adopted.

It was some days after the skin was removed from the carcass before we received it, and as the skin had not been properly cared for, we were not able to save the front feet, except the claws. From that time on Bruin apparently stood with his front feet buried in the moss and leaves in which he was standing. As a matter of fact, the front feet were buried about where the Newberg Friends Church now stands. The interment was without ceremony and rather hastily performed, I myself wielding the shovel with more pleasure than mourning.

The rest of the skin was treated with preservative chemicals while we prepared a frame for the body. The frame was composed of iron rods and heavy wire, padded with cotton, excelsior and burlap, and was mounted on a board. After its chemical treatment, the skin was not quite so disagreeable to handle and, as we had been careful in our measurements, it was fitted onto the body with very little modification.

While Bruin was being cared for, preparations were being made to move the Academy buildings to the present college campus so that Pacific College would be able to open in the fall of 1891. I am not certain about this statement, but I believe that Bruin traveled from one campus to the other inside one of the buildings. At any rate, the chemical fumes had all summer in which to evaporate, so Bruin was with the stuffed birds and squirrels in the little museum when Pacific College opened on September 9, 1891.

After a few years as a museum specimen, moths and other agencies caused Bruin to lose his charm. In fact, he looked more like a tramp than like the gentleman he had always been. So Bruin went into the discard and was sent to the basement to be cremated in the furnace. However, his iron frame presented a problem and he was put in a corner and forgotten.

Old Bruin made one more notable public appearance before becoming the object of more or less friendly class encounters. One Halloween some students took Bruin from his nook in the basement just to show him the changes in the city since he took his last ride down the street. The fact that there was a meeting in progress in a lodge hall that evening suggested that Bruin might meet some of his old friends there. So Bruin, still mounted on his original board, was stationed in front of the door in such a manner that a string attached to the door would cause him to move forward to meet the person coming out. The report of the encounter says that the yell with which he was greeted could have been heard the full length of Main Street.

Bruin returned to his nook in the furnace room, there to remain until he became the center of certain strenuous student activities with which my assignment, "The Origin of Old Bruin," is not concerned.

1928-29 basketball team. Front row: Harold Smith, Bill Woods, Dick Everest, Bill Sweet, Ben Huntington, student manager. Back row: Fred Harle, Frank Cole, Coach Emmett Gulley, Dick Haworth, Bob Bissett.

nation would end poverty by outgrowing it. No one could have predicted the critical period the nation faced.

The college board decided that year to concentrate on Portland in another major financial campaign. It set the goal at $100,000—about four times the school's annual payroll. Yet within three years depression-induced national unemployment had skyrocketed from 3.2 to 24.1 percent, while the nation lost more than half its Gross National Product.

In addition, the funding campaign faced logistical problems. The board asked President Walter Dexter of Whittier College to assist in a kickoff banquet, but he declined. Since no comparable substitute was available, Levi Pennington volunteered to take charge himself.

The financial drive failed. Plagued by the developing depression, many prospective donors could not pledge; others promised but defaulted. J. Henry Scattergood of Philadelphia pledged $12,500 on condition that it would complete a $300,000 endowment. When the campaign collapsed, he refused to give the money.

Nevertheless, President Pennington and the board exhibited remarkable optimism. Near the end of 1930 they discussed another fund drive, this one to be undertaken only if all the supporters responded enthusiastically. The constituents showed scant enthusiasm—in the first two months they donated only $600 in cash, $1,000 in pledges, and some produce.

Operating expenses so outdistanced income that the next summer college officials took a drastic step—they

PACIFIC COLLEGE

Levi T. Pennington
PRES.

NEWBERG 1930

dipped into the precious, hard-earned endowment funds. They also considered but rejected a proposal to enlarge the board to include several potential contributors outside the Friends Church. Meanwhile, many students could not pay the $100 annual tuition charge. The administration reluctantly decided to continue the longstanding policy of withholding academic credit from students with unpaid bills.

Still undaunted by the deepening depression, the board agreed in 1931 to take bold action. Upon receipt of an optimistic letter from Irene H. Gerlinger, a friend of the College, the trustees named her vice-president in a specific attempt to broaden the College's constituency, with emphasis on solicitation among eastern Friends.

"If I could be assured of the whole-hearted cooperation of the college administration, trustees, and alumni," Gerlinger wrote, "I would be willing to undertake a campaign of education of Oregon people through which I believe we could over a period of three to five years achieve our goal [completion of $300,000 endowment, pay past liabilities and some current operating expenses]. When we had gained some momentum here, I believe Friends in the other parts of the country would be rallied to our support.

The campaign would be one of peaceful penetration into people's consciences and pocketbooks and one in keeping with the best traditions of the Friends. It would not be a hurry-up, expensive affair like the usual professionally conducted ones with which we are familiar."

Gerlinger experienced some success, but not enough to provide solvency. She also produced some new ideas, including a proposal to rename the school "Herbert Hoover College," in order to broaden its appeal among Quakers and other constituent groups. The board declined the name change and a suggestion to initiate a "vanishing chain program" for raising income.

However, it accepted her proposal for a nationwide Pacific College Auxiliary and temporarily employed an office manager who received 20 percent of the collections. Unhappily, this idea also achieved limited success. Gerlinger produced little more than her cost to the College, so in 1934 the board decided to terminate her services. However, when she responded with an offer to continue at $1 a year, the trustees retained her temporarily.

Nevertheless, the College's longstanding policy of seeking eastern Quaker money began to lose credibility. Some wondered why the College should seek their support, since economic problems were endemic to the whole nation. As one Philadelphia Friend remarked, depression hit the East as hard as the West. Perhaps the Newberg school should be helping others rather than continually begging money.

PRESIDENT PENNINGTON proposed a plan in 1933 to raise $10,000 in one year by establishing four $2,500 quotas: Newberg, Portland, Salem, and one combining the rest of Oregon and eastern Friends. Again, the program achieved only limited success.

Later that year, Virgil Hinshaw traveled as field secretary on the College's behalf. Board member Laura Hammer spent the summer of 1934 visiting the Herbert Hoover family in California and Friends in the East. She reported a very cordial reception, with many people expressing real interest in the school's welfare, but not much new money.

The next year, the College hired Herman O. Miles as financial secretary and sent him east "to interview wealthy Friends." He died suddenly, however, before completing a year at the College.

Each effort raised some money, but not enough to balance the budget. Undaunted, the board in 1935 established a six-year goal for increasing the endowment to $500,000. A $25,000 award from Eldridge A. Stuart of Los Angeles (connected with the Carnation Foundation) brought much initial encouragement and provided scholarship aid. However, the campaign committee found no other major donors. By the end of Pennington's presidency in 1941, the total endowment had reached about $275,000—an increase of a little over $50,000 since the school's standardization in 1925.

EVEN BEFORE the depression, Friends Pacific Academy became a casualty. Early in 1929, the board sponsored a public meeting in which long-time supporters Chester A. Hadley, W. W. Silver, C. A. Dimond, C. Aebischer, and others discussed the issue. They concluded that the preparatory school, whose enrollment had declined to 60 from its 1922 peak of 86, represented a liability that could not be continued.

In their official minutes, the managers pointed out that in addition to the financial burden, the Academy's rivalry with Newberg High School brought antagonism and a loss of support from Newberg patrons; few Friends students from outside Newberg attended; standardizing agencies uniformly recommended against college preparatory departments; every inspector under the United States Bureau of Educational Standards recommended the action; and every other four-year Quaker college in America had already discontinued its preparatory department. The school closed that spring, except for nine seniors who stayed to complete their preparatory careers at the Academy.

Ⅰɴ 1932 THE COLLEGE faculty took sacrificial action: Emma Hodgin, Alice Meyers, and Hubert Armstrong resigned. The teachers recognized that the resignations not only interrupted three careers, they also increased teaching loads and eliminated some course offerings. However, the faculty felt the financial exigencies impelled a drastic response.

The teachers took an even more drastic step, revealed in this message to the board:

"To the Board of Managers of Pacific College.
Dear Friends:
As members of the Faculty of Pacific College we are keenly conscious of the serious financial situation in which the college finds itself, and we sympathize deeply with you in the financial problem which faces you in these

Class of 1932 at the Friends Church. LaVerne (Hutchens) Moore, Dorothea (Nordyke) Hart, Lincoln Wirt, Levi Pennington, Eliza (Hadley) Hall, Elinor (Whipple) Stickney, Doris (Gettman) Allen.

> *"We are convinced that Pacific College has a mission to fulfill, and we desire to offer you every possible cooperation in seeking to fulfill this mission. To this end, we are united in offering as a gift to the college one-tenth of our next year's salaries."*
> —Letter from the faculty to the board in 1932.

---

extremely difficult times. We are aware that if the college is to continue its usefulness, it will be necessary for those most closely connected with it to contribute to its support to an extent involving genuine sacrifice.

"We are convinced that Pacific College has a mission to fulfill, and we desire to offer you every possible cooperation in seeking to fulfill this mission.

"To this end we are united in offering as a gift to the college one-tenth of our next year's salaries.

"In doing this we are venturing to hope that the members of the college board and other friends of the college, who, as it seems to us, should be as much interested in the

maintenance of the college as we are, may feel the challenge to similar sacrificial giving.

> On behalf of the faculty for 1932-33,
> Levi T. Pennington, President
> Mary C. Sutton, Secretary"

The board applauded this generous offer from teachers already receiving what President Pennington called the lowest faculty salaries in Oregon. (Full-time salaries at Pacific College ranged from $1,200 to $1,750, about half that paid to Oregon state system college teachers, and presumably somewhat lower than other private schools.) The faculty requested that the board use the savings to assist needy students, thereby providing 20 greatly needed $100 full-tuition scholarships.

The board and constituency apparently did not immediately "feel the challenge to similar sacrificial giving." Not everyone gave the College ten percent. Still, Oregon Yearly Meeting's gift income remained impressive for a 3,000-member, depression-wracked religious body. Gifts routed through the Yearly Meeting—not including those paid directly by individuals—totaled $4,602, $7,618, and $4,815 for 1933 to 1935.

Even with the faculty reduction, the College could not meet its payroll. The board adopted a policy in 1933 guaranteeing faculty only 60 percent of their salaries, "the balance to be raised and paid if at all possible, but no salary indebtedness beyond the 60 percent to be carried over to the following year."

Faculty members discussed the new policy and reluctantly agreed that under the emergency circumstances, they had no choice but to accept. Few realized, however, that the practice would continue for a decade. For ten years the College paid only 60 percent of its contracted payroll—and sometimes failed to meet even that figure.

Although budgeted an annual salary of $3,000, Levi Pennington recalled many years later that for a time during the depression his monthly paycheck was $57.50, "and two Decembers in succession there was no check at all—Merry Christmas! My secretary got nearly 50 percent more pay than I did, for the law required that janitors, secretaries and other employees of the College be paid in full, but mere presidents and faculty members could work for nothing if they wanted to—or had to."

The College's 1939-41 "Cash Disbursements and Receipts" book reveals that Levi Pennington received salary payments of only $969 during his final year as president. The same source shows that the faculty averaged less than $700 annually.

Faculty members regretted the missed paydays, and with reference to their colleague Oliver Weesner, who doubled as college treasurer, lamented with dry, sympathetic humor:

"Christmas came and Christmas went,
But Weesner never paid a cent."

Faculty representatives met regularly with the board and also on a joint faculty-board-administrative subcommittee that considered financial problems. They therefore never suffered the loneliness of sacrifice without full comprehension. Knowing all the facts and recognizing that the board sympathized, personnel maintained positive morale through the depression years. Despite the obstacles, most stayed on, year after year.

considered an attempt to secure New Deal government funds for an addition to the gymnasium but found the plan to be unfeasible.

In 1939, chemistry teacher Laurence Skene and custodian Harlan Jones directed a major remodeling of Kanyon (Minthorn) Hall, which included moving the main entrance from the building's west to south side. Field Secretary Veldon Diment raised $6,500. Faculty and friends donated material and labor. At the same time, workers extended River Street through the campus, connecting it with North Street.

IN THIS ERA, the College continued to emphasize the spoken language and produced successful forensics teams. Esther (Miller) McVey won several honors, including first place in the Oregon women's extempore speaking contest. As a member of the Oregon Forensic Association, Pacific fielded annual debate teams and engaged in after-dinner speaking contests, the Old Line Oratorical Contest, and regional and national peace oratorical contests.

The Trefian Literary Society celebrated its 25th anniversary in 1940. Esther May (Weesner) Thomas and Irene (Swanson) Haisch served as presidents during that year.

As a teacher at Pacific from 1932 to 1935, Annice Carter directed 12 three-act plays and several other dramatic events. In 1935, over 40 students participated in the Gilbert and Sullivan opera *Trial by Jury*, with Helen Lou (Povenmire) Baker, Ray Hansberry, and Eugene Coffin singing the leading roles. The same year, Emmett Gulley directed *El Si De Las Ninas*, starring Harvey Campbell, Doris (Darnielle) Sics, and Dick Wilcox. Two years later, Veva (Garrett) Miller, who earned an excellent reputation as drama coach, directed—and Howard Harrison and Esther May (Weesner) Thomas starred in—Booth Tarkington's *Clarence*.

With the approach of World War II, the College produced a World War I drama, *The Enemy*, which, according to the 1938 *L'Ami*, "dealt with the insanity of war." The same year, Howard Harrison and Ruth Hodson starred in the light-hearted *Charley's Aunt*. Drama director Marian Sanders featured A. A. Milne's *Dover Road*, with David Michener and Corinne (Rickert) Wenrick, and Heinrich Ibsen's *The Master Builder*, starring Howard Harrison and Helen Robertson, in 1940.

Alexander Hull completed his 25 years at Pacific College in 1935. A nationally known composer recognized in *Who's Who in America* as both musician and writer, Hull brought the College distinction during his long tenure. Several Pacific College chorus members also sang with the Portland Junior Symphony. By Hull's final year, the chorus included 39 voices.

Frank and Genevieve Cole honored at May Day, 1930, and with Governor's Volunteerism Award, 1990.

Carl Sandoz in 1990, wearing letterman's sweater from his illustrious athletic career (1928-1934). He won five college letters as a Pacific Academy student, then 12 more while in college. His 17 letters, for football, basketball, track, soccer, and tennis, are thought to be the most Pacific College letters won by any student.

Music production slumped slightly in subsequent years, but Joseph Finley and Florence Murdock served creditably as directors. In addition to the chorus, Pacific annually produced a glee club and orchestra. In 1937, musicians formed the Adelphian Music Club to study classical and modern composers, opera, light opera, and folk songs. The students elected Esther May (Weesner) Thomas and Ivan Makinster as first Adelphian presidents.

THE COLLEGE temporarily discontinued football in 1926 and initiated soccer the next year, beating Reed College 2-0 in the first match. *The Crescent* reported another win that year over Linfield College. The Wildcats arrived with only eight players, but "the Quakers kindly loaned them enough men to make a team." President Pennington refereed at least one game, a 3-0 defeat of Reed College. Reed's president kept time.

The 1929 soccer team had by far the best record in the Northwest, finishing undefeated and yielding only one goal all season. That squad capped a three-year soccer dynasty that included but one loss. *The Crescent* commented about the second half of a win over the University of Oregon:

"Oregon, outweighing and perhaps passing a little more smoothly than the P.C. boys, became exasperated and played a little rougher game. Time out was called when Bob Bissett received six kleet [sic] marks in the stomach, but Bob showed his gameness, as did several other Prune Pickers who were injured, and limped back into the game.

47

"At the start of the last period the P.C. team had a five-second pep rally in a huddle, and the old Pacific spirit could not be denied. Darkness seemed to aid the pickers of dried plums, and Green and Moore were successful in spilling continually the Oregon halves, leaving the fulls alone in front of those star forwards, Cole, Sandoz and Harle.

"Finally, with a perfect example of teamanship [sic], those same three got directly in front of the goal, Cole and Sandoz spilled the goalie, the ball rolled out of the pile, and Harle shoved it in the pen. P.C.'s joy was unbounded, though the rooters didn't know it was scored till a minute later. Oregon was demoralized, and, just to show it wasn't an accident, Cole, on a pretty piece of dribbling, slipped it through the goalie's legs and into the net.

"A moment later the game ended, leaving eleven weary players, crazy with joy, at the hands of a mob of noisy, wild, spectators."

Two years later, a joint committee of the Men's Athletic Council and the Faculty Committee on Athletics decided to discontinue soccer and reinstate football. A successful campaign raised $400 for equipment and Coach Hubert Armstrong issued new uniforms to 18 aspirants. Several games were canceled, however, and the 1931 season produced only two losses and a 13-13 tie, the latter with Reed College.

The Crescent commended the team's leading rusher, Carl Sandoz, quarterback Denny McGuire, right halfback Chet Weed, left halfback Gene Coffin, and Jim Haworth, who "was so tough he never wore a helmet. The opposition, being human, were more affected by his appearance than they would have been if Jim had hidden part of his face beneath a mask."

The newspaper also applauded among others, Tom Howard, Link Wirt, Don Larimer, Harry Christie, Carl Withers, Curt Morse, and Willie Post.

The gridders improved little the next two years. Pacific College experienced an especially dismal 1932 season, making only one touchdown in four games. However the lone touchdown, scored by Ronald Hutchens, came in a 6-0 homecoming win over Reed College.

The 1933 eleven won three, lost three, and tied one, with Carl Sandoz and Gene Coffin starring. The 1934 squad won two, lost three, and tied one. *The Crescent* colorfully reported that "the spearhead of the Pacific offensive all season was Captain-elect Louis Sandoz, but it took the flaming spirit of Captain Eugene Coffin to keep the attack from faltering when the road proved rough."

Two years later Coach Hal Chapman's gridders won five, lost two, and tied two behind the stellar play of Clyde Vinson, Jack Mahoney, and Alfred Bates.

Students raking leaves. Front: Eva Hart, Helen Wehrley, Elizabeth (Aebischer) Edwards. Standing: Angus Henrickson, Helen Lou (Povenmire) Baker, Eugene Coffin, Charles Henrickson, Garnet Guild, Elwood Egelston, Howard Richards.

Hal Chapman also coached the basketball squad, which in 1934-35 won the Willamette Valley Conference title. The starting lineup included forwards Delmer Putnam and John Haworth, center Walt Johnson, and guards Allen Hadley and Howard Karbel. Two years later Chapman's squad took the championship again, climaxing the season with a 24-22 victory over Oregon Institute of Technology. Starters included Delmer Putnam, Louis Sandoz, Ned Green, Eldon Bush, and John Dimond. Carl Sandoz participated six years (including two as an academy student but playing for the College), earning 17 letters in football, basketball, track, soccer, and tennis. His brother, football and basketball standout Louis Sandoz, also starred in track, establishing a school javelin record of 151 feet, 10 inches.

By the 1930s the College increasingly emphasized women's sports. At first it featured volleyball and tennis. The 1934-35 volleyball team won four and lost one, with Elizabeth (Aebischer) Edwards, Garnet Guild, and Eva (Hart) Carter leading the way. In 1937-38 the school added women's basketball, and the team showed "lots of enthusiasm" behind student player/coach Lois McCurley.

Tennis had long been an important sport, with Frank Cole, Charles Beals, and Winifred (Woodward) Sandoz among the stars. Pacific accepted a 1935 invitation to join the newly organized Intercollegiate Tennis League, composed of men's and women's teams from the area colleges. Thelma (Jones) Weatherly, Mary (Brooks) Dimond, Rachel (Pemberton) Gettman, Dora (Bales) Cronyn, and Corilda

Women's volleyball team, 1935. Front row: Marguerite Nordyke, Janet Jack, Jean (Gardner) Coffin. Middle row: Pearl (Kivett) Pearson, Violet (Braithwaite) Richey, Marjorie (Seeley) Hiatt. Back row: Elizabeth (Aebischer) Edwards, Isabella (Wilson) Ruggles, Garnet Guild, Eva (Hart) Carter.

(Stewart) Grover starred. Jim Haworth and Eugene Coffin stood out among the male players.

The Oregonian reported in 1933 that "the old idea that athletes were poor students was blasted by a statement issued recently by Emmett W. Gulley, director of physical education at Pacific College." According to the news release, the lettermen for the preceding five years earned average grades of 86.20, compared to 85.41 for non-letter winners. Tennis boasted the highest average, followed in order by basketball, track, football, and baseball.

MOST PACIFIC students during the late 1920s were Quakers and, like their theological forebearers, sometimes responded to the world in a manner that put them well ahead of their time. When in 1928 the United States sent troops to suppress a revolution against Nicaragua's pro-American military government, the Pacific College student body unanimously voted to send this message to the Secretary of State:

"The student body of Pacific College wish to express deep regret that the United States government has felt it necessary to exercise armed intervention in Nicaragua; and to express the hope that in the future if intervention in any countries of the western hemisphere shall seem necessary, for any reason, this shall come about through the action of the Pan-American congress or some other council of nations rather than by the individual action of the United States.

> On behalf of the student body,
> Wendell Hutchens, President
> Velda J. Livingston [Sweet], Secretary"

Pacific College organized an International Relations Club in 1931 as part of a new affiliation with the Carnegie

49

1935 graduating class. **Front row:** Eva (Hart) Carter, Eugene Coffin, Howard Richards, Ruth Jacobs. **Middle row:** Helen (Wehrley) Jackson, Elizabeth (Aebischer) Edwards, Clarence Moore, Garnet Guild, Helen (Povenmire) Baker. **Back row:** Wendell Mills, Charles Henrickson, Angus Henrickson.

Endowment for International Peace. The international relations emphasis proved important at Pacific College, influencing many students.

Elmore Jackson, a 1931 graduate, became the first Quaker representative to the United Nations. He successfully negotiated the Friends Middle East refugee work accompanying the Israeli-Arab wars of the late 1940s.

One of his books, *Middle East Mission*, describes his 1955 negotiations involving Egyptian Prime Minister Gamal Abdel Nasser and Israeli leaders, including David Ben-Gurion.

George Fox College named Jackson its Alumnus of the Year in 1976, citing him for "distinguishing himself in international peacemaking."

THE ADMINISTRATION occasionally encountered student discipline problems. The foremost occurred during the 1925-26 school year, when the faculty charged several students with various offenses, mostly smoking.

The teachers considered the matter for several weeks, giving each offender opportunity for rehabilitation; five apparently signed statements that they would discontinue smoking and were retained, although with continuing supervision. The board eventually expelled three young men and one young woman.

Against one of the men, faculty minutes charge: "For many offenses, confessed and proven, breaches of discipline, violation of college requirements, foul talk, etc., for a general evil influence and unwillingness to profit by the opportunities presented here, and for confessed immoral conduct . . . ."

One expelled young man—whose offenses included failure to submit *The Crescent* copy to the faculty representative—later appeared with his father, who denied that his son had broken any rules and charged that the faculty had failed to provide adequate warning of the impending penalty's seriousness. The faculty felt the father and son presented no new evidence to justify reopening the case, however, and enforced the expulsion order.

The following February the college board commended Pennington and the faculty's handling of the disciplinary matters. It expressed its "fullest confidence in, and appreciation of President Pennington."

Some students, however, continued to question the College's parental role. Even a few parents objected to the long-standing regulation extending beyond the campus the ban on social dancing, card playing, smoking, and drinking.

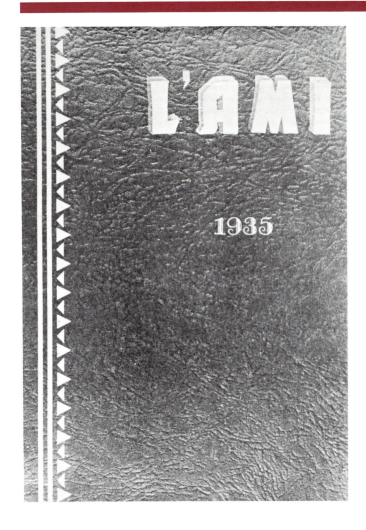

The board in 1939 approved an administrative recommendation that college authorities discontinue responsibility for off-campus conduct regarding social dancing, card playing, and smoking. However, the school maintained the general ban on the use of alcoholic beverages, off as well as on campus.

Some students still criticized the regulations. The board met with them but did not further modify its position. It soon approved a statement by President Pennington endorsing the College's long-standing aims and ideals.

Some student complaints yielded results. For example, in 1940 a group formally expressed misgivings regarding the girls' dormitories and food service. A board-appointed "Committee for Consideration of Dormitory Problems" investigated and found "constant unrest and discontent on the part of students because of the poor quality and lack of variety in meals." College authorities alleviated this problem without increasing costs by a change of cooks and, according to board minutes, improved utilization of local fruits and vegetables, careful buying, and wise menu plan-

ning. The board also employed the new cook part-time that summer to supervise students in canning fruit and vegetables.

IN SOME WAYS, the Pacific College students and their parents reflected Oregon Yearly Meeting, where divisive theological undercurrents had been developing for years. Many constituents who opposed reversing the ban on some off-campus behavior saw board action as evidence that the school had drifted from its evangelical moorings.

To a degree, the issues reflected tensions that had existed in American Quakerism and the broader church for a century and more. Resulting divisions hurt the College considerably and significantly eroded its constituent base. The source lies deep in the Yearly Meeting's history.

In his first report to the Yearly Meeting in 1912, Levi Pennington depicted a united, common purpose as even more important than finances. Sadly, during much of his long presidency, the college constituency lacked that broad consensus. Deep within the very fibres of the school, of Oregon Yearly Meeting, and of Quakerism—indeed, of Protestantism in general—divisive seeds grew.

In 1887 Orthodox, Gurneyite Friends had entered into an organization called "Five Years Meeting of Friends," comprising 12 yearly meetings across the United States. Oregon Yearly Meeting participated in a unified statement called the "Richmond Declaration of Faith," as historic Quaker orthodoxy adapted to the pastoral system and evangelistic modes. Nineteenth-century revivalism had influenced all these Friends; virtually all emphasized the Bible as God's revealed Word, and Jesus Christ as the living Word and Redeemer.

Some felt uneasy, however, with the emotionalism, nationalism, and militarism of many evangelical Protestant churches; others disdained any association, even in name, with theological liberals. Although much common ground existed, these positions were subject to potential polarization as, in the 1920s, the broader Protestant church fractured into "Modernist" and "Fundamentalist" camps.

Divisive symptoms appeared as early as 1919, when Yearly Meeting attenders heard rumblings of discontent with Five Years Meeting of Friends. Complaints centered around the "liberal interpretation of Scripture tending toward destructive criticism" and Five Years Meeting's endorsement of literature "whose authors are known to hold in question the authenticity, historicity, and integrity of the Bible."

Further concern focused on what some Oregon Yearly Meeting Friends saw as a disproportionate emphasis on social and political change "to the neglect of the teachings of the Bible on the redemption from all sin through the merits of the shed blood of our Lord Jesus Christ."

Five Years Meeting's executives responded with reassurance, affirming that its leaders "have saving faith in our Lord Jesus Christ, which we recognize as the prime requisite for Christian service...." However, after five contentious years, Oregon Yearly Meeting withdrew.

Levi Pennington opposed the separation. Like two previous presidents (Thomas Newlin and Edwin McGrew), he had served as presiding clerk of Oregon Yearly Meeting (1914 to 1924). In his opposition to secession, Pennington retained the spirit of the Oregon Yearly Meeting's early history. A different mood conditioned the 1920s, however, as tolerance often gave way to dogmatism on both sides.

For example, although Oregon Yearly Meeting had championed the founding of the American Friends Service Committee (AFSC) to counter the effects of World War I, many became hostile during the 1920s. In 1938 the Yearly Meeting officially left AFSC over issues parallelling those that tore Oregon Yearly Meeting from Five Years Meeting.

Meanwhile, some members of Oregon Yearly Meeting questioned the spiritual condition of a few Pacific College faculty members. The gradual reduction in Oregon Yearly Meeting's support of the College provides clear evidence of the developing disaffection. In 1921, 73 percent of Pacific College's students were Quakers. When Pennington left the presidency 20 years later, that figure had plunged to less than 44 percent. By 1939, only 21 percent of Idaho's Greenleaf Friends Academy graduates attended Pacific College. Many others opted for Bible schools and evangelistically oriented colleges.

Most Northwest Friends had become associated with the "Holiness Movement," a post-Civil War renewal impulse involving revivalist Quakers and other denominations. By 1900, Holiness had become identified with Wesleyan theology. Its doctrine promised a radical destruction of the sin nature through the spiritual experience called sanctification. Contrary to Wesleyan and Quaker antecedents, however, the movement in the 20th century neglected political and economic justice.

Levi Pennington resisted the trend. For years he had been a leader among Friends who, while solidly Christ-centered personally, tended to encourage Quaker ecumenism and de-emphasize overt evangelicalism. Like his predecessors, he identified with the broader Quaker movement.

Pennington's nemesis in the Yearly Meeting was an outstanding Holiness leader named Edward Mott. Like Pennington, Mott grew up with both programmed and unprogrammed Friends meetings in the eastern United States. He accepted Jesus Christ in a non-Quaker revival

1936 graduating class. Front row: Ruthanna (McCracken) Hampton, Charlotte (Coleman) Sanderman, Lera (Rice) Toft, Maxine (Mason) Brandt, Marjorie (Seely) Hiatt, Violet (Braithwaite) Richey, Isabella (Wilson) Ruggles, Margaret (Coulson) Dicus. Back row: Rex Hampton, Harvey Campbell, Virgil Hiatt, Clayton Hicks, Ronald Sherk, Ray Hansberry, Ernest Kaster.

meeting and later reported: "The light I received at that time had a permanent effect upon me and I had a consciousness of saving grace which has never been lost."

Also like Levi Pennington, Edward Mott esteemed his early Quaker forebears and was a deeply convinced religious pacifist. However, whereas Pennington devoted his primary antiwar efforts to solving the war-inducing problems of injustice, oppression, and militarism, Mott tended more toward introducing people to Jesus Christ in the conviction that only redeemed people can prevent war.

Although Pennington did not resign his position as presiding clerk, the Yearly Meeting named Mott to replace him in 1924. Mott served for the next 21 years. Thus, he was clerk in 1926 when Oregon withdrew from Five Years Meeting. (Pennington later contended that Mott conducted that decisive meeting unfairly, forcing Oregon Yearly Meeting out when the actual sense of the Yearly Meeting was in doubt. However, Oliver Weesner, who clerked the committee that recommended the change, believed secession was the will of Oregon Yearly Meeting, although he personally opposed the decision.)

After many years as a Friends pastor and Bible school teacher, Edward Mott served from 1922 to 1933 as president of North Pacific Evangelistic Institute (later renamed Portland Bible Institute, then Cascade College). This school had been started in 1918 in Portland's Piedmont Friends Church by Quakers who were strongly influenced by the Holiness Movement. They expressed concern that there was "no such school within easy reach of the young people of Oregon and Southwestern Washington."

THE DESIRE for a Bible school was not unique to Northwest Quakers. It reflected also a division of thought in many denominations, one that in Quakerism separated such institutions as Whittier College and Huntington Park Training School for Christian Workers, William Penn College and Vennard College, and Friends University and Friends Bible College.

For 40 years, therefore, Pacific College's primary competition came from Portland Bible Institute/Cascade College. Ironically, for 11 years, two of Oregon Yearly Meeting's outstanding leaders, Pennington and Mott, headed colleges that directly competed for the same Quaker students.

By the end of the 1930s, as many Oregon Yearly Meeting college students attended Cascade College as Pacific College.

By that time, most members of Oregon Yearly Meeting identified closely with the Holiness Movement. Quakers came to resemble Free Methodists and Nazarenes. For some constituents, no significant difference existed.

This left Oregon Yearly Meeting and its college increasingly oriented toward preaching and evangelism, at the expense of human service.

The body put more emphasis on eliciting conversions and providing preparation for the hereafter and less on reforming unjust political and corporate structures. Concern for one's fellowman in the "here and now" gave way to the fear that social action would be counterproductive to the primary goal of winning souls for Jesus. In this they deviated significantly from the early Quaker and Wesleyan conviction that conversion and social concern are inseparable parts of the same spiritual experience.

Levi Pennington found his leadership increasingly frustrated by these changes. Those who deemphasized social action and disdained cooperation with less overtly evangelistic Quakers treated the president with suspicion and sometimes open hostility. They reacted similarly to such stalwart Pacific College faculty members as Emmett Gulley, Russel Lewis, and Perry Macy, and board chairmen Thomas Hester and Hervey Hoskins, who maintained ties with the American Friends Service Committee and the broader Quaker movement.

IN 1940, 65-year-old President Levi T. Pennington submitted his resignation. It took effect the following June, at the end of the school's first half century. The retiring president submitted a long letter, ending with this paragraph:

"I cannot tell you with what feelings I look forward to the change I have suggested. It seemed to me, as I first faced it as a possibility for the near future, that it would be like giving up those I love and surrendering life itself. But I shall hope that the change may be brought about happily

The Yearly Meeting assisted in the salary of Gervas Carey, a highly regarded former Friends University Bible teacher and Newberg Friends Church pastor. The College immediately doubled its Bible and Christian education offerings.

Gulley, the trustees, and other Yearly Meeting leaders targeted prospective Friends students. Ed Harmon, an Oregon Yearly Meeting pastor/evangelist and Pacific College student, became a part-time student recruiter. A women's trio—Marguerite (Barney) Brown, Kathleen Smith, and Elenita (Mardock) Bales—traveled with Harmon and his wife, Lois, a Pacific College English instructor, to churches and summer conferences.

The effort yielded positive results. Friends enrollment leaped to 62 percent Gulley's first year, then increased gradually to 74 percent in 1946. About 44 percent of Oregon Yearly Meeting's college students attended Pacific in 1943. Four years later the percentage had grown to 57. The enthusiasm of Yearly Meeting superintendent Joseph Reece, recruiter Ed Harmon, and several pastors attracted the Friends students.

Total enrollment jumped from 86 in 1940-41 to 129 the next year. Although World War II intervened, attendance soon rebounded despite a tuition increase from $100 a year to $150, and then $170. A Veteran's Administration G.I. Bill contract helped boost enrollment to 161 in 1946-47.

THE COLLEGE REQUESTED a special $25,000 Yearly Meeting donation in 1944. An Oregon Yearly Meeting committee—Carl Byrd, Paul Cammack, Harlan Smith, Dillon Mills, Richard Kneeland, and Clark Smith, chairman—reported having "prayerfully and carefully" investigated the matter and concluded:

"In view of the splendid progress made by the college in the past few years in spiritual values, in academic standards, and in financial stability, the committee is recommending that the loan and gift be made by the Yearly Meeting to the amount of $25,000. The committee believes that it will be an effective method of bringing about closer cooperation between the Yearly Meeting and Pacific College."

Nevertheless, grave internal problems remained. The issues that separated Oregon Yearly Meeting from Five Years Meeting continued. Progress toward evangelical goals only strengthened those Friends who feared "modernistic" trends. With momentum on their side, they set about to free their College from spiritually subversive influences.

They became disappointed, however. While recognizing some movement toward their goals, they felt the administration impeded rapid progress.

They analyzed the situation accurately. Although a sincere agent of reconciliation, Emmet Gulley could never endorse the overtly revivalistic trend. Nor could the conservative local leaders ever fully accept the president's humanitarian philosophy. Given the era's tendency toward polarization, eventual impasse seemed almost inevitable.

Gulley's long association with the American Friends Service Committee, from which Oregon Yearly Meeting withdrew over doctrinal differences in 1938, symbolized the problem. Only one year after the OYM-AFSC division, Gulley temporarily left his Pacific College teaching post to join the Service Committee's work in Spain and Cuba. Two other administrators during Gulley's presidency—Vice President Laurence Skene and Academic Dean Lewis Hoskins—also associated with the AFSC, making them equally suspect. When the more revivalistic wing decried tardy progress toward their goals, they easily found a scapegoat in the college administration.

The anti-Gulley movement accelerated in 1945. At the midyear ministerial conference early that year, the pastors of Oregon Yearly Meeting recommended that the trustees consider terminating Gulley's presidency. At the next board meeting, the president responded by offering his resignation. The trustees persuaded him to reconsider, however.

Faculty in mid-1940s. Front row, from left: Perry Macy, Genevieve (Belz) St. George, Herschel Thornburg, Mary Sutton, Ed Harmon, Alice Roberts, Laura Doble, Charlotte Macy. Back row: Burton Frost, Roy Clark, Roy Knight, Gervas Carey, George Moore, Emmett Gulley, Laurence Skene, Russel Lewis, Oliver Weesner.

Encouraging closer cooperation, the board appointed Charles Haworth, Harlan Smith, and Allen Hadley to study the relationship between the College and Yearly Meeting. That spring the committee returned a discouraging report. At the June 1945 Yearly Meeting session, the college board withdrew the $25,000 gift request.

Yet at the corresponding Yearly Meeting sessions, the official visiting committee commended the school for its "deep spiritual tone in many of the college activities." President Gulley wrote an optimistic annual report, noting that "Pacific College wishes to be of great service to Oregon Yearly Meeting and the kingdom of God and wishes to maintain at all cost a real Christian educational institution. To this end we seek divine guidance and blessing."

Gulley emphasized the "remarkable unity and cooperation between faculty, student body, Board, people in the Newberg community and the Yearly Meeting," and expressed appreciation for constituent prayers. He did note that one Yearly Meeting group had expressed dissatisfaction with his administration, but did not elaborate. The college board accepted the report "with appreciation."

Nevertheless, the next day President Gulley resigned. The trustees accepted, but gave him "a unanimous vote of confidence." The board minutes do not give the specific reason for the resignation, but the *Newberg Graphic*'s next issue included:

"It was understood that Gulley's resignation came at the request of a small group of ministers and others of Oregon Yearly Meeting and of the Friends Church during recent sessions.

"While Gulley had stressed the necessity of having a Christian educational institution, some demanded that they make the school even more evangelistic, it is said."

The next month, the trustees bowed to considerable pro-Gulley pressure from faculty, Yearly Meeting, and Newberg elements. They rehired the president for a five-year term, with Laurence Skene reelected as vice president. At the same meeting, the administration backed an attempt to remove the Yearly Meeting's veto and reduce its corporation nominations from 50 to 40 percent. However, the board rejected the initiative by an eight to four vote.

The next *Newberg Graphic* reported the board's confidence in Gulley policies and noted that he would continue the effort to make Pacific a strong Christian educational institution. The newspaper added that local businessmen, who had become more closely associated with the College in recent years, welcomed President Gulley's return.

Tension continued, however. Later in 1945 the college board approved a minute requiring faculty members to conform to Oregon Yearly Meeting's spiritual standards. At the same time, the board commissioned Paul Cammack to interview one faculty member "in regard to rumors that are being circulated by members of the Yearly Meeting." Although Cammack found the rumors of "unorthodox teaching" untrue, the board decided it would be unwise to renew the teacher's contract.

Constituents increasingly perceived the president as outside the Yearly Meeting's Holiness emphasis. Discontent mounted. Some students disdained Gulley's response to their request for on-campus revival meetings: He told them Pacific was an educational institution, not a camp meeting.

Meanwhile, the trustees added evangelical stalwarts Herschel Thornburg, Roy Clark, Roy (Pop) Knight, Charlotte Macy, and Ed Harmon to the faculty. The president's caution notwithstanding, the 1945-46 school year saw a renewed emphasis on evangelistic efforts. Pacific College participated in week-long campaigns led by Nathan Pierson, Carl Byrd, and J. G. Bringdale (the latter in cooperation with Newberg Friends Church). The school emphasized deputation, with several student groups regularly serving the region's churches.

During the summer of 1946, 25 Pacific College students at Twin Rocks youth camp signed a petition calling for "more frequent spiritual chapels" and "administration and faculty who will take the lead spiritually, socially and educationally." The document, submitted to the board and to Oregon Yearly Meeting Superintendent Joseph Reece, also requested that student body representatives attend the November board meeting. The board decided to invite all the college students to express their concerns.

Fifty-five students, one third of the student body, attended that decisive meeting. They reported the need for more spiritual vitality. Further, they rather idealistically called for accreditation and an increase of Ph.D.'s on the staff.

During the subsequent discussion, President Gulley explained that he had contacted a number of Ph.D.'s but found none willing to come. Lack of funds to pay acceptable salaries and the lack of doctorates on the staff hindered accreditation, the embattled president reported.

After Board Chairman Hervey Hoskins dismissed the students, a heated discussion ensued. Faculty and board factions charged that Gulley's presidency kept financial support and some Ph.D.'s from the school. Someone predicted that if Gulley resigned, five or six Ph.D.'s would accept contracts almost immediately and donors would underwrite salary increases to $2,400 for the M.A. and $3,000 for the Ph.D.

Emmett Gulley then announced his willingness to step down. After much debate, the board voted six to five to accept the resignation, to take effect the following June.

Gulley presented a written statement at the next board meeting, which included:

"Current controversy among Pacific College supporters revolves around the relative position of religion in the school. There is a demand among the board members that the Quaker institution be made more evangelistic, while the President has maintained, during his administration, that Pacific College should be primarily an educational institution with the Christian point of view."

Financial Secretary George Moore observed that no one should impute ulterior motives to those representing either side of the controversy. He emphasized the need to train Christian public school teachers, businessmen, and professional workers. "It is not our intention to make Pacific a seminary," Moore added. "We believe that it is possible for a college to be aggressively Christian, and at the same time maintain the highest type of scholarship which will stress the evangelical note."

Within one month of Gulley's resignation, 29 students, eight faculty members, and 46 townspeople unsuccessfully petitioned the board to reconsider. The professors (Laurence Skene, Mary Sutton, Rachel Aldrich, Galen Miller, Perry Macy, Lindell Hockett, George Berreman, and Russel Lewis) submitted another petition the following month, again without satisfaction.

By March, eight teachers had resigned, some apparently in protest. Donors had withdrawn library construction contributions totaling $4,000. Immediately after Gulley's resignation, Ferd Groner wrote: "Since you have resigned as president of Pacific College I have withdrawn my support and have changed my will . . . ." Gulley estimated the canceled bequest at $250,000.

Home economics class in the Wood-Mar basement. Jean White, Professor Helen (Willcuts) Street, Betty (Street) Hockett, and Margaret (Dickson) Magee. (Unidentified young lady seated.)

Most of the Yearly Meeting endorsed the board's action, however. By March of 1947, Oregon Yearly Meeting constituents had pledged $15,000 in an attempt to attract faculty with doctorates.

In his final report the following June, President Gulley reviewed his six-year administration, noting that the endowment had been increased by $125,000, accreditation was anticipated "in the very near future," and "the standing of Pacific College both among the supporters of the institution, the school men of the Northwest and the people of this community was raised to one of the highest peaks in the history of the college." Gulley then expressed profound regret for what he saw as action that would prevent further progress.

THE COLLEGE FACED MANY additional problems, mostly financial. Enrollment declined sharply during the war, and the board had difficulty paying the bills. In 1943 the school could not even afford to hire a janitor.

Early in his term, President Gulley projected a living endowment campaign. He made two fundraising trips to the East Coast, one with Levi Pennington, the other with Lewis Hoskins. Newberg Friends Church gave the campaign a significant start, pledging over $1,500 for each of the following five years.

In 1944 the college administrators proposed visitations to local Friends churches. They hoped to raise $100,000 for salaries, a gymnasium, and debt retirement. The campaign started well, but foundered in the College-Yearly Meeting controversy. The next January, a discouraged Gulley wrote to Levi Pennington regarding Friends in eastern United States: "I can well believe that a good deal of

knowledge of the difficulty here spread east—chances of gaining help there greatly lessened."

The year before Gulley took office, the school had 82 students, with annual tuition at $100; in 1947, 161 students remitted $170 tuition fees. Even with this increase, the students paid only 40 percent of their educational costs. Therefore, the board decided to raise 1947-48 tuition to $200; as costs increased, however, the percentage the students paid went down even more.

The College rescinded in 1944 its depression-induced practice of paying only 60 percent of the stated faculty salaries. The board set a firm $1,050 minimum, rising to $1,800 for department heads "when funds are available." Two years later the trustees proposed a $1,800 minimum, with $400 additional for summer involvement in study, research, travel, or work for the College. Lack of funds killed this dream, however.

DURING WORLD WAR II several Pacific College students performed military service; others, probably a minority, served as conscientious objectors in Civilian Public Service camps. Refusal to obey conscription preceding the war led to the arrest of one professor, Edwin A. Sanders. According to the *Oregon Journal*, he would have been 4-F anyway, but he refused to register and the Selective Service System charged him with draft evasion.

"The conscription act flouts my whole philosophy," Sanders proclaimed. On December 7, 1940, a federal court convicted and sentenced him to one year in a work camp. The College provided active support and unsuccessfully sought his release. The following September the Yearly Meeting sent him "a carefully formulated message of love and sympathy."

Few College and Yearly Meeting men took such a firm position, however. Available evidence suggests that nearly two thirds accepted combatant military service. As in World War I, freedom of conscience reigned.

FOR STUDENTS AND FACULTY, Pacific College embodied a participating community. Just as the entire group picked prunes together in 1929, the populace of the 1940s and 1950s picked up filberts to aid the College. Arthur Roberts, graduate of 1944, later recalled one such community experience:

"For many years the College had a tradition of two campus cleanup days. Everyone got into the act, even the fussy dean of students, Mr. Diment. Malingerers lost face. We raked the lawns, hauled away trash, swept the furnace room (four-foot slabs of wood provided heat in Wood-Mar) and we cleaned windows with newspaper. This was a new one for me. For some reason I associate this method with the chemist, Professor Skene. Usually our labors were rewarded by some kind of goodies, cookies and apples, perhaps. This egalitarian approach had its values. Work was a social leveler, although there weren't many wealthy students. No government aid was available, either, to use for paying work-study assignments."

The College maintained an active cocurricular program. The chorus toured 1,500 miles in 1941-42, giving 18 concerts before 4,000 people. Following wartime curtailments, the school developed noteworthy music and deputation ministries throughout the Northwest.

Forensics achievements included Jack Willcuts' oration entitled "Christianity vs. Nationalism," which won at several regional tournaments. Norval Hadley won the state speech contest championship in 1947, and Priscilla (Doble) Jeffery took the after-dinner speaking state championship two years later.

"The Four Flats," a quartet that twice won the Original All Northwest Barber Shop Ballad Contest, attracted major public attention. The group consisted of Norval Hadley, Ronald Crecelius, Harlow Ankeny, and Dick Cadd, with Roy Clark, Glenn Koch, and Randall Emry each participating on occasion. Following their graduation from the College, the

Basketball team in 1943-44. Front row: Everett Craven, Jr., David Thomas, Jack Willcuts, Terrill Repp, Allen Thomas. Back row: student coach George Bales, Arthur Roberts, Don Brash, Orrin Ogier, Quincy Fodge, Don Bowers.

1946 football team. Front row: Bob Cadd, Jim Moore, Jack Cadd, Bert Kiefer, Dick Cadd, Gene Smith, Melvin Veale, Verne Brightup, Dave Fendall, Wayne Antrim. Back row: Coach Kelsey Hinshaw, Glen Moor, Ben Franklin, Bob Armstrong, Bob Hurford, Rollo Upton, Art Cole, Earl Craven, Norval Hadley, Dale Parrish, Clare Smith, student manager Jack Martin.

Four Flats represented Youth for Christ full time. Later, as the World Vision Quartet, they appeared with Bob Pierce, Billy Graham, and other evangelistic teams and made a trip to the Far East.

Beginning in 1950, the College sponsored an annual quartet festival that drew enthusiastic crowds of over 2,000 people. Eight radio stations broadcast the event. Roy Clark served as master of ceremonies, with the Four Flats often the feature attraction.

College publications report numerous other activities, including the annual May Day celebration, with Maypole winding and a baseball game; *Crescent* book reviews; a regular *Crescent* feature by history professor Mackey Hill entitled "The World Is My Campus"; Pacific Coast trips and retreats; special prayer and campus work days; an annual freshman initiation week; and a yearly freshman class presentation of skits, one-act comedies, and music for the entire student body.

UNDER STUDENT COACH George Bales, the 1943-44 basketball team won eight and lost four games in the only intercollegiate sport played that year. Football resumed with a six-man version in 1945, but the gridders played only two games and lost both to Reed College. Robert Hurford captained the team.

Due to the lack of a gymnasium, the basketball team played at the junior high school in 1945-46, winning seven and losing five behind captain Arnold Booth. The 1947 *L'Ami* states that "a new inspiration to the fellows was the new gymnasium." However, success required more than inspiration; the Quakers lost the first home game to Lewis & Clark College, 58-13, en route to a 4 and 14 record.

The 1947-48 school year included a heavy sports slate, with the 11-man football team going two and four under student coach Earl Craven. The basketball quintet won only one game (Reed) of a 25-game slate. Norval Hadley was GFC's top scorer.

The women's basketball squad won five and lost four, with Dorothy Barratt scoring 132 points. Gladys Engle and Gertrude (Haworth) Ankeny served as team captains.

Local businessman and former professional player Barney McGrath coached the baseball team without remuneration from 1942 through 1955. Pitchers William Hayes and Darwin "Cub" Grimm stood out.

George Bales, a Newberg High School state wrestling champion and GFC graduate, returned in 1948 and for six years produced successful football teams.

The 1949 gridiron eleven, one of the best in GFC history, won four, lost two, and tied one. The following year, fullback Harold "Spud" Ankeny scored 56 points and gained 712 yards on 122 carries enroute to a four-and-four team record.

Bales' basketball squads consistently finished near the top of the Metropolitan Collegiate Conference. Led by Waldo Haworth's 240 points, the 1949-50 Quakers went five and three in the Metropolitan Collegiate Conference.

The next season the Balesmen won 14 and lost seven behind all-conference forward Nigel Shockey and team captain Gene Hockett.

George Bales, one of the
most successful coaches
in GFC history.

1950 Gold "Q" officers: Leona (Harmon) Lyda, Marjorie (Larrance) Weesner, Betty (Street) Hockett, Margaret (Weber) Winters, Gladys (Carolyn) Engle.

The 1951-52 team, composed of Nigel Shockey, Elmer Kendall, Bill Field, Gerald Lemmons, and Verne Martin, won the championship and ended the season with a 16-8 record. Shockey, an all-conference forward, averaged 20 points a game to lead the league. After a victory over Reed College that year, the 400-pound victory bell, which had hung since 1885 in the Hoover Hall tower, crashed from its moorings—from unaccustomed overwork, students claimed. Overall, Bales' basketball teams won 71 and lost 52.

Fullback Dick Zeller emerged from this era as one of the best football players to don the Old Gold and Navy Blue; among his accomplishments was a 41-yard punting average in 1954, ranking him third in the nation behind two National Collegiate Athletic Association (NCAA) kickers. That year Verne Martin received the Robison "outstanding senior athlete" trophy for his sparkling four-year basketball and baseball career. In addition to its own sports program, the College for a time served the area by organizing and hosting an elementary school basketball tournament.

MEANWHILE, LEADERS TRIED to improve the school academically. Recognition by the United States Bureau of Educational Standards had been a magnificent accomplishment in 1925. It opened the door to significant progress. In subsequent years, however, a regional accrediting agency, the Northwest Association of Secondary and Higher Schools, emerged. Pacific did not meet its standards, so lost recognition as an accredited college. President Gulley submitted a preliminary inquiry to the Northwest Association in 1944, but it discouraged formal application, citing the significant debt (although $18,000 was repaid that year), inadequate salaries, absence of a gymnasium, and lack of Ph.D's.

Most colleges accepted Pacific College transfer credits anyway. The State Department of Education gave teacher education graduates emergency certificates. In the midst of the 1947 turmoil, however, the Newberg school district dealt the College a major blow by refusing to accept Pacific students for cadet teaching. Newberg Superintendent of Schools Hubert E. Armstrong, a Pacific graduate and former teacher, listed the official reasons as excessive teaching loads on his staff, lack of Newberg teachers' preparation to supervise cadets, Pacific's uncertain ability to meet the program's financial obligations, and fear that the relationship would jeopardize Newberg's accreditation. Further, "the uncertainty as to who will be president of the college and who will constitute the staff adds to the feeling on the part of the high school board that they are not certain as to the kind of training the cadet teachers will have received in preparation for assuming obligations as teachers in our classrooms."

DESPITE THE OBSTACLES, the College maintained a surprisingly strong faculty. For example, George Moore supervised the teacher education program while doubling as financial secretary. Although stretched too thin by overwhelming responsibilities, he inspired students by his zeal for knowledge and his optimism about the future. A superb motivator, he challenged students toward service.

In his pending autobiography, Arthur Roberts commends Moore and several other faculty. He remembers President Gulley as a "practical Quaker" who did not disdain physical labor:

"His example helped me avoid the pitfalls of 'white collar' snobbery.... One summer Gulley and I retarred Wood-Mar Hall. This was a hot, messy job, and during

61

Mary C. Sutton, one of most respected and best-loved teachers, taught science and German and also served for many years as Registrar. Her 52 years as a full-time teacher was the longest during the College's first century.

intervals between applications we held spirited discussions.... He refused to separate the ordinary realm of life from the spiritual. And more than the substance of our philosophical arguments...is the fact that college president and sophomore student could work together tarring the ad building without either of them feeling that the experience was demeaning or out of synch with reality."

Roberts speaks also of Bible professor Gervas Carey, "an articulate teacher and meticulous scholar":

"I can see him yet sitting at the desk, his eyes flaming from that sharply chiseled face crowned with iron grey hair.... I felt intimidated by Dr. Carey at first, and then inspired. He was not a gushy person, but in time the professor-student relationship yielded to that of mentor-mentee, and then to friend and friend.... Carey was a moderate, a strong and disciplined Christian who did not flow with the tide, whether that tide be revivalism or modernism. His course in theism showed how rationally credible the Gospel is. His Bible courses reinforced for me that

the Quaker understanding of the Gospel made good sense...."

Roberts had postponed the required science course until his last semester and had to spend graduation morning searching the canyon for flowers to classify:

"Otherwise Miss Sutton wouldn't let me graduate. She showed tough love, forcing academic discipline on the students, but holding out for mercy in administrative deliberations over suspension or expulsion for moral miscreants. Later I learned she wept in prayer nightly over those who failed, that they might find their way back to God and to personal integrity."

Students knew mathematics professor Oliver Weesner for his patience and reiterated explanations. Arthur Roberts recalls that along with Mahlon Macy, Deane Roberts, and Jack Willcuts, he lived in the Weesner home (later willed to the College and named Weesner House):

"Mrs. Weesner washed our clothes and put up with our shenanigans...[such as] racing through the front door

62

(1952-54)—found this impossible with available funds. The College rejected some prospective faculty due to their theological liberalism; others would not come to a non-accredited school; still others, some who met the spiritual and academic qualifications, felt unable to work for the $3,000 offered those with doctorates.

One outstanding Bible teacher, Paul Mills, did come. Although lacking a doctorate, he fulfilled the desires of

---

"People are waiting to see if the college will fold before they extend their support. If they wait, it will."
—Gervas A. Carey, President, 1947-1950

---

many who wanted to emphasize a strongly biblical Friends position. His helpful booklet, "The Bible and War," has gone through several reprintings and serves those who seek to understand Jesus' teachings regarding human relationships in wartime.

Gervas Carey did not want to be president. He accepted only after refusals from several men, including Dr. Walter R. Williams, Jr., a Quaker professor of education at the University of Florida, and Harold Kuhn, another Quaker Ph.D.

Carey attended Cleveland Bible Institute (later renamed Malone College), earned an A.B. from Friends University and a B.D. from Princeton Theological Seminary. In 1939 Friends University conferred a Doctor of Divinity. Before coming to Pacific in 1940, he had spent most of his career as a Quaker pastor, including several years at Newberg Friends Church.

The new president faced the future with grim determination, but without great optimism. "People are waiting to see if the college will fold before they extend their support," he lamented. "If they wait, it will."

The school's academic weakness concerned Carey. He wondered how long a college might survive when graduates could not get teaching credentials and the history professor and librarian didn't even have bachelor's degrees in their specializations. Carey hired Mackey Hill, with an M.A. in history, and Mrs. Malcolm Armour, who held bachelor's degrees in library science and theology.

Walter R. Williams, Jr., evaluated the College in 1948. He recommended a greater attempt "to provide the excellence of a Christian, Quaker environment in a manner that avoided any possible coloring of 'intolerance' or 'radicalism.'" He also warned that the College's financial

with Bruin Jr., only to have it torn in half by pursuers.... Clothes weren't much of a problem. We didn't have many. Dirty white corduroy pants (sometimes with pencil sketches) were standard collegiate attire in those years."

The College honored Oliver Weesner in 1953, after he retired from serving the school 43 consecutive years as mathematics professor and sometimes treasurer. (Weesner continued seven years in a part-time role.)

EMMETT GULLEY'S resignation narrowed the already tenuous support base and contributed to a long, difficult period. At the very moment Oregon Yearly Meeting demanded a more evangelistic spiritual emphasis, it also demanded accreditation and professors with doctorates.

The top administrators following Emmett Gulley—Dr. Gervas Carey (1947-50), Dr. Paul Parker (1950-52), and an administrative committee headed by Donald McNichols

base must be immediately broadened for the institution to survive another generation. "The crucial test of Pacific College is financial. It is at this point that the institution will succeed or fail."

Williams proposed an increase in faculty salaries, maintenance of low tuition, and an annual contribution of $25,000 from Oregon Yearly Meeting.

Soon thereafter, President Carey presented a plan to raise $550,000 over six years, with $100,000 to clear indebtedness, $300,000 for dormitory construction, and $150,000 for operating expenses. The Yearly Meeting would contribute $25,000 annually. The plan failed. However, the GFC trustees did attempt to raise $25,000 annually through 1,000 memberships in a special "living endowment" fund, called a $25 Club. This program enjoyed some success; by 1953 the club reached a peak membership of about 700, which yielded nearly $15,000 annually.

Williams' thorough report enumerated several strengths, notably the core of teachers who had given many years to the College, the loyal tradition that had developed over the years, and the wholesome Christian atmosphere and influence.

THE RAPID ENROLLMENT increase after World War II created a need for new buildings. In honor of former board chairman Thomas W. Hester (trustee 1917-43, chairman 1933-43), the College built a new gymnasium in 1946-47.

Years later, Emmett Gulley recalled the original gymnasium, which "was really two old barns shoved together.... It was not adequate, was poorly heated, drafty, and had too few seats for spectators." The new gymnasium (termed "Hester Dome" by students) brought marked improvement.

Gulley described the construction. Although the College faced hard times and financial problems, "courage was plentiful and the need was urgent." Gulley and Roy (Pop) Knight drew the plans. The president then convinced a cement block company to sell materials for a low price. However, the stone mason charged too much, claiming to be the only one capable of laying the blocks. Gulley reported that he replied:

"I'm sorry you feel that way. I know how to lay blocks and there are some able and willing students here who would be glad to earn the money and do the work." Gulley then trained himself, selected several students, taught them how to lay blocks and "they did a first rate job."

Clyde Thomas (grandfather of Clyde Thomas, who in 1990 became Director of the Physical Plant) did the wood-

Hoover Hall in the 1940s. The left half was the original "Academy Building," built in 1885 and moved to the present campus in 1892, when the other section was added. The building was razed in 1954. The trustees returned the bell to almost exactly the same location when the Centennial Tower was built in 1990.

work. The College built the gymnasium, Gulley emphasized, literally by "blood, sweat and tears."

In 1945 the school purchased for $6,000 a house on the corner of Hancock and River streets, opposite the original, still-standing Ezra H. Woodward house. The College used this building, first named Edwards Hall and later McGrew House, as a dormitory until 1964, then donated it to the city for fire department practice. (The school later constructed Winters' Apartments on the site.)

64

Oldest School Building Comes Down

Meanwhile, the College purchased at low cost, and transported from Camp Adair near Corvallis, several units that had been military barracks during the war. These "vet houses" became the dining hall, music, and art buildings. Others served as the school's principal married student and faculty housing. At one time, these former military units served more than half the Quaker campus's building needs.

Fire dealt a damaging blow in 1946, partially destroying Hoover Hall, one of the two buildings moved to the campus in 1892. The structure housed the men's dormitory, music and art departments, typing and shorthand room, biology laboratory, a darkroom, and a large recitation room. Insurance covered all but $1,500 of the $75,000 damages. The school repaired Hoover, but razed it in 1954 when architects deemed it unsafe for continued use.

Wood-Mar's southwest corner room served for several years as a library until, in the 1930s, the school moved its books to Wood-Mar Room 14, along the east side of the main floor. Then, in 1947, the College reconstructed a veterans' building into a temporary library. ("Temporary" proved to be 15 years.) Under the direction of librarian Loyde Osburn, students spent the 1948 Easter vacation transporting books in V-shaped wooden troughs built for the purpose. Meanwhile, board member John Brougher in 1947 financed a science building that now bears his name.

FOR YEARS THE DESIGNATION "Pacific College" created much confusion. Several other institutions shared the name, including Pacific University in nearby Forest Grove. Board chairman Walter P. Lee reported being introduced as "president of the board of Pacific University"; the same error sometimes occurred when Pacific College students won newsworthy honors.

The trustees therefore solicited proposals for a new name. By 1949 they had gathered a long list, including Newberg Friends College, Chehalem College, Northwest Friends College, Pacific Quaker College, Friends Pacific College, Herbert Hoover College, Barclay College, Friendswood College, Peace College, and George Fox College.

After discussion, the board turned the matter over to Loyde Osburn, Joseph McCracken, and Robert Nordyke, who recommended the name "Friendswood College."

However, the board rejected the committee report after studying a long, persuasive letter in which alumnus Arthur O. Roberts argued that the name "George Fox College" had compelling historical and religious significance. The board then unanimously adopted the name "George Fox College."

Board member J. A. Dunbar, who personally favored the name even prior to Arthur Roberts' letter, later reported some dissatisfaction from various Idaho Friends who feared overidentification with politically and theologically liberal "Eastern Friends." Although he requested reconsideration, the board maintained its decision.

In a letter to the alumni, President Carey analyzed the new name:

"Pacific means peaceful. George Fox exemplified that spirit to a remarkable degree. However, his character and experience were far broader than his peace testimony. Out of this relationship with God there came also his testimony to the unity of the race, the love of God for all men, the Divine call to Christian service, and the desirability of Christian education."

IN 1948 GERVAS CAREY adamantly demanded retirement from the presidency. The trustees again offered a contract to Walter Williams, who returned two propositions: "(1) that the board consider someone else instead; and (2) if the board felt Williams had a service to render the College, he would accept a three-year appointment on the condition that the University of Florida grant him a three-year leave of absence."

The trustees unanimously accepted the second proposition and invited him to come July 1, 1949, at a salary of $4,800 (compared with the $7,500 he made as a professor

GFC'S VICTORY BELL

The original bell tower in Hoover Hall, Dave Adrian and Gene Hockett ringing the bell in 1980, and the bell's permanent location in the Centennial Tower.

THE ANCIENT VICTORY BELL—long a campus centerpiece—returned to near its time-honored location with the erection of the Centennial Tower in 1990. Pealing from Hoover Hall's tower, the bell for nearly 70 years called students to class and celebrated athletic victories, academic and forensic triumphs, and financial campaign successes.

The bell adorned the building upon its construction in 1885 and moved to the permanent campus seven years later. Only once in the next 62 years did it leave its home. That occurred when several enterprising 1950s students—including freshman Sam Farmer, who years later became GFC vice president for development—

dismantled it. With Farmer as lookout below, the other three students lowered it by rope.

"I was explaining to Dean Donald McNichols what we were doing out there when, unfortunately, the rope broke," Farmer lamented. "It made a terrible BONG when it hit the side of Hoover, then buried itself in the ground below. The next day the junior class dug it up, hauled it off and eventually mounted it on wheels in the gym."

The College razed Hoover shortly thereafter, so the bell remained on wheels, later to be placed in the school museum. Former dean Kenneth Williams recently revealed what happened when two boys stole the bell

66

and hid it in Myrtle Best's house, where they lived while in college:

"Mrs. Best came to Arthur Winters (business manager) to tell him the boys had a door jammed so she could not open it. Mr. Winters understood students quite well. He came into my office correctly predicting the missing bell's location. So one night when the boys were gone, he, Harvey Campbell (registrar) and I dragged the bell out of Mrs. Best's house, took it to Mr. Winters' place, and hid it in his stack of baled hay.

"I called the boys the next morning to tell them we knew they had the bell, and we expected it to be returned immediately. They confessed that they had had the bell, but someone had stolen it from them. I insisted that since they had taken it, they were responsible to get it returned. I called them in several times to see if they were making any progress in getting the bell back.

"Of course they were not, but I kept the heat on them for about a week. Then we three culprits went out and retrieved the bell, put it in its proper place and said nothing about it. The boys discovered it had been returned and came in to report that "someone" had returned the bell. Arthur, Harvey and I had many good laughs about that, but didn't tell anyone what had happened."

In 1959 Reed College students stole the bell and took it to Portland—probably as retaliation against George Fox students burning the letters "GFC" in the Reed campus lawn. After some time President Milo Ross demanded that the bell be returned.

A few weeks later the Reed culprits displayed George Fox's victory symbol during a basketball halftime and nearly set off a riot. George Fox students chased the miscreants from the Reed campus and caught them at the Hawthorne Bridge.

According to *The Crescent*, GFC stood by its "pacifistic stance" and attempted nonviolent persuasion. However, Gary Brown, who later became director of alumni relations, remembers "a scuffle." Whatever the confrontation, the bell slipped from the Reedsters' grasp and disappeared with a splash into the Willamette River.

GFC president Milo Ross issued a stern letter to the Reed president, demanding the bell's hasty return. The Portland school paid to have the river dredged. This work, according to Brown, required "all kinds of divers and equipment." In due time the offenders returned the bell to Newberg to await its permanent position in the Centennial Tower.

of education in Florida). However, the University of Florida president refused to grant Williams a leave. Gervas Carey therefore continued as president a third year. After consideration of several other possibilities, the board selected Dr. Paul E. Parker in the spring of 1950.

Paul Parker earned a bachelor's degree from Arizona State University and the M.A. and Ph.D. from the University of Arizona. He came to George Fox after 11 years as an elementary, high school, and college teacher, and 10 years pastoring Friends churches.

Parker fought impossible obstacles. Finding the need for austerity so great, the president often walked the campus at night, making sure no water taps were running and all unnecessary lights had been turned out. Staggering under a $120,000 indebtedness, the administration refrained from some maintenance and from watering the campus during summer months. Through these measures, Parker heroically managed to balance the budget one of his two years in office. A tuition increase from $250 to $300 in 1951 helped to accomplish this objective.

Paul Parker accepted the presidency because he wanted to help students. Years later, one 1951 sophomore recalled his inability to pay the next semester's $150 tuition. Dr. Parker called him into the presidential office, spoke encouragingly of the young man's future, then confided that an anonymous friend wanted to pay the $150. The student never learned the source, but remembered the kindness. He managed to graduate, later earned advanced degrees, and eventually returned to teach and befriend similar young people at George Fox College.

Wanting to provide a benefit to underpaid faculty, the board in 1951 extended to the teachers' unmarried children the long-standing policy of partially remitting tuition for ministers' dependents. Two years later it broadened the policy to include missionaries.

THE LACK OF REGIONAL accreditation clouded the College's future. The Northwest Association's 1944 recommendations had been partially met, so in 1951 the College submitted another application, this one primarily President Parker's personal work.

In response, the Association applauded the Newberg school for constructing the gymnasium. It noted that George Fox was "clearly committed to worthy objectives in the area of education," adding that "the concern of staff and students for the realization of both Christian and Quaker objectives is readily apparent."

The committee emphasized, however, that "the academic program was definitely subordinate to the realization of the Christian requisites of life." It pointed to major deficiencies in library, salaries, and maintenance. Further, the College's academic program and financial base remained very weak. The Northwest Association delivered a punishing blow to the College and President Parker, as it again denied accreditation.

President Paul Parker resigned in February of 1952, citing intense stresses that caused doubt as to his suitability for the presidency. The board expressed appreciation for

"This college is built primarily on sacrifice."
—Donald McNichols
Administrative Committee Chairman,
1952-1954

---

his contribution, citing specifically his faith, personal sacrifices, humility, efforts to gain financial stability, unselfish devotion to Christian education, promotion of high ideals, and confidence that the College would continue to be a place where God had His way.

THE TRUSTEES WORKED for two years to find a successor. Meanwhile, Dean Donald McNichols, Bible professor Paul Mills, and public relations director Harlow Ankeny administered the College. They did well, considering the obstacles.

Like Parker, the new administrative team balanced the books one of its two years. McNichols described this as "a modern miracle," adding: "This college is built primarily on sacrifice."

Such fiscal conservatism during those years reduced the debt slightly, to under $115,000 in 1953. Board chairman Ivan Adams noted that if 115 people pledged $250 a year, the debt would be paid in four years. Dean Donald McNichols added that a student joining the $25 club would remit annually until 1972 before completely repaying the College for the cost of education above that paid by tuition.

McNichols, a highly gifted literature professor, earned the respect of the college constituency, as did Mills and Ankeny. However, they could not raise enough money to provide solvency. At the conclusion of a 1952-53 drive that produced over 100 new $25 Club memberships, McNichols noted that although this progress was somewhat encouraging, it represented only one half the anticipated total and one fourth the amount needed.

THE COLLEGE, in an attempt to remain orthodox and evangelical, found itself in a difficult competitive position during the 1941 to 1954 period. While educational costs

rose rapidly, the Oregon Yearly Meeting constituency dropped slightly. Furthermore, the school received a decreasing percentage of the Yearly Meeting's college students—from approximately 57 percent down to 30 percent between 1948 and 1954. (Based on the 45 churches reporting in 1954, 43 Yearly Meeting students attended GFC, 30 enrolled at other church-related colleges, and 70 attended secular schools.)

Although fewer Oregon Yearly Meeting students enrolled, the percentage of Quakers at the College increased. In 1948-49, 126 of the 171 students were Friends (73 percent). The next year 151 enrolled, 118 of them Friends (78 percent). By 1954, of the 98 students at GFC, 79 were Quakers (81 percent).

Some Yearly Meeting members expressed concern that the College teach more about Quakers and Quakerism. The school already offered Friends doctrine and Friends

history, but it began to require Quaker students to take the doctrine class.

Some desired that college representatives visit local churches regularly. Many wanted the Yearly Meeting to assume a more active financial role. However, the first six months of the 1953-54 school year, Oregon Yearly Meeting constituents contributed more than 60 percent of the $11,000 gift income. Although inadequate records prevent complete verification, this probably was not unusual.

Yearly Meeting constituents occasionally recommended changes. For example, some argued that the school needed a Dean of Men and Dean of Women in order to tighten discipline. This soon occurred.

A few constituents complained that in a Christian institution, female basketball players should not wear shorts. Board members argued, however, that the women had worn shorts when playing basketball in high school, and the college could not reasonably prohibit them—they might have to drop the sport, since it wouldn't be sensible to play in any other clothing. GFC women continued playing basketball—while wearing shorts.

MEANWHILE, THE TRUSTEES sought a president. Among others, they considered Lowell Roberts, Richard Chambers, Donald Spitler, Arthur Roberts, Mahlon Macy, Sheldon Jackson, and Jack Willcuts. Many felt Willcuts, a 1944 Pacific College graduate, would be ideal; however, he felt God's leading to a second term on Oregon Yearly Meeting's Bolivian mission field.

The board decided in August of 1953 to invite Eugene Coffin, a Quaker from California. The minutes report "a wonderful sense of unity that he is the man." However, Coffin declined, saying he wanted first to complete a master's degree at University of Southern California, then possibly a Ph.D. The Board again considered 1944 graduate Arthur Roberts and Richard Chambers of William Penn College, then turned once more to Eugene Coffin.

In late November of 1953, a unanimous board agreed to offer Coffin a contract for 1955-56. In the intervening year, the College would pay him $3,000 while he pursued the doctorate. Again Coffin declined, this time firmly shutting the door. Next, the board asked highly respected, long-time Friends pastor Charles Beals. He also refused.

By this time, Oregon Yearly Meeting Superintendent Dean Gregory and Administrative Committee Chairman Donald McNichols emphasized that hiring a president had become an urgent priority. Gregory even specualted that the Yearly Meeting would be willing to accept a president from outside Quakerism, assuming the candidate met the other qualifications. The board then studied several non-Quakers without success.

Meanwhile, a Friends pastor named Milo Ross had been undergoing a career change necessitated by his wife's terminal illness. In February 1954, Ross sought work at the College and was hired for three months to solicit students.

THE COLLEGE'S problems mounted. Since 1941, the school had moved toward the more aggressively evangelical position favored by most Yearly Meeting constituents. By the early 1950s, half the students majored in Bible, reflecting the major's strength and the concern for a biblically educated ministerial leadership in the Yearly Meeting.

Yet chief administrators Gulley, Carey, and McNichols all warned against reduction of the liberal arts emphasis. Carey cited students who had gone on to seminary and "discovered they hardly had a college education." Although he had come to Pacific College to enhance Bible offerings, Carey deplored the results: "I have a feeling that we have been giving too much work in the Bible department in undergraduate work." It was easier, he noted, to do deputation and attend prayer meetings than to study science. "A minister needs history and literature and cannot get too much of it."

By 1954 the boost from World War II veterans had run its course and enrollment dipped to 98, only 19 of them non-Quakers. The unaccredited, highly religiously oriented College attracted few outside the denomination. The number of Quaker students had declined from 126 in 1948 to 79 in six years, as most Friends in the Northwest sent their children to less expensive state schools or accredited religious institutions. To make matters worse, no qualified person seemed willing to be president.

With enrollment receding and indebtedness mounting, the College faced its nadir. The board momentarily flirted with a Madison Avenue approach—find and promote a positive slogan, such as "Knowledge on Fire" or "The World's Most Unusual Christian University"—but quickly thought better of it.

The members of George Fox College's 1954 graduating class expressed their confident support in a tangible manner: All 21 graduates joined the $25 Club. It would take more than that, however, to keep the College alive for their children.

Chapter Five

THE NORTHWEST ASSOCIATION of Secondary and Higher Schools accredited George Fox College on December 2, 1959. Without this credential, the school had little prospect of celebrating a 100th birthday—or perhaps even a 75th.

Two years earlier, accreditation seemed inconceivable. An indebtedness that approached $150,000 headed a long list of liabilities. Yet from 1957 to 1959 a remarkable debt liquidation campaign breathed new life into the institution and impressed the accrediting association with the school's long-term viability.

Debt elimination required a dedicated, united, confident constituency. That Oregon Yearly Meeting regained that confidence is perhaps the most significant story in the College's first century. From this renewed constituent support came the strength to develop academic quality worthy of accreditation.

Symbolically and actually, the recovery process relates closely to two personnel decisions: the hiring of Arthur O. Roberts and Milo C. Ross.

In October of 1952, Oregon Yearly Meeting Superintendent Dean Gregory journeyed to New Hampshire to confer with Roberts, a Friends pastor completing his Ph.D. in history of Christianity at Boston University. A graduate of Greenleaf Friends Academy, Pacific College, and Nazarene Theological Seminary, Roberts agreed to teach religion and philosophy for $3,000 a year.

With Fern and their three children, Roberts moved in 1953 at age 30 from the academic intensity of Boston and Harvard universities to a North River Street "vet house" apartment and a Wood-Mar Hall classroom. A brilliant scholar who became an internationally heralded Quaker thinker, Roberts provided stability and a deep Friends conscience. He served for 35 years as a teacher and administrator before becoming "Professor-at-Large" in 1988.

In March of 1954, after spending two years considering at least 15 prospective presidents, the George Fox Col-

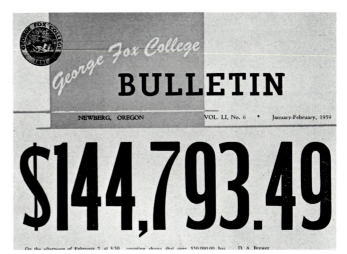

Announcing one of the outstanding events in the College's history.

lege board unanimously appointed Milo C. Ross at a salary of $3,800 with a $720 housing allowance. (Like Roberts, the new president first lived in a "vet house.") The trustees hired Ross with Oregon Yearly Meeting's full approval, evidenced by positive letters from representative leaders such as former Greenleaf Academy principal Arthur H. Winters, Newberg Friends Church pastor Charles Beals, and Idaho businessman J. Allen Dunbar, a GFC board member.

With the hiring of Roberts and Ross, the Yearly Meeting and other constituents felt a united confidence in the College's leadership. The dominant theme was faith in a work that Ross, Roberts and the other faculty, the board, and the Yearly Meeting firmly believed to be God's will. The common goal of a high-quality, Christ-centered liberal arts college unified the academic community that would serve Northwest Quakerism and evangelicalism generally.

Ross and Roberts led the school's climb to heights previously unparalleled. The confidence they inspired led to Oregon Yearly Meeting's renewed support, the successful debt liquidation campaign and, consequently, full accreditation by the Northwest Association of Secondary and Higher Schools.

The two symbolized the College's dual emphasis of that era: increasing evangelical Friends support and developing academic strength. Oregon Yearly Meeting respected both men, and the larger Quaker community recognized them as bridgebuilders and eloquent evangelical spokespersons. Roberts' intellect commanded respect; Ross's fortitude and social nerve inspired confidence. Intellectuals and spiritual leaders listened, and the College advanced.

Milo Ross's upbringing contributed to his understanding of Quaker issues. Reared in a Friends home in Salem, Oregon, he grew up fully conscious of the intellectual/

Fall Regular Student Enrollment, 1954-1968		
1954—109	1959—144	1964—336
1955—133	1960—179	1965—344
1956—122	1961—197	1966—358
1957—142	1962—230	1967—387
1958—142	1963—298	1968—392

theological battles that prompted Oregon Yearly Meeting's withdrawal from Five Years Meeting of Friends Church.

Profoundly influenced by the ensuing surge of evangelical enthusiasm that spawned the Christian Workers' League, Oregon Yearly Meeting's mission thrust into Bolivia, and the movement for a more evangelically oriented college, young Ross sought a deep, profoundly Christian experience. In the summer of 1929, he answered God's call to Christian service at Twin Rocks youth conference on the Oregon coast. For a time he considered a missionary career.

Along with many other young Friends who looked toward full-time Christian service, Ross bypassed Pacific College in favor of Portland Bible Institute (later renamed Cascade College), where he earned a Bible diploma. He eventually received a bachelor's degree in Spanish and the secondary teaching credential from Willamette University. In 1934, while still a university student serving as part-time pastor, Ross married Helen Ritter. Even before the ceremony, they appeared before the mission board to announce their willingness to serve in Bolivia if God so directed.

God did not lead the Rosses to Bolivia. Instead, Ross became a Quaker preacher, serving churches in Rosedale, Oregon (1933-1936); Greenleaf, Idaho (1936-42); Medford, Oregon (1942-1949); and Seattle, Washington (1949-1953). He also moonlighted for the postal service, a fruit cannery, and in construction as a union carpenter. For several years he was the unpaid radio voice of the *Quaker Hour*, which broadcast to hundreds of thousands in seven states.

Milo Ross did not move easily toward college administration. In fact, at first he had little interest in the College. As he later pointed out: "It came as a creeping surprise to me . . . that my interest kept growing in George Fox College." He felt inadequate with only a bachelor's degree. "I questioned if I could teach, and I didn't want to embarrass the

---

*"I have made a rule never to let a day go by
without asking for money."*

—Milo Ross, president, 1954-1969

---

board further—my impressions were that small colleges had too many ill-prepared misfits already. But all the while I became more interested."

In 1953 the Rosses' oldest son, Stephen, decided to enroll as a freshman at George Fox. Shortly thereafter, Helen Ross's chronic illness, from which she was to die in 1954, forced a move from the pastorate in Seattle to Salem.

Milo Ross faced a career change. "Almost in a weak moment, I let Ivan Adams [chairman of the trustees] know of my interest in coming to work at the College," Ross noted later. Within a few weeks he accepted a part-time job assisting in student recruitment.

Meanwhile, the board searched for a president. The administrative team, headed by Dean Donald McNichols, had performed admirably under severely distressing circumstances. However, by 1954 enrollment dipped to 98. To many onlookers, the College's life seemed limited. The stormy 1940s had taken their toll. The board simply could find no qualified individual willing to face creditors and uneasy constituents in what some thought a hopeless cause.

Yet the College's original mission continued to inspire constituents. Recognizing that a reasonably high-quality educational program still existed, many in Oregon Yearly Meeting maintained a supportive, hopeful attitude. Perhaps given strong, competent, confidence-inspiring leadership, the College had a future. Many expressed surprise when the board chose Milo Ross as president early in 1954. Yet putting his very considerable energy and creativity into the work, he set out to *make* the College succeed.

ALTHOUGH MILO ROSS had been a successful pastor and church planter, few thought him qualified to head the

College. Most agreed with Ross himself that a 43-year-old pastor with only a bachelor's degree and no training in college administration had scant presidential qualifications. How could a pastor with no doctorate inspire respect from a faculty full of academics? he wondered.

Years later someone asked Milo Ross whether his experience as a Friends pastor had provided adequate training for the college presidency. He responded negatively, noting that Friends churches traditionally had no pastors, and those that eventually adopted the system carefully avoided pastoral control:

"How different this was from the administrative function of a college president! On my first day behind the desk, I was besieged with a volley of questions from faculty and students, all of whom demanded immediate answers. Decision making had never been considered or discussed in any ministers' conference I had ever attended!

"... In over twenty years of pastoral experience, I had never had a church office, let alone a secretary. Now over forty years of age, I had never dictated a letter! ... I was given to snap judgment, often biased by a lack of full or balanced information. I must have been more afraid of myself than others were of me, but going to my office as early as possible ... I had my devotional quiet time, asking

God for wisdom, and especially that we should all be protected from error, mistakes in the college in particular. And time after time, as difficult decisions had to be made, they were often wiser and more equitable than my human wisdom alone could have dictated."

Ross immediately asked the board to appoint Donald McNichols, Arthur Roberts, and himself as an administrative committee. Effective leadership required consultative decisions involving scholars with wisdom shaped by the academic and administrative cauldrons, he believed. He read rapidly and retained data and interpretation. He felt comfortable with scholars and at home with the arts.

Although a part of Oregon Yearly Meeting's evangelical impulse, Ross had no defensive anti-intellectualism and feared neither secular academics nor "liberal" Quakers. He immediately set out to improve his abilities and to establish relationships with potentially helpful people. He took a reading class with Arthur Roberts in Friends history and doctrine. He developed warm, beneficial friendships with the presidents of Reed, Lewis and Clark, Linfield, Willamette, and other neighboring institutions, and with Quaker colleges such as Guilford, Whittier, Malone, William Penn, Earlham, and Swarthmore. "Perhaps, almost by osmosis, a person picks up 'know-how' from those who know more than he and who have had experiences which they are willing to share."

Previous administrations quite naturally had exercised extreme austerity in attempting to balance each annual budget and avoid increasing the burgeoning debt. This impeded creativity. Ross took another approach: Be creative and build attractive programs, he reasoned, and morale will improve, students will come, donors will give and the bills will be paid. Long-term progress requires short-term improvements. The College's image and its reality must be of growth and increasing programmatic strength.

In other words, Ross believed that constituent acceptance required immediate improvements. A flurry of activity brought several innovations; some had a price tag. As a result, during Ross's first three years, the administration and board added more than $40,000 to the debt. They increased underwritten scholarships from one to seven, raised salaries, initiated a faculty rank and tenure plan, and added majors in art (in cooperation with the Museum Art School in Portland), music education, and psychology-sociology.

They also boosted tuition from $300 to $350 annually, enlarged the Board of Trustees from 15 to 30 members, inaugurated a special financial drive called the "George Fox College Advance" (which netted over $20,000 the first year), and enrolled 86 members in the "Century Club," a

Students enjoying the newly completed Student Union, 1958. Included are Jerry Pierce, Meredith (Richey) Morse, Paul Morse, and Jack Hoskins. The dining hall is in the background.

group that pledged $100 annual donations. In addition, they explored official relationships with other Friends yearly meetings.

The creative flurry even included hiring an architect, Donald Edmundson, to analyze the potential for campus construction. With amazing prescience, the trustees projected a library, music hall, chapel, dormitories, married student housing, a house for the president, and parking. Although they did not pursue these ideas immediately, the school clearly had renounced negativism for a vision of greatness.

In 1956 the board planned a modern dormitory to be financed with federal funds; it was not completed, however, until 1962. In 1958, a gift from the family of recent

graduate Dick Mott and an increase in student body fees provided a student union building. According to Ross, George Fox was the smallest college in the United States with a full-fledged student union. The SUB, he soon reported, "has done more than any one thing to raise morale, elicit community support, and produce a situation of satisfaction."

Beginning in 1954, the "chemistry" was right for this sudden upsurge in George Fox College's fortunes. For the first time in a great while, the Yearly Meeting constituents accepted the College as totally parallel with their own mission and themselves as active participants. Without this

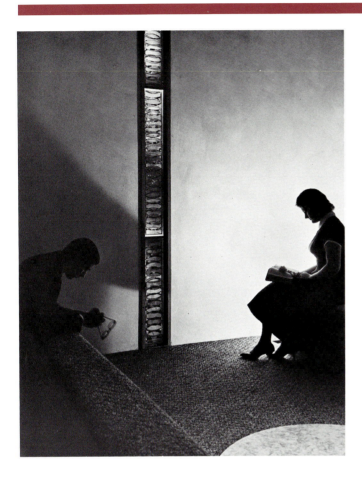

rejuvenated support, the College could not have moved forward. Buoyed partly by increased scholarships and a deferred tuition payment plan, enrollment increased by 36 percent during Ross's first two years (from 98 to 133).

Longtime rival Cascade College also played a positive role. In 1957 it awarded President Ross the Doctor of Divinity degree. Three years later Cascade's dean, Phillip S. Clapp, served as half-time visiting dean, helping GFC develop its curriculum.

HAD THE NEW administration opted for fiscal austerity and debt reduction in 1954, it probably would have failed. Continued inadequate programs could not have caught the imagination of the faculty and students; few potential donors would have committed themselves to a debt reduction drive seen only as anointment for burial.

In 1955, appreciative Oregon Yearly Meeting executive committee members recommended strong OYM support of the College's budget. One year later, they set a $20,000 annual goal and almost succeeded: The Yearly Meeting's 5,000 members contributed $15,776, $19,892 and $16,528 the next three years. After three one-year terms as presi-

dent, a unanimous board enthusiastically extended Ross a five-year call.

Donald McNichols left the College for further graduate work in 1955. By 1959 the administrative team included Kenneth Williams, dean of the faculty; Denver Headrick, director of development; James Bishop, public relations officer; Arthur Winters, business manager; and Harvey Campbell, registrar. George Moore replaced Williams as dean of the faculty in 1961.

Each man contributed significantly to the school's progress. Williams, who initially served as dean of students, enforced stringent rules that brought several expulsions due to smoking; however, the amiable Dean provided a positive, optimistic atmosphere in the student body. Headrick effectively contacted hundreds within and outside the Yearly Meeting. Campbell served as an effective part of a progress-oriented team. Winters proved adept at relating positively to students and faculty while making decidedly limited resources stretch to cover the school's necessities.

DONALD McNICHOLS had laid an excellent foundation for advancement toward accreditation, but the Northwest Association seriously doubted whether 5,000 Quakers could support a college. The overwhelming indebtedness made accreditation seem out of the question.

When Ross first became president, he made a thorough study of accreditation history at George Fox and neighboring colleges. The Northwest Association would not accept the school, he concluded, without improved salaries, programs, constituent support, and significant

75

debt reduction. Although Ross himself contributed to the indebtedness by deficit spending calculated to restore optimism, he realized that the college obligations had to be faced before they got completely out of hand.

In January of 1957, Oregon Yearly Meeting Superintendent Dean Gregory reported to the board that significant Yearly Meeting sentiment favored an effort to liquidate the entire $144,000 indebtedness. He recommended a campaign to complete the task by 1960. In the discussion, John Brougher, a Vancouver physician and staunch College and Yearly Meeting supporter, started the program by pledging $10,000. An anonymous donor pledged another $10,000.

During the next two years, repeated contacts to Friends churches, alumni, Newberg residents, and other constituents brought remarkable success. The soliciters completed the campaign February 2, 1959, eliminating the entire debt a year before the target date. Afterward, the George Fox College *Bulletin* described the campaign:

"On the afternoon of February 2, at 3:30 President Ross received a long-distance call which confirmed the last pledge of $2,000 putting the Debt Liquidation Campaign 'over the top.' Born in a prayer meeting held in the home of one of the board members in the winter of 1956-57, the drive has progressed over the intervening months to embrace every segment of the college constituency: board members themselves, faculty and staff, pastors of supporting churches, alumni in many parts of the world, Friends, townspeople and Newberg business houses, Oregon corporations, and foundations.

"The organization was full-orbed, too. The board authorized the creation of sponsors and regional committees, the alumni association organized itself by chapters and graduating classes, Denver B. Headrick gave a major portion of his time and energy to the cause, and during the last year the City of Newberg itself rose to the occasion through the Chamber of Commerce, a speakers' bureau and door-to-door solicitation. Thousands of pages of literature went out from the college offices, hundreds of inches of newspaper space were freely granted, and we enjoyed the cooperation and enthusiastic support of friends, both old and new."

The American Association of Colleges awarded President Ross a "citation of merit" for "having the best debt liquidation drive of its kind in the United States." Newberg citizens, who contributed $25,000, named Milo Ross their "Man of the Year"—an honor that would have been out of the question for any George Fox College president a decade earlier.

During the final campaign year, Oregon Yearly Meeting led the nation in constituent support for colleges. The

Council for Financial Aid to Education reported that OYM's $8.76 per member contribution more than doubled any other denomination's aid to its college.

Debt liquidation may be the hardest money to raise. Yet the campaign inspired Oregon Yearly Meeting. The church accepted the objective, however distasteful, as a means to an end: accreditation. This reawakened constituency gave new life to the College, like a stricken patient rising from the deathbed.

THE ACCREDITATION PROCESS began with a 170-page self-evaluation report in 1957-58, written by Arthur Roberts and Kenneth Williams. The report detailed the College's history and mission, its strengthening academic programs, and its optimistic anticipation of the future. It showed that despite low salaries and a substandard library, the College effectively educated its students; for example, GFC graduates earned advanced degrees proportionate to those from accredited schools. In April of 1959, the examining committee visited the College. Afterward, it re-

ported some deficiencies to be met, notably in library, faculty salaries, and institutional control of majors and teacher loads.

President Ross appeared before the Higher Commission in Spokane December 1, 1959. He reported significant progress toward meeting the deficiencies cited eight months earlier. The improvements pleased the commission. The next day—December 2, 1959—it granted George Fox College a two-year accreditation. Thus, the school attained its most significant milestone since 1925, when it had gained recognition by the then-extant U.S. Bureau of Educational Standards.

The report carried some stipulations, however, notably an immediate and sustained increase in faculty salaries. The committee also advised elimination of some small enrollment courses, criticized the College for overloading its administrative staff, and again encouraged library improvement.

According to its recorded minutes, the college board reacted to accreditation in this manner:

"This report was received with a deep sense of gratitude to our Heavenly Father for His answer to the many prayers which have been offered by friends and constituency through the years, and to President Ross, the college administrative committee, and the faculty for their unswerving devotion to the cause of accreditation. This spirit of rejoicing and thanksgiving was accompanied by a recognition that difficult tasks still lie ahead and that dedi-

cation and deep devotion on the part of the trustees are essential if the college is to continue to progress and fulfill the divine purpose for which it was instituted. The members of the board entered into this business session in a spirit of humility and utter dependence upon God, and our Savior, Jesus Christ, for Divine wisdom and guidance."

Following this, trustee Eugene Coffin offered a motion, unanimously adopted by a spontaneous standing vote, commending the president for his "excellent public relations" and "fine representation of the college" before its various publics. Three years later the board again expressed its thanks to God and its esteem for Ross, pointing to the College's "growth and spiritual progress" and the president's leadership among the wider bodies of Friends and the educational community across the United States.

Milo Ross accepted the accolades graciously. Yet the president knew those around him deserved significant credit. Even before accreditation, Ross had told the board of his appreciation for the faculty, noting that "the loyalty, concern, consecration, and service of our entire faculty and staff are amazing. Many could work in institutions where the salaries are greater, and many have. We presently have people on our payroll who left positions in larger institutions, and where the salary was anywhere from $500 to $3,000 more than George Fox pays. It is a source of humbling joy to work with such people."

IN FACULTY RECRUITMENT, Ross and the board followed two fundamental principles borrowed from the president of Harvard University and the founder of Oberlin College: (1) Agree on the best person in the world for the particular position, then go after him or her; and (2) pray specifically about that person, anticipating that the college and candidate would together ascertain God's will.

Milo Ross's account of hiring Cecilia Martin in 1954 reveals much about this era. He later told of unsuccessfully trying until late that summer, his first in office, to secure a Spanish teacher. Then one day a visitor asked if the College had any open positions, revealing:

" 'My field is languages. I like English literature, but I can handle others as well.'

'What others?'

'French, German, Spanish, Italian, Greek, Latin, and Hebrew.'

"This was already too good to be true. But I had a sneaking suspicion that that kind came high. Our salaries were rock-bottom.... I made some more sounds about Spanish and that it was an orphan with us, half-time, and all that, but her answer still left me with a little hope when she claimed that she and her husband had but recently

Faculty and staff in early 1960s. Front row: Edna Williams, Sarah McCracken, Cecelia Martin, Helen (Willcuts) Street, Mary Sutton, Harriett Storaker, Mary Hazelle. Middle row: Kenneth Williams, Mackey Hill, Helen Ross, Dilla Tucker, Genette McNichols, Marie Tieleman, Hector Munn, Evan Rempel (with Lady). Back row: Denver Headrick, Arthur Winters, Milo Ross, Earl Hazelle, Paul Mills, Arthur Roberts, Harvey Campbell, Floyd Weitzel, Jim Bishop.

moved to Newberg, that he did not want her to work full time, but she hated to allow all her education and experience to be wasted. So I asked what her training consisted of. A bachelor's and a master's degree, together with a full doctorate from the University of Washington. Later I was to learn it was a Phi Beta Kappa!"

Cecilia Martin's presence doubled the faculty Ph.D.'s. First half time, and later full time, she gave excellent service for 19 years. As a devout Episcopalian, Dr. Martin reinforced the school's Christian impact on world culture. "I have marveled ever since," Ross confided. "I had no other applicants for any subject, let alone Spanish. My prayers had been answered exactly."

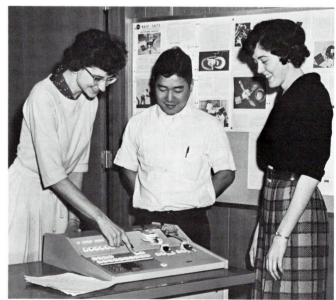

Professor Dorothy Oppenlander demonstrating GFC's first computer, a PDS-1020. The students are Hideo Osakabe and Linda (Davenport) Swenwold.

78

Paul Mills teaching a Bible class. Students are Darryl Nordyke, Seung Kyu Kim, Dick Lakin, Jan (Burnett) Schmeltzer, Edgar Madrid, Charles Mylander, Daniel Cammack, and Ron Stansell.

The College progressed remarkably in the attempt to upgrade its academic standing. The board tried to attract faculty members with doctorates and encouraged young faculty to continue their educations. Between 1954 and 1969, faculty doctorates increased from one to nine, with several others in process. The College attempted to balance young scholars with mature teachers such as home economist Helen (Willcuts) Street, who served a total of 16 years; Paul Mills, who retired in 1974 after 27 years; and Laurence Skene, who served 21 years.

George Moore, one of the new doctorates, headed the faculty as dean. After suffering severe disappointments while a Pacific College teacher/administrator in the difficult 1940s, Moore earned a Ph.D. in education from the University of Iowa. In 1961, Milo Ross invited him back to the place of shattered dreams, made him a partner in the school's sparkling achievements, and pronounced him "one of the ablest leaders in the field of Christian higher education." Moore complemented Ross's personality, contributing greatly to the optimistic planning and staffing of an improving College. He served as dean and professor of education and psychology until 1968. After retirement from administration, he continued to teach until 1976.

Years later, the personable dean remained fondly in students' memories; many recalled his "Thisa-and-thata" chapels, in which he would deal with assorted academic and spiritual concerns. Upon his retirement, the students dedicated the *L'Ami* to his honor. Long after his death in 1984, the faculty remembered him for his genuine collegiality and famous pancake breakfasts.

Hector Munn taught science at George Fox from 1958 to 1962, and again beginning in 1967. He completed the Ph.D. at Oregon State University in 1969 and served the school creditably through the remainder of its first century, as registrar after 1977.

Myron Goldsmith, an outstanding religion and Greek professor, came to GFC from a career as a Friends pastor in North Carolina. Arriving in 1961, Goldsmith added much strength to the increasingly significant Bible and religion emphasis. He wrote his Ph.D. dissertation at Boston University on Oregon Quaker pioneer William Hobson.

Goldsmith contributed significantly to Oregon Yearly Meeting by giving leadership to pastors' short courses, workshops for church leaders, service as Yearly Meeting/College archivist, leadership on various committees, and coauthorship with Jack Willcuts of a book entitled *Friends in the Soaring Seventies*.

Dennis Hagen, a gifted music teacher, arrived in 1964 and also remained through the conclusion of the first century. His instrumental groups brought credit to the College. During the 1980s the versatile Hagen spearheaded the Champoeg Historical Pageant and became known as Oregon's leading authority in pageantry, assisting in historical pageants throughout the state. In 1988 he completed a public school administrator's credential and became an important part of the College's teacher education program.

Bob Gilmore also joined the faculty in 1964 and served past the end of the College's first century. His versatility allowed him to teach Spanish and direct the school's Instructional Media Center. With his wife, Maurine, Gilmore provided remarkably efficient audiovisual services in spite of numerous adversities.

Mackey Hill, with an A.B. from the University of California, Los Angeles, and an M.A. in history from the University of the Pacific, served from 1949 to 1974, usually as the entire history, political science, and economics departments.

As needed, he also taught reading and conference classes in sociology and geography. Meanwhile, he took graduate classes when possible and for several years pastored concurrently at the Carlton Free Methodist Church, about 12 miles from Newberg. He and his wife, Bertha, reared six children, all GFC attenders. His former students hail Professor Hill as a Christian gentleman who served cheerfully and faithfully under intensely adverse circumstances.

The College awarded the third honorary degree in its 70-year history to Mary Sutton at the completion of her 52 years of service. During her long career, she taught German and biology while serving as the college registrar and faculty secretary. Former students uniformly praise her for her keen mind and demanding classes. The Mary Sutton Residence Hall, constructed in 1977, memorializes her enormous ministry at George Fox College.

Other GFC faculty merit mention, among them longtime art teacher Pete Snow, scientists Elver Voth, Dale Orkney, and John Brewster, each who came to the College during the 1960s; the latter three earned doctorates while at GFC. Marjorie (Larrance) Weesner coached in 1953-54, then returned a decade later to begin a career that extended through the College's first century. Known affectionately as "Doc," she completed the Ph.D. in 1971 while coaching and teaching physical education.

Psychologist Sheldon Louthan came in 1963, after five years at Los Angeles Pacific College. Louthan, George Moore, and David Myton materially strengthened the teacher education program.

Considering the size of the school, George Fox succeeded in attracting an exceptional teaching corps. Without it the College could not have maintained its accreditation and improving reputation.

YET THE FACULTY and staff were woefully underpaid—a problem that worried the board and college personnel. In 1954, five years before accreditation, the faculty salary committee of Arthur Roberts, Helen (Willcuts) Street, and Paul Mills proposed a schedule allowing $3,000 for beginning instructors and $6,500 for full professors with extensive experience. While admitting that resultant salaries would be somewhat higher than for most small colleges (which averaged $2,743 for instructors and $4,800 for professors), the committee members defended the plan. The scale could be reached in four stages, they argued, each remitted by a 15-student enrollment gain and a 75-member $25 Club increase.

The board ruled against tying salary increases to $25 Club memberships, however. It also decided the plan could not begin without a balanced budget, which required 140 students. So the faculty struggled through the 1950s at salaries ranging from $2,100 to $3,000, with six members occupying "vet houses"—the army surplus housing units that had occupied the campus since World War II. Some faculty expressed discontent, noting that the average GFC faculty member received $2,000 less than the Linfield counterpart, $1,250 below the average at Lewis and Clark, $1,000 below Seattle Pacific, and $500 below Northwest Nazarene College.

80

In February 1956, the board adopted a salary minimum of $2,400 for a beginning bachelor's degree and a $4,900 maximum for a Ph.D. with extensive experience—all contingent on the school's ability to pay. The College paid the salaries, however, by borrowing $4,000 that summer and $2,500 the next.

Always responsive to opportunity, President Ross chose the first board meeting after accreditation to recommend immediate compliance with the Higher Commission's stipulations.

He suggested three blanket $500 annual salary increases. However, caution overcame the euphoria. The board approved only the plan's first year.

Nevertheless, significant progress followed. Between 1954 and 1969 minimum faculty salaries increased from $2,100 to $6,200, with maximum salaries up from $3,000 to $10,000.

Although partly financed by enrollment gains and tuition increases, the faculty also benefited from foundation support. For example, in 1962 the Calder Foundation gave $25,000 for faculty assistance, including a well-deserved $2,000 Holy Land and European study tour for Bible professor Paul Mills.

THREE MONTHS AFTER ACCREDITATION, Dr. Thomas E. Jones, former president of Earlham College who had become Administrative Consultant for the Association of American Colleges, thoroughly analyzed the College. President Ross later asserted that his close friend and adviser's evaluation represented "the best $150 we ever allowed!"

After recommending broader general fund support, Jones stated that "the remarkable success of George Fox in lifting an indebtedness that had been hanging like a pall for some years, and the universal spirit of good will of alumni, students, Newberg businessmen, churches and colleges in the Portland-Willamette area have made possible a new era. Too great a proportion of the current support of the college comes from student tuition and fees.... [It] is scarcely fair from the standpoint of a church which expects the college to carry its heritage and spread its point of view in a growing industrial and cultural section of the country....

"George Fox College has taken on new life. It is well located, has an increasing clientele, the backing of the Northwest Association of Secondary and Higher Schools, and the good wishes of its educational neighbors. It must increase the plant, the quality and compensation of faculty, design a more exciting program, and work with the church and community to develop a high grade Quaker college."

The following year Professor Jones wrote that "a great Quaker institution is aborning in the Northwest." The Higher Commission renewed accreditation in 1961. Its chairman commented: "Now you have a college of some eminence."

ACCREDITATION OPENED some long-closed doors. George Fox College immediately joined the Oregon Colleges' Foundation and the Oregon Independent Colleges' Association. The next year alumni support increased by $5,000, to a total of $40,500; board members donated $10,800. Long-time plant services employee Isaac Smith and his wife, Esther, gave their $25,000 house. The Calder Foundation of New York City, parent of Publisher's Paper Company in Newberg, supplied another $25,000.

Earlier, the federal government contributed through the post-World War II G.I. Bill. In 1959 the government initiated National Defense Education loans; one decade later it contributed well over $100,000 annually. Other federal programs in the 1960s provided $118,000 for

"The remarkable success of George Fox in lifting an indebtedness that had been hanging like a pall for some years, and the universal spirit of good will of alumni, students, Newberg businessmen, churches and colleges in the Portland-Willamette area have made possible a new era."

—Dr. Tom Jones, Administrative Consultant for the Association of American Colleges, 1961

Calder Center, $3,300 for audiovisual aids, construction loans for Pennington Hall, Edwards Hall, Weesner Village, and Heacock Commons, and money for student employment. The College benefited mightily from the infusion of federal aid.

GFC soon launched the Diamond Jubilee, its primary fundraising vehicle during the 1960s. The brainchild of Denver Headrick, this successful drive set as priorities money for faculty salaries, scholarships, buildings, and endowment.

Headrick later reported personal visits with 250 corporations; 80 percent had never heard of George Fox College. He cited three essential words for success: "Work, work, and work."

Milo Ross also put it directly: "I have made a rule never to let a day go by without asking for money."

Gilbert and Olive Shambaugh provided the College's most significant gift to that time. In 1960 they donated $275,000 for library construction. Gilbert Shambaugh graduated from Earlham College and taught briefly at Pacific before 1920; Olive Johnson Shambaugh graduated from Pacific College. New Mexico land holdings made them wealthy late in life.

The Shambaughs became interested in supporting the College through her niece, the president's efficient secretary, Gwen Winters. In a letter, Shambaugh asked many detailed, technical questions about the school's philosophy, structure, legal status, and financial position. To respond, Ross had to secure legal information, interview trust officers of two banks, and solicit written opinions from the Internal Revenue Service. In a few days Gilbert Shambaugh responded, in part:

"Dear Dr. Ross:

"I knew all the answers. I wanted to know if you did...."

Over the months the parties exchanged several letters, requiring extensive research by the board and president. Finally, Ross interviewed the Shambaughs in Albuquerque. Before he left, members of Newberg Friends Church held an all-night prayer meeting.

Milo Ross tells more:

"All was arranged, when a letter came only five days before our departure, reading in part: 'We suggest you do not come. We do not have the available money to go ahead with the library project. Your coming will only be a mutual embarrassment. Sorry.'

"Letters, of which this is a sample, are the reasons why college presidents go to early graves! But I couldn't stop. I had too much momentum. We simply had to proceed, but in some reasonable manner and without offense. I immediately answered it, trying not to show too great disappointment, but telling of our firm program to come as far as southern Colorado [on another matter], where and when on a certain afternoon, I planned to call long distance. Of course, I told no one of the problem, except my secretary.

"That phone call from Alamosa was one of the most difficult I ever made. It took courage for me even to lift the receiver. But, wonder of wonders, from the other end I heard Mr. Shambaugh's pleasant voice and the words, 'Come right on down. We have an apartment ready. We can hardly wait!'

"...I was never grilled so long and so astutely by anyone before or since about George Fox College. For several hours into the night and again the next morning, we ranged in animated discussion from questions of the con-

nection with the church to the academic plans for the future, to the calibre of the Board of Trustees, to student life, to the support by the city of Newberg. His questions were piercing and almost devastating....

"Admitting... that George Fox may not have been strong, an infusion of ready funds could make a dramatic change for the better. And while money in itself cannot guarantee excellence and future greatness, given a strong board and administration, and a keen faculty with ability, imagination, and willingness to innovate, adequate funds could make their dreams come true....

"My clincher came in an effort to have him face up to the opportunity he had to become the 'angel' for George Fox. As others had helped one college after another, why should he not come forward for George Fox? He saw the light! Rather, he saw it all the time. He was probing to see if the other party in the conversation had a glimmer or two."

One month later the Shambaughs visited the campus to discuss technical details and finalize arrangements for their gift. According to Milo Ross, GFC students challenged

Foreign students, 1962. Front row: Seung Kyu Kim, Korea;
Andrew Waweru Muune, Kenya; Hideo Osakabe, Japan; Sayed
Habibollah Kazerunian, Iran. Back row: Ki Hong Ryu,
Korea; Sang Jeung Kim, Korea; Julius Wafula, Kenya; Edgar
Amilcan Madrid, Guatemala; Bowers Chasia Ukiru, Kenya;
Myung Tok Pae, Korea; Won Geum Gym, Korea; Sang Tok Pae,
Korea. (Not pictured: David Liu, Taiwan).

Shambaugh's skepticism about college young people. While
in Newberg, the couple attended the Christian Endeavor
(youth meeting) at Newberg Friends Church. Ross reported
that Shambaugh "was happy to see in excess of a hundred
college students enthusiastically singing rousing choruses,
engaging in earnest impromptu prayers, and a number giving thrilling accounts of answers to prayer and evidence of
divine intervention in providing for their return or coming
to college.... I recalled his having been especially critical
of youth when we had conferrred in his home less than a
month before, but the George Fox collegians, innocent of
the biases of the crippled gentleman who sat in the rear of
the church, atypical of the average American youth, to be

sure, had accomplished for their college what no amount
of formal statements or protestation in brochure would
ever do."

As a result, Gilbert and Olive Shambaugh gave George
Fox College almost enough holdings to completely finance
the Shambaugh library, an absolute necessity for the College's developing prosperity.

IN 1964 Headrick and Ross approached the Louis Calder
Foundation regarding a much-needed classroom and
laboratory building. The Newberg-connected foundation
had already given smaller gifts, but invited Ross to New
York City in 1964 to present plans for a science building.
Once again, Newberg Friends Church members supported
the trip with an all-night prayer meeting.

Ross arrived in New York, checked into an inexpensive
hotel with no available room containing a bath, "and
thereon hangs a tale," the president later revealed. Then
he faced the foundation executives:

"I was pretty nervous.... I knew I had their tacit
approval from the looks on their faces. They were very
pleased, indeed, with the sketches. They all liked them
immediately.... We talked on for an hour or more before
Mr. Dreher asked the fateful question. I had to answer, 'At
least $300,000,' which was the figure given me by
[architect] Don Lindgren. I saw the men look at each other.
Then Mr. Dreher spoke for the three: 'We will give you
$300,000....'

"We had won! What I did not know until much later
was that the Calder board had put the ceiling on their possible gift at $200,000 prior to my coming. But, seeing the
very clever plans, they had upped it by common consent
another $100,000. The argument over whether or not a
good architect pays for himself has its answer as far as our
experience is concerned....

"We parted, as may be imagined, on the best of terms,
with my walking across mid-Manhattan to my hotel. I
began to feel ill and as I went along, a nausea and stomach
distress hit me. I was barely able to get to my room. And
there I was without a bath! I was so ill that I could hardly
lift my head off the bed. During the night I made fourteen
trips to the public bath, down the length of the long cor-
ridor where my room was, across the entire front of the
hotel, and back along a far side—I couldn't have been farther away! ... Such are the occupational hazards of a college president."

Milo Ross revealed another personally embarrassing
incident. On one trip from the East Coast he stopped in
Dearborn, Michigan, with but $5.00 remaining—only to
discover that the airport was in Ypsilanti, 30 miles from his

destination. Discovering that one-way bus transportation cost more than $5.00, the unflappable president paid $3.95 for a ticket that got him part way, then "walked the last three or four miles into the American Road Offices, arriving hot and hurried without much time to spare." After the interview the host gave Ross a Dearborn Museum tour. Ross thoroughly enjoyed it, albeit nervously wondering how he would get to the airport. With less than two hours before flight time, the host asked the same question.

"That was a hard one! It might not be to the best interests of higher education and George Fox College in particular if he were to know that I was down to $1.05. So I thought up a fast one. In a wink I responded, 'Oh, I came in on the Greyhound.' I don't think he caught on, but I shall never know. At least, he didn't show it. He carried on instead by saying, 'That's a long, tiring trip, what with the evening traffic and all; let me call my chauffeur. He can get you there in half the time.' With that he summoned a liveried driver, and I was whisked away to the airport in a black Thunderbird! You can add your own moral. If you want more, it is simply the saying among college presidents, 'No one will give money if he knows your college needs it.'"

George Fox College did need it. Ross and Headrick kept asking. Sometimes they succeeded. For example, in 1965 the College constructed a dining hall with funds given by Everett and Bertha Heacock and other donors.

THE COLLEGE'S NEWLY WON status also made low-interest federal construction loans available. As a result, in 1962 the College constructed Pennington Hall (a dormitory named in honor of Levi and Rebecca) with a $594,000 government loan. The same year, the school built Weesner Village (honoring Oliver Weesner, who taught at the College for 50 years) with $130,000 of Housing and Home Financing Agency funding. The 32-apartment complex served married students at first; later, as enrollment mounted, the College used it as overflow singles housing.

George Fox College constructed Edwards Hall, another dormitory, in 1964. M. Lowell Edwards, a Pacific College graduate who invented the heart valve (son of Clarence Edwards, Pacific's first graduate, and grandson of Jesse Edwards), provided $18,000 for furnishings. Noting that 89-year-old President Emeritus Levi Pennington interested Edwards in giving to the College, the board sent the long-time president this resolution:

"The Board of Trustees meeting in an all day session has considered the recent significant developments in connection with the interest of M. Lowell Edwards; and it has been brought to our attention by President Milo C. Ross and others that much of this interest can be traceable to

Pi Gamma Sigma scholastic honorary, 1964. Barry Hubbell, Del Meliza, Sheldon Hinshaw, Howard Macy, Ron Stansell, Carolyn (Hampton) Stansell, Esther Mae Hinshaw, Lon Fendall, Raelene (Barnes) Fendall.

your contact with Mr. Edwards. We are...pleased with this...donation for the furnishings of Edwards Hall. We wish to thank you and pray for God's richest blessing upon you."

Lowell Edwards later gave the College its first computer, $160,000 in stock for the endowment fund, and an amateur radio station which was placed with its antenna extending 81 feet above Brougher Hall (called by students "Brougher Tower"). Developed by ham operators Evan Rempel and Dan Hill, the radio station contacted missionaries in South America and reported on the GFC-OIT basketball game.

THE COLLEGE'S RESURGENCE could be called a miracle. The Edwards' gifts symbolize the most miraculous aspect of it all—the miracle of healing. The bitterness from the 1920-1950 divisions was abating. That the old Quaker names such as Edwards and Pennington adorned newly constructed buildings symbolized the miraculous healing of memories. The issues of "Modernism" and "Fundamentalism"—once replete with name calling—no longer created so much disunion.

Oregon Yearly Meeting and its College had found a way to bridge chasms and speak a clear evangelical Christian message without the fear, anti-intellectualism, and intolerance that had characterized earlier years. Not all the deep wounds had been healed, but the Great Physician was being allowed to work.

Right: Bill Hopper scores
42 points in one 1956
game, breaks school rec-
ord of 40 set by Delbert
Replogle 40 years earlier.

Cutting the ribbon at the opening of Hobson Hall. Milo Ross, Jack Willcuts, Dorlan Bales, Homecoming Queen Merilyn Pang, and Robert Lauinger are pictured.

Heacock Commons is completed in 1965.

The GFC students honored Levi Pennington in 1967, dedicating *The Crescent*'s "Diamond Jubilee" issue to the longtime president. His name "so far outshadows the rest that it is almost synonymous with the old name of Pacific College," the citation announced.

Pennington died eight years later, at age 99. Then president David LeShana expressed the College's esteem, characterizing Pennington as friend, leader, humble man, and humanitarian. LeShana concluded: "How does one describe such a man, such a giant among men? The words of the Old Testament prophet, Nehemiah, are appropriate: 'He was a faithful man and he feared God.' He was faithful to his God, to his family, to his calling, and like Enoch of old, he walked with God."

Further evidence of the rapprochement occurred when the College invited Gulley to speak at "Nostalgia Night" in 1977. Gulley could not attend, but sent prepared remarks, including: "We rejoice at the good reports that we get from George Fox College . . . and I am glad to have been able to make a wee contribution when it was needed."

DRAMATIC PROGRESS in many areas notwithstanding, the administration still had difficulty meeting annual budgets. In January 1962, the president sought advice from the board: Should he pay salaries or federal taxes? The board decided to continue its long record of meeting the payroll and let the government wait temporarily.

The College never missed a payroll, but economic problems continued. In order to correct a "dilemma of great magnitude" the board in 1965 studied possible "drastic" cost-cutting reductions in the school's programs. Board members selected from a list of items that might be eliminated or greatly reduced. However, they made few cuts.

Frank Cole, an experienced businessman, became business manager the next year and warned the board to reduce expenditures or risk great danger. The College therefore eliminated intercollegiate wrestling and the home economics major, and increased annual tuition from $580 to $660.

Total assets in 1969 were $4,765,797, compared to $615,000 fifteen years earlier. By 1969 the endowment stood at $1,215,000, up from $274,000 in 1954. The College's operating budget in 1954 totaled $119,000; by 1969 the figure had grown to just over $1,000,000. Although with the school's improvement and the postwar baby boom, enrollment increased from 98 to 392 and tuition from $300 to $990, the additional income failed to cover mounting expenses. (Tuition in 1954 paid 50 percent of each student's educational costs; in 1969 it paid 55 percent.) When Ross left office in 1969, the college indebt-

85

1964 students whose ancestors attended Pacific College. First row (third generation): Ken Simmons, Nancy (Nordyke) Mylander, Cheryl (Morse) Johnson, Juanita (Astleford) Johnson. Not pictured: Darrell Nordyke and Robert Craven. Others are second generation, including, Second row: Jon Bishop, Brian Beals, Kent Thornburg, Howard Macy, Jerry Sandoz, Dean Thompson, John Baker. Third row: Evangeline Green, Jacquelyn (Smitherman) Mylander, Marcia (Dillon) Caldwell, Suzanne (Harmon) Livingston, Patricia Hill, Roberta (George) Tuning, Joyce (Roberts) Owens, Karen (Thornburg) McConaughey. Fourth row: Phyllis McCracken, Linda (Gulley) Bloodgood, Carolyn (Hampton) Stansell, Mary Alice (Hampton) Maurer, Mary Church, Margaret (Church) McCormick, Anne (Thornburg) Roberts, Raelene (Barnes) Fendall, Carolyn (Harmon) McDonald. Not pictured: Marion Clarkson, Judy (Geil) Schubert, Carol Hibbs, Marilyn (Hill) Pruitt, Phil Morrill, Dale Rinard, Jamie Sandoz, Harold Thomas, Lois (White) Jones, James Hamilton.

which, although written in the male gender, extended to women also:

"We seek to offer to each athlete the opportunity to participate in his favorite type of activity, while letting him explore and enjoy others that might be new to him. In doing this we offer to him the opportunity to develop self-realization, emotional growth and maturity, a winning attitude, physical development, and an atmosphere that challenges him to his fullest potentiality."

Through the 1960s, women participated in volleyball, basketball, and softball. The school reinstated women's tennis in 1965 and added field hockey the next year. Although not highly organized, the lady Quakers fielded small track teams. In 1964 Janet (Johnson) McClurg won the 100 and 220 at the U. S. Track and Field Federation meet. The GFC team took third behind the University of

Oregon and Oregon State in the Women's Collegiate Recreation Association, composed of all Oregon colleges and universities. Janet (Johnson) McClurg placed first in the 100-yard dash and the standing broad jump.

In a banner year, both the 1965 volleyball and basketball teams went undefeated, and the softball squad lost only one game. The Quakers took the Women's Conference of Independent Colleges championship in volleyball, basketball, softball, and track. Marjorie (Larrance) Weesner coached the volleyball, basketball, and softball teams; Randy Winston coached track.

The championship volleyball team included Ilene (Haskins) Beeson, Cynthia (Chong) Petersen, Nancy (Crockett) Findley, Jan Gaithright, and cocaptains Linda Moore and Janet (Johnson) McClurg. According to Coach Marge

Weesner, Janet Johnson was "probably by far the best athlete GFC has had. She had *amazing* natural ability."

The basketball dynasty extended to include championships in 1966, 1967, and 1968. The Lady Quakers also took the conference softball title in 1968 and 1969.

From field hockey's inception in 1966 until its demise over a decade later, GFC's teams proved successful. League all-stars included Barbara (Jones) Ireland, Marjorie Brood, and Nancy (Perry) Hodson in 1966; Barbara (Jones) Ireland and Mafi (Faletau) Downs in 1967; Kathy (Jensen) Magee in 1968; Sharon Smith and Betty Phillips in 1969; and Betty Burbank and Nancy (Phillips) Frey in 1970. Three years later, Betty Phillips took second in the conference 100-meter dash and set a record in the the long jump.

Sports columnist Peter McHugh, in his "Pete's Patter" for May 5, 1967, commented enthusiastically about coach and director of athletics Earl Craven, departing after four years at GFC:

"...Who would have dreamed in 1963 that the little Quaker college in Newberg would soon...participate in seven different varsity sports?...Or that our athletic teams would be traveling up and down the coast, meeting competitors from Los Angeles to Anchorage, Alaska?

"But Earl Craven had the vision of developing a good collegiate athletic program with facilities to match. It takes more than just a vision to build something from nothing. It takes planning, organization, and an ability to transmit and sell ideas, topped with plenty of hard work. Students and faculty who are familiar with the activities around the gymnasium can testify to his industrious nature and drive to get the job done."

Coach Craven's resignation, prompted by disappointment that the school failed to make a major commitment to football, impaired the athletic program.

Two years later, the College withdrew from the Oregon Collegiate Conference and dropped a football program that, except for five years in the late 1920s and the World War II period, had existed three quarters of a century. However, the Quakers remained in the NAIA and became a regional basketball and track powerhouse in subsequent decades.

THE COLLEGE ALSO attempted excellence in forensics, music, and other cocurricular areas, often using deputation as an outlet. In 1954-55 the Deputation Committee arranged for 150 special services, with 25 students serving as assistant pastors, Sunday school teachers, youth leaders, and musicians. A typical team consisted of Orville Winters, evangelist; Roland Hartley, song leader; and Margaret (Hancuff) Lamm, pianist.

The school also had a women's quartet, trumpet trio, trumpet duet, at least two ladies' trios, and at least one men's quartet. Several campus organizations cooperated in these activities, among them the Student Christian Union, Music Club, Student Ministerial Association, and Singing Men. Carl Reed's a cappella choir that year toured Northwest churches.

Ross Stover, William Koenig, Harriet Storaker, and Ernest Lichti each served a year or more as choir director following Reed. Tours often included either southern Idaho or southern California.

The vocal format emphasized soloists, trios, and quartets. Instrumental groups included a sax quartet, a small band, at least one jazz combo, and an organization promoting music appreciation, called Opus II. The Singing Men continued to sponsor the annual Quartet Festival for several years.

Dennis Hagen's concert bands and Jerry Friesen's a cappella choirs received plaudits during Pacific Coast tours in the late 1960s. In 1965 Hagen formed a brass choir, consisting of 12 to 15 performers. Friesen established the oratorio program, which combined college and community singers and the college orchestra in annual performances.

The College typically performed at least one major and one or two minor dramas each year. For example, Bob Byrd starred in 1955 as Teddy Brewster in *Arsenic and Old Lace*; Kara (Newell) Wilkin and Lois (Burnett) Miller played his sisters, with Margaret (Shattuck) Lemmons directing. That year, Lois (Burnett) Miller and Larry Ross received the Actorator Club's best actress and actor awards.

Two years later the student body performed *Tomorrow the World* at GFC and *The Other Wiseman* in area churches. Dilla (Tucker) Winslow directed Shakespeare's *The Merchant of Venice* in 1959, with Bob Church, Floyd Chamberlain, Howard Morse, and Lyla (Bury) Hadley in leading roles. The following year the school performed *The Big Fisherman*, with Francis Whitaker as Simon Peter and Edward Peacock directing. Clara Axie Dyer directed *The Little Minister*, *Our Town*, and *Antigone*. In 1965 the drama society, Delta Psi Omega, gave Nancy (Forsythe) Thomas and Clark V. Adams best actress and actor awards, with Adams and Phil Roberts chosen best codirectors.

Jo (Kennison) Lewis directed an outstanding dramatic achievement, *Skin of Our Teeth*, in 1968. One spectator, Austin J. Simpson, wrote that he had performed in the same play on Broadway, directed it in a three-year professional tour, and seen it given by 100 different college groups over the years. Nevertheless, Simpson applauded the George Fox performance, saying: "I have never seen an amateur group do a better job than yours. The secret was,

The Board of Trustees, 1964. Front row: Milo Ross, Olive Shambaugh, Ivan Adams, Arnold Owen, Emil Swanson. Second row: John Brougher, Charles Beals, Eugene Coffin, Gervas Carey (not board member but former president). Third row: Homer Hester, Floyd Bates, Glen Rinard, Dean Gregory, Wayne Roberts. Fourth row: Gerald Dillon, Fred Jarvill, Frank Colcord, Walter Lee, Philip Martin. Back row: Fred Baker, Wilbert Eichenberger, Clare Willcuts, Allen Hadley, Wayne Antrim. Not pictured: Mark Hatfield, John Farner, Glenn Koch, Forrest Holmes, Lloyd Hinshaw, Dwight Macy, Walter Wilhite, Dorwin Smith.

I believe, that your young people believed the message of the play: that the mercy of God is the hope of the world . . . ."

Simpson was right. George Fox College students did tend to be different. They were not all angels, however—at least not all the time. Three normal human college students make the point: Ralph Cammack, Chuck Tuning, and Dave Wing installed a speaker in Wood-Mar Auditorium's electric organ, wired to a microphone in the basement furnace room. During a recital, the three delivered messages to the organist. The incident sparked a minor campus revival. Some students encountered "spiritual beings"; one met the "devil" and defied him.

In chapel the next morning, Dean Kenneth Williams suggested that anyone who knew about the wired-in speaker should contact the dean. The miscreants soon came to Williams's office, bowed, and greeted: "Good morning, Father Confessor." According to Cammack, Williams "laughed so hard his bald head turned red." However, the dean, while applauding the ingenuity, scolded the young men, assuring them that embarrassing their fellow students was not appropriate behavior. The offenders good-naturedly agreed to apply their energies in more positive ways.

FROM HIS FIRST YEARS at George Fox, Arthur Roberts sought to develop special incentives for advanced learners. He initiated in 1958 the "intensified studies" program, which still continued at the end of the College's first century. A faculty committee selected outstanding students to participate in a special seminar and to do research over a two- or three-year period.

In the early years, this program was funded by a grant. Sometimes the group took study tours, including New York City, Washington, D.C., Victoria, B.C., and San Francisco. Participants reported their research in chapel. The program stressed academic quality without elitism.

John Johnson did the first senior Intensified Studies project, entitled "Leplace Transforms." Over 60 others presented papers in the following 30 years. Among the first were Howard Morse, "Estrogen in Pigeons"; Nancy J. (Forsythe) Thomas, "Dios Y Los Ninos"; Anne (Barager) Stenberg, "The Nature of the Masque and its Use by

90

Shakespeare as a Dramatic Device"; and Stephen Gilroy, "Effect of *In Vitro* Tissue Culture upon Antibody Formation of Transferred Rat Spleen Cells."

THE NORTHWEST ASSOCIATION of Secondary and Higher Schools originally accredited George Fox for two years and renewed it in 1961. Three years later the committee reported a pleasant return visit: "The physical progress is nothing short of amazing" and "the new library is a joy." The accrediting body continued to strike familiar negative themes, however, noting serious salary and library resource deficiencies.

The College gained a modified approval for an elementary education program through a 1954 joint degree arrangement with Oregon College of Education. Secondary credentialing lagged, however. Although after a ten-year lapse the Newberg school district in 1959 reinstated the College for secondary practice teaching, the State Department of Education still refused to accredit George Fox. For another decade, secondary education students therefore either transferred or completed requirements after graduation.

The College began a major effort to obtain secondary certification in 1966. It hired David Myton, who held a Ph.D. from Ohio State University, as associate professor of education and director of the teacher education committee. In cooperation with Dean George Moore and education teachers Sheldon Louthan and Paul Cammack, Myton in 1966-67 developed an intensive self-study, followed by professional education courses for juniors. That spring an advisory team visited and made recommendations.

The next year the College offered senior-level professional courses. Myton wrote a 161-page self-study based upon Oregon's standards for accreditation of secondary teacher education programs. A professional team soon evaluated the College and, in 1969, approved teacher education in health and physical education, biology, and mathematics. The next year it added music and followed with language arts, physical science, and social studies endorsements in 1971.

SHORTLY AFTER Ross's arrival, the Board of Trustees attempted to reach other yearly meetings by increasing its own size from 15 to 30 members. Then, in 1964, it increased to 42. The bylaws stated specifically that all nominees "shall be in harmony with the Constitution and Discipline of Oregon Yearly Meeting of Friends Church."

With the increase to 30, the bylaws required 24 to be Friends; of the 42, at least 30 had to be Quakers. All others were Christians with a particular interest in George Fox College and higher education. Northwest Yearly Meeting approved all members.

During this period, the largest vocational category on the board—11 of the 28 members listed in the 1959 accreditation report—was "Friends minister." Five executives, two businessmen, three professionals, two ranchers, one farmer, one teacher, and three workers also served. At that time, the board included only white males, although several women served in earlier and later periods, including Olive Shambaugh, who was named in 1964.

THE COLLEGE CONTINUED to attract many Quakers. During the 1959-60 accreditation year, 107 of 144 students were Friends (74 percent). Nine years later, the percentage had dropped to 48.2, although the total Quaker enrollment had increased to 189 (of 392 regular students).

About 56 percent of Oregon Yearly Meeting's 1956 undergraduate students attended George Fox College. This dropped to 44 percent by 1969. However, Milo Ross still reported that more Quaker students attended George Fox than any other college except Earlham in Indiana. He noted further that more Friends instructors worked at George Fox than at any other college in the world.

According to a 1965 study, 20 percent of all North American Quaker young people preparing for Christian ministry attended George Fox College. Ross contended in 1967 that GFC was more closely identified with its church than any other Friends college.

The president demonstrated tangible loyalty by, some years, preaching or lecturing in over 100 Friends churches. While at GFC, Ross preached at least once in each of the Yearly Meeting's nearly 50 local churches; he also spoke to most of those in California and Rocky Mountain yearly meetings. Several faculty members also served the church directly; for example, Myron Goldsmith, Paul Mills, and Arthur Roberts pioneered a "school for elders," providing training for local church leaders.

Nevertheless, some board members believed even stronger ties should be established. Also, some in the Yearly Meeting expressed concern that rapid progress might lead the school away from its evangelical doctrine. For example, one board member feared accreditation's influence on faculty and student spiritual life. In its 1963 sessions, Oregon Yearly Meeting constituents officially expressed a similar concern; for example, the official visiting committee regretted that some students studied on Sunday.

Milo Ross foresaw another danger. He feared that burgeoning enrollment and need for money might compromise the College's emphasis on pacifism and social justice. Growth in enrollment and financial support might come disproportionately from Christians hostile to emphases that Ross saw not merely as Quaker distinctives but central Christian doctrines that the larger church had generally neglected.

Ross felt, however, that given proper emphasis, the College could grow to 700 students with nearly 50 percent Quakers. He also believed the school could find donors who shared its spiritual position. For example, the president reported one couple's delight on learning that GFC promoted biblical pacifism:

"When they made their first trip to the college, it was our happy privilege to prove to them our active position. Professor Paul Mills met with them, pointing out from the New Testament the basis of our stand. We prepared figures to show the proportion and number of our students who were conscientious objectors, beginning with

World War I. We claimed to be the only college anywhere which offered an academic class in sociology entitled "Peace and War." After having shown them the complementary situation between our stated aims and our active program with a bias toward Christian pacifism, they proceeded to name George Fox as the principal beneficiary in their estates."

A S GEORGE FOX COLLEGE moved into the late 20th century, inadequate finances continued as its foremost problem. During Ross's 15-year tenure, tuition and enrollment gains matched faculty salary increases, but funds remained inadequate.

The school had strengthened measurably. No longer did anyone doubt its continued existence. Yet much remained to be accomplished. In the next decade, George Fox College made remarkable strides toward fulfilling its potential.

92

Hester Gymnasium

Dining Hall

Fine Arts Building

Vet Houses

Library

Edwards (McGrew) Hall

Chapter Six

Lathering up in the fountain. Squeaky-clean students are Russell Schmidt and Alan Stokesbary.

WHILE PRESIDENT, Milo Ross insisted that the board look for an eventual successor. As early as 1961, David LeShana's name appeared. Three years later, the trustees addressed the subject more seriously and again discussed LeShana. Another three years elapsed before he came to GFC as a one-year "acting president."

Born in India of Methodist missionary parents, David LeShana came to the United States to attend Taylor University in 1949. There he met Becky Swander, a Quaker undergraduate. They married in 1951 and, after he completed a master's in education at Ball State, moved to southern California. He pastored at Long Beach Friends Church and earned a Ph.D. at the University of Southern California. The Barclay Press published his dissertation in 1969 under the title *Quakers in California: The Effects of 19th Century Revivalism on Western Quakerism.*

David LeShana's keen insights, dedication, and dynamic speaking ability gave him an unusually commanding presence. One George Fox faculty member later remarked: "Had he chosen politics, Dave LeShana would have been a great U.S. Senator."

While projecting LeShana as a long-range prospect for the GFC presidency, the board attempted to secure his services in 1965 as director of development. LeShana declined. One year later, however, Milo Ross reiterated that he could not indefinitely maintain the frenetic pace. When he requested a vice president to take some of the burden, LeShana's name quickly emerged as the foremost possibility.

By 1967, David LeShana was ready for academia. Although already offered several other positions, he consented to an interview. In LeShana's presence, the board's executive committee held a lengthy discussion regarding GFC's future leadership. Milo Ross offered to take an unpaid one-year leave to provide LeShana a salary. Academic Dean George Moore offered to do the same the following year, again to provide a salary without increasing administrative costs. The board anticipated that by the third year, funds would be available for the new administrator to continue at the College, perhaps as director of development. Given all these assumptions, the board offered LeShana the title "vice president," but with presidential duties.

Under this plan, the trustees asked LeShana to accept what might be considered regressive steps: successive years as acting president, vice president, and director of development. However, Milo Ross had asserted that he wanted to groom LeShana for an eventual presidency, and the board concurred.

After much prayer, LeShana decided to come to George Fox College at a salary below several other offers. His duties the first year included the full responsibilities of the president's office, administrator of development and public relations, and administrative committee chairman.

LeShana succeeded as acting president. Therefore, with Ross's return the next year, the board had two men uniquely qualified for the presidency—amazing, since finding even one seemed impossible only 15 years earlier.

The trustees named LeShana executive vice president when Ross returned. The College enjoyed another outstanding year, with Ross and LeShana serving amicably as almost copresidents. Ross maintained final responsibility, reporting to the board and overseeing the development program. The deans reported to LeShana, and he to Ross.

LeShana oversaw the general fund finances, alumni, public relations, and studies for a potential cluster-college arrangement with Warner Pacific and Cascade colleges. Then, in the fall of 1969, Ross resigned to become chancellor of the Associated Christian Colleges of Oregon (ACCO), which was exploring the cluster-college concept.

Few exit leadership as gracefully as Milo Ross. Although some constituents wanted him to continue, he believed that he had led the College to a point where it should be guided by someone with better academic

Fall Regular Student Enrollment, 1969-1981		
1969—406	1974—481	1979—734
1970—472	1975—556	1980—746
1971—443	1976—627	1981—743
1972—432	1977—708	
1973—463	1978—715	

credentials. From afar, Ross foresaw that day and did everything he could to prepare the best possible successor. Then he found a way to bow out skillfully at only 58 years of age.

The board quickly and unanimously chose David LeShana as his replacement. LeShana later revealed that Milo Ross originally persuaded him to come to GFC, and recalled: "No president anywhere has had the support, love, and care that Milo gave me. I often asked his advice, but he absolutely refused to interfere or influence my decisions. He took great delight in our successes, almost like a grandfather. He didn't have a jealous bone in his body. He was always a help and never a problem."

Accepting the presidency, David LeShana wrote to the trustees:

"The days ahead will not always be easy. Change and progress often carry a high price tag! Yet I am confident of God's blessing and presence as we follow Him. There is much to learn, new areas of involvement to explore, new dimensions of effectiveness to discover. To this end, I commit myself, and commend my task to you for your prayer and patient understanding."

In his December 1970 report to the board, LeShana identified academic and spiritual excellence as the "twin goals of distinction." He emphasized four keys: understanding God's Word, openness to His Spirit, common commitment, and authenticity. LeShana stressed the importance of attracting other evangelical groups while still maintaining the school's Quaker distinctives.

LeShana first faced the college indebtedness, which, although liquidated in 1959, had rebounded to $375,000, due partially to the building spurt. In 1970 the College therefore initiated a program called the Valiant 500—an attempt to raise $500,000. The name came also from the early Quaker "Valiant 60," who spread God's light in the 17th century English countryside.

Director of Development Maurice Chandler oversaw a remarkably successful effort. For the second time in 15 years, its constituents rescued the school. Oregon (renamed Northwest) Yearly Meeting again rallied around and supported its college, with significant assistance from key businesses and foundations.

The campaign received a major boost when the Collins Foundation promised a $50,000 matching grant. When finally completed early in 1972, the half-million dollar Valiant 500 effort eliminated the entire indebtedness and added $125,000 to help balance the 1971-72 operating budget. This marked the beginning of another significant forward thrust.

Throughout GFC's history, many administrators served because a need existed—dedication outweighed expertise as the primary criterion for service. During the LeShana era, the College became larger; its administration more formalized and professional. The decision-making process increasingly emphasized proven management principles. The administrators who surrounded LeShana illustrate this point.

Frank Cole, who had served as business manager since 1966, recommended four years later that the board replace him with someone more experienced in accounting and finance. Late in 1971, the College hired Donald J. Millage, senior audit manager and former national director of professional development (in charge of training audit staff members throughout the U.S.) for Price Waterhouse's Wall Street office in New York City.

Cole then became assistant to the president for long-range planning and budgeting, a position funded by the federal government's Title III program. The board gave Cole a strong affirmation and a standing vote of appreciation.

Don Millage grew up in southern Oregon and spent 15 years in business before coming to George Fox. At each board meeting, members listened appreciatively to this gifted CPA's articulate, businesslike, wit-punctuated

reports; they repeatedly thanked Millage for his systematic, clear explanations. In subsequent years, many other colleges sought the George Fox business manager's counsel; each accrediting team commended the College for his work.

Arthur Roberts served as academic dean from 1968 to 1972. Although a visionary curriculum planner, his primary talents lay in the scholarly brilliance that made him a revered philosopher, teacher, writer, and poet. Roberts returned in 1972 to his first loves of teaching and writing.

The College hired William Green from Malone College in Ohio as its new academic dean. Green had earned a bachelor's degree in theology from Malone (and was 1973 alumnus of the year), a bachelor of arts from Taylor University, a master's from Western Reserve University, and a doctorate in education from the University of Tennessee. He served 13 years as a faculty member and 10 as academic dean at Malone College. Although offered a Malone vice-presidency at a higher salary than George Fox could pay, he accepted the GFC position because he felt the Lord had called him to the Newberg school.

Green served George Fox with distinction until his retirement from administration in 1984 and from teaching in 1989. Included was one year, 1982-83, as the College's interim president. When he retired from full-time employment in 1984, George Fox College conferred on William Green a doctor of humane letters degree.

Building on his predecessors' efforts, Green devoted much attention to orderly curriculum development based on student flow, and to faculty development. He also promoted GFC's profitable membership in the Christian College Consortium and recommended a contingent salary plan, providing bonuses when tuition income allowed them. In addition, he helped develop several administrative initiatives, including faculty salary and fringe benefit improvement, full-time secretaries for most divisions, and standard office furniture for all faculty.

Although businesslike and efficient, Bill Green enjoyed humor, even at his own expense. For example, one year the faculty discussed a name change for "The Faculty News." One member recommended "'The Dean's Bulletin'—because it can easily be nicknamed 'Bill's Bull.'" The congenial dean joined in the laughter, although not without a threat to repay in kind.

Harold Ankeny, George Fox College's superb "utility player," served as dean of students from 1968 to 1974. At that point he stepped aside for Eugene Habecker, a young man highly motivated toward a career in higher education. Habecker, with a Temple University law degree, served four years before leaving to work on a Ph.D.; he soon became president of Huntington College in Indiana and later president of the American Bible Society.

Julie Hawley, with a master's degree from Azusa Pacific and experience as GFC's associate student life director, served during 1978-79. Lee Gerig then took the position for seven years. A former dean of admissions at Seattle Pacific University, Gerig held two bachelor's degrees and a master's in counseling from Indiana University. Recognized in *Outstanding Young Men in America* and *Who's Who in the West*, Gerig continued the tradition established by Habecker and Hawley. During part of the Habecker-

97

Administrators Don
Millage, George Moore,
Gene Habecker, and
Maurice Chandler prepare
for 1978 commencement.

Bottom: A familiar pose
for Barry Hubbell.

Hawley-Gerig era, the College required dormitory head residents to have master's degrees in student services.

Other new administrators contributed to the school's development. In addition to Millage (1972), Green (1972), and Habecker (1974), the College hired Jim Settle as director of admissions (1973). These men complemented the work of LeShana and Maurice Chandler, who had become assistant director of development in 1966 and director of development in 1969.

WHILE DAVID LeSHANA served as president, the College's annual operating budget grew from just over $1 million to more than $5 million—a 90 percent increase in real dollars (discounting inflation).

During the same period, the endowment principal stayed at approximately $1 million, with its average annual yield nearly $100,000.

At first the LeShana administration found budget balancing exceedingly difficult. In 1966-67, the year before LeShana became acting president, the College spent $100,000 over budget.

In 1968-69, the school transferred part of a $92,000 gift from Lowell Edwards to balance the budget; two years later the College endangered its credit rating before finally borrowing $100,000 from endowment to pay the bills.

Board meetings frequently became prayer meetings as the financial crisis deepened. Yet they also often became praise meetings; in June of 1971, at Director of Development Maurice Chandler's suggestion, the board sang the doxology to celebrate donors' gifts totaling $100,000 more than the previous year.

The College in 1971-72 projected a large deficit, but the $125,000 operating income supplement from the Valiant 500 helped balance the budget. Also, Don Millage, who became business manager that January, immediately initiated expense reductions. At the board meeting that spring, Millage thanked the faculty for its cooperation.

The Valiant 500 debt liquidation and Millage's fiscal expertise enabled the College to turn a financial corner. The newly engendered optimism and confidence in the school's fiscal integrity led to some immensely important, previously unanticipated gifts.

Donors responded to a school that could eliminate a $375,000 debt and that showed a determination to live within its means.

Other factors also contributed. The school raised new income from the federal government, constituent gifts, foundation grants, and increased tuition prices. Enrollment growth from 406 in 1969 to 743 twelve years later provided a major income increase.

Director of Admissions
Jim Settle introducing a
new student to David and
Becky LeShana, 1977.

GEORGE FOX COLLEGE received almost $7.9 million from the federal government (including student and construction loans) and an additional $1.8 million from the state between 1958 and 1980. During the 1970s, about 32 percent of all student tuition and fees came from federal and state grant and work-study funds. Guaranteed student loans from private banks comprised another 25 percent. In 1977, the trustees sent a resolution thanking Oregon's congressional delegation and other federal officials for the financial assistance.

Former Director of Financial Aid Harold Ankeny concluded that GFC benefited greatly from federal and state assistance: "It is safe to say that . . . [the] college has been strengthened immeasurably, perhaps even salvaged from extinction by the infusion of almost $10,000,000 into its operation. . . . It is sound public policy to support private higher education with public funds."

Ankeny continued: "Without a doubt the federal assistance provided the impetus for the college to 'make it.'"

The State of Oregon's financial contribution dates from 1969, when the PESIC (Purchase of Educational Services from Independent Colleges) program began. The state reimbursed private colleges for all except religious education. The first year, George Fox benefited by $24,000; by 1979, annual PESIC income had grown to $225,000, before reduction to $130,000 by 1982.

JAMES AND LILA MILLER of Cascadia Lumber Company gave the College $600,000 in 1973—one of the most important gifts the school has received. The Millers' son, Paul, graduated from GFC in 1969 and married fellow student Judy Warner. Greatly impressed with the College's impact on their son's life, the Millers asked how they might help financially.

President LeShana responded with several suggestions, including a new physical education-athletic complex. Jim and Lila Miller enthusiastically endorsed the sports center idea, but placed no restrictions on the use of their funds.

The Miller money literally proved to be a godsend. Reserving $500,000 for a sports center, the administration immediately spent $50,000 on existing obligations and another $50,000 for various maintenance and operating expenses, effectively covering the 1972-73 operating deficit and sparking a long period of financial stability.

The Miller gift inspired a campus master plan and a successful campaign to complete funding of the $2.2 million, 55,000-square-foot sports complex. The family of Coleman H. Wheeler, former Willamette Industries chairman, gave over $400,000.

At the December 1975 board meeting, David LeShana announced that capital campaign funds exceeded $2.7 million. Two days earlier, the total had been $1.2 million, the

---

"Without a doubt the federal assistance provided the impetus for the college to 'make it.'"

—Harold Ankeny, Former Director of Financial Aid

---

president reported, but he had received a late afternoon telephone call revealing a $1.5 million gift from the M. J. Murdock Trust.

The board sang "Praise God from whom all blessings flow . . ." and David Leach offered a prayer of thanks. President LeShana gave the credit to God's goodness. In this gift and the entire capital fund campaign, he noted, God had rewarded many people's prayers and years of faithful service.

The College named the building, completed in 1977, the Coleman H. Wheeler Physical Education and Sports Center. It contained athletic administration and faculty offices, along with staff, class, weight, multipurpose, dressing, and equipment rooms. The east wing housed two handball/racquetball courts.

The gymnasium section, named to honor James and Lila Miller, featured a 116- by 174-foot playing surface with three basketball courts and potential seating for 2,500 spectators. The floor could also accommodate three volleyball or ten badminton courts.

Prayer before an athletic
road trip.

Bottom: Mike Wirta, the
No. 1 Bruin fan, with
basketball coach Sam
Willard.

The College then constructed the Milo C. Ross Fine Arts Center in the old Thomas W. Hester Memorial Gymnasium's shell. Completed in October 1978, the $1.5 million building housed classrooms, the music and religion faculties, and practice and recital areas.

Meanwhile, George Fox officials erected the Herbert C. Hoover Academic Building, primarily with funds donated by the J. Howard Pew Charitable Trust. They also added to Heacock Commons. The boom continued with the Charlotte Macy and Mary Sutton Residence Halls in 1977 and the Gervas Carey Residence Hall in 1980. The College also purchased several residences for student housing.

With a 1978 grant from the M. J. Murdock Charitable Trust, GFC constructed a television center for broadcast-quality production of video courses and programs for use across the country. The original purpose was "to extend our educational program to the average citizen at a competitive price...through the medium of video cassettes." Mel Schroeder, Allan Hueth, Rawlen Smith, and Warren Koch put several college courses on tape. Some filled a significant need, still being used across America over a decade later. Market limitations prevented significant expansion in that area, however. Subsequently, the TV Center functioned primarily as a teaching station for GFC students and eventually became the foundation for a valuable telecommunications major.

George Fox College still needed an adequate auditorium. The 420-seat, 70-year-old Wood-Mar third floor proved inadequate for performance and chapel. For a time, the fire department condemned its use for large crowds. The College therefore began a $2.5 million campaign for the second phase of the Milo C. Ross Center.

The drive succeeded remarkably. Northwest Yearly Meeting attenders gave nearly $400,000; the Collins Foundation added another $400,000, and a GFC student's parents contributed $250,000. In the spring of 1981, the Kresge Foundation pledged $150,000 if the gift would complete the funding drive by Feb. 15, 1982.

Led by Director of Development Maurice Chandler, the College developed a "Buy-A-Seat" campaign, in which donors "bought" seats for $500. This plan raised more than $250,000.

However, less than two weeks before the February 15 deadline, the campaign still lacked $225,000. In what LeShana termed "a miracle of the Lord's answering our prayers," the College completed the drive in time to assure the Kresge money. Numerous small gifts supplied $125,000; one donor pledged another $100,000; another gave a $115,000 trust to provide a reserve fund.

GFC band director Dennis Hagen later recalled the "great relief in our hearts when David LeShana announced

the final $125,000 was raised, assuring the $150,000 from Kresge. It was barely under the wire. We felt the tension and the relief. Praise God!"

The College named the new chapel/auditorium in honor of William and Mary Bauman. Not only had he served the school 21 years as a trustee, but the couple provided a sizeable contribution to the campaign.

The William and Mary Bauman Chapel/Auditorium provided a full stage, dressing rooms, greenroom, orchestra pit, lobby, art exhibit hall, and ticket booth. The building won immediate acclaim as a fine facility for major productions, including some by the Oregon Symphony.

During construction, the Hobson I men held an all-night "slumber party" among the gravel and concrete foundations. They wanted to be the first students to sleep in chapel.

100

THE GFC BRUINS
AND BRUIN, JR.

In keeping with their Quaker values, early Pacific athletic teams did not hide behind ferocious titles like Tiger, Bulldog, or Bearcat. Letting their prowess on the field speak for itself, they called themselves, simply, "P.C."

This tradition continued until 1934, except for brief intervals when an occasional sportswriter popularized a title such as the "Quakers" or "Prune-Pickers"—the latter springing from a fundraising venture in nearby orchards.

"Prune-Pickers seems a fitting nickname for such a notorious college," one writer asserted in a 1929 *The Crescent*. "A record of eighteen hundred boxes of prunes in one day and now a year of the most enjoyable athletics that Pacific has ever known."

As their reputation grew, the P.C.s eventually became known as "the Quakers." "Quakers," however, did not lend itself easily to a mascot.

Decals, mugs, and T-shirts eventually sported a fox (dubbed Foxy George by *The Crescent* cartoonist Will Howell in 1962). A little bear also gradually found his way onto newspaper and yearbook pages in the 1960s. The students and faculty voted in 1970 to change the athletic teams and mascot officially to the "Bruins."

Though the name "Bruin" contradicts such unassuming titles as "Quakers" or "Prune-Pickers," a bear had acted as unofficial mascot since the old Pacific Academy days when an academy student tamed a bear (it was later killed and its skin donated to the campus museum). In the 1930s when the beloved old bearskin known as Bruin ended up in the furnace, students quickly constructed a small canvas replica called "Bruin Jr."

Tradition held that each year's senior class would enjoy Bruin and then bequeath him to the junior class upon graduation. The mascot accompanied many classes on senior outings. In 1930 the junior class was not content to wait for Bruin and absconded with him in the middle of the night.

After that, the tradition became more openly competitive. Bruin Jr. may be in the possession of any class. At regular intervals he is "flashed," and the chase is on. Students have been known to chase each other through town, even stopping traffic. Ron Crecelius recalls several students climbing right through the back seat of a car stopped at the streetlight. Other flashings included dropping Bruin Jr. from a helicopter onto the football field and flashing him on the Willamette during the annual raft race. Each time a fight ensued.

Early versions of the mascot may be found in the George Fox College museum. One canvas Bruin Jr. was tattooed for posterity by victorious classes: "Retrieved by '44"; "Purloined by '46"; and "Garbaged by '47."

Brawls over Bruin Jr. have occasionally involved campus administration. Levi Pennington, it is said, used to "charge into the fray" in an attempt to keep excited students under control. One year, Chaplain Ron Crecelius dropped Bruin Jr. from Wood-Mar's third story, and a fight broke out immediately. "One senior in a suit disappeared in the mud," Crecelius chuckled, "and ended up looking like three miles of bad road."

The class in possession of the bear hides it for safekeeping. Previous hiding places have ranged from the heat register in front of the Wood-Mar stage to a rock quarry on Rex Hill.

In recent years, the Bruin symbol has added even more life. Each year a student is selected to wear a bear suit and represent Bruin as a part of the rally squad.

SHORTLY AFTER DAVID LeSHANA came to George Fox in 1967, he asserted that "the college is a good ten years ahead of its public image." Conscious that the school's success depended on public awareness, and seeking a new fundraising technique, LeShana, Chandler, and Director of Alumni and Church Relations Gene Hockett instituted a series of promotional dinners. They held the first in March 1968 at southern California's Disneyland Hotel. For ten years the College held annual dinners in Anaheim.

Chandler and Hockett arranged the dinner meetings in cooperation with California Friends churches, which provided lists of interested persons and gave logistical support. Local constituents invited the parents of high school juniors and seniors as special guests. David LeShana later reported that these dinners helped establish a strong, continuing relationship between California Yearly Meeting of Friends Church and George Fox College.

Early success inspired similar efforts in GFC alumni centers throughout the Northwest. Entertainment usually included a high-quality multimedia presentation, a musical group, guest speakers such as Senator Mark Hatfield, Governor Tom McCall, astronaut James Irwin, and entertainers Art Linkletter, Norma Zimmer, and Pat Boone. In 1970, the Disneyland Dinner drew 450 people and raised

DEAN WILLIAM GREEN and the faculty developed a future-oriented curriculum. Green emphasized the need for an increasingly heterogeneous student body that could relate to international and urban problems. This required improved academic offerings and pedagogical techniques. The dean advised his faculty to "make an overt effort to present other options to our students than they have considered so they have a true academic freedom: an opportunity to view all options.... We need to innovate, and continually look at curriculum in a fresh light."

In 1978 the faculty debated a general education revision. When finally completed, general education courses accounted for approximately 40 percent of the requirements, with the rest divided about equally between the major and electives. During this time, the College remained on the three quarter system, with summer offerings limited to special studies and field experiences. The school offered about 25 majors.

Bill Green also initiated an annual one-week September miniterm. The first focused on "The Christian Liberal Arts College." In 1974, National Black Evangelical Association President William Bentley led over 60 students in an eye-opening "Black Experience Week." The next year, 127 students and townspeople flew to Washington, D.C., for an exceptional learning experience in the nation's capital. Tom Sine, former GFC dean of students, and alumnus Carl Haisch led a futures seminar in 1976; the following year the group studied Francis Schaeffer's *How Then Shall We Yet Live*; in 1978 the program focused on biblical views of creation.

Many George Fox students joined others from Christian College Coalition schools in a one-semester American Studies Program in Washington, D.C. Conveniently housed on Capitol Hill, the program provided enriching classroom experiences and internships in a wide variety of Washington public and private agencies.

In 1977, history professor Lee Nash initiated a biennial Herbert Hoover Symposium. This program, originally underwritten by David Packard, invited internationally recognized Hoover scholars to study George Fox's most illustrious alumnus, the nation's 31st president. In addition to the college community, attenders included historians, Hoover buffs, and high school advanced placement American history students.

IN 1975 NORTHWEST YEARLY Meeting gave the Tilikum Center for Retreats and Outdoor Ministry to the College. Located seven miles from the main campus, Tilikum comprised 77 meadowed, wooded acres and a 15-acre lake.

By the end of the 1970s, the land, donated by Russell and Irene Baker, housed six buildings where director Gary Fawver offered classes, camping experiences, and a variety of camping services to area churches. Fawver's leadership soon led to accreditation by the American Camping Association.

IN ITS EARLY years, the Associated Christian Colleges of Oregon progressed hopefully. Then Cascade withdrew, leaving only Warner Pacific and George Fox. Milo Ross's 1969 appointment as ACCO chancellor signaled a movement toward a cluster-college arrangement, with contiguous

campuses in Newberg. For a time it appeared that Warner Pacific and perhaps as many as three other small Christian colleges might make the move, probably occupying land north of the Southern Pacific Railroad tracks (centering in the eventual location of Spaulding Oaks apartments).

By sharing some buildings and athletic fields, combining small classes, and allowing students to elect courses offered from each school's specialties, officials foresaw significant cost savings, investments from donors, federal grants, and a healthy intercampus rivalry in the context of authentic Christian community.

The concept could, they believed, provide large-college benefits while maintaining each small school's unique individuality. At one point, Warner Pacific appeared ready to make the transition, but some setbacks, including a premature announcement of the Portland school's pending decision, derailed the proposal.

THE LeSHANA ADMINISTRATION enjoyed the continued goodwill and active support of Northwest Yearly Meeting (Oregon Yearly Meeting had been renamed in 1968) as the confidence engendered in the Ross period continued. In 1971, the board rejected David LeShana's proposal to broaden the potential financial base by allowing more non-Friends board members. The bylaws continued to require board membership to be five-sevenths Friends, of whom two thirds-had to be from Northwest Yearly Meeting. Through the 1970s, Quakers comprised an exact minimum of the first requirement (30 of 42).

Norval Hadley, superintendent of Northwest Yearly Meeting, emphasized that the best way to relate to the

church was to help it. The church and the College adopted this approach—that both were best served by mutual cooperation.

All was not always harmonious, however. The George Fox community represented a mixture of conservative and activist social values. Typical of many colleges, the trustees generally reflected the more conservative position, while the faculty included an element of the socially and politically progressive.

During these years, board composition changed considerably. When the College first gained accreditation, 40 percent of the trustees were Friends ministers. Twenty years later, that category had shrunk to less than 10 percent—four of 42 members. The 1979 board also included 18 executives, five businesspersons, two educational administrators, nine professionals, two college teachers, one rancher, and one United States senator (Mark Hatfield).

This did not mean the board became less spiritual. It was, however, more professional, affluent, and business management-oriented. Although lack of data on the earlier period prevents political comparisons, polls taken during the 1970s reveal that about 90 percent of the board registered Republican and gave Republican presidential candidates about 80 percent of their votes.

LIKE THE BOARD, all faculty at George Fox shared a belief in God and commitment to Him through a personal saving faith in Christ Jesus. All displayed a human concern, albeit expressed in various ways. Undoubtedly, all George Fox College faculty members considered themselves theologically conservative, but they disagreed about how to express it politically.

For example, in 1980, non-Quaker faculty voted strongly for Ronald Reagan, while Quakers split about evenly among Reagan, President Carter, and independent candidate John Anderson. When in 1978 capital punishment appeared on the Oregon ballot, non-Quaker faculty, staff and administrators favored the death penalty, while Quakers overwhelmingly opposed it.

Although diverse politically, this competent, dedicated faculty uniformly expressed a strong commitment to Jesus Christ. About 60 percent were Quakers; all were Christians who aspired to as much scholarship and pedagogical excellence as their heavy schedules allowed.

THE VIETNAM WAR and discrimination against non-white Americans sparked protests on campuses across the nation. Compared with many colleges of that era,

George Fox seemed rather placid. The situation remained so calm that at a promotional dinner several years later, a speaker assured prospective GFC parents that "during the 1960s there weren't any demonstrations on the George Fox College campus." However, reflecting another view, one professor retorted privately: "I can hardly imagine a greater indictment of a college: to remain uninvolved while other campuses are speaking out against the war and injustice."

Although no major protests erupted, several students did participate in peace marches in Portland and Salem. The College became involved in at least one 1969 moratorium, holding special forums and prayer meetings, and setting aside time to remember Larry Wheeler, a GFC alumnus killed in action in Vietnam. Many students skipped lunch that day and raised $150 for the World Relief Commission's Vietnam work.

Like the U.S. as a whole, the GFC community clearly did not agree on the proper attitude toward the Vietnam War. Although the student body criticized Vice President Agnew's "flippant and disdainful attitude" toward the moratoriums, ex-Marine Jim Tusant and 115 student and faculty cosigners wrote President Nixon of "our approval and backing of your efforts to make peace in Vietnam."

O N SOME CAMPUSES, the protest movement ended with cessation of the military draft. Yet many Christian college students in the postwar period found their consciences quickened, activated by the desire to speak out against injustice.

Part of the Black Student Union, 1980. Front row: Earl Flemming. Middle row: Shavon Dennis, Jacquie Williams, Jacque (Davis) Coleman, unidentified, Michelle Jones. Back row: Saundra Burns, Corliss (Bausley) Martin.

Many GFC students projected a human concern that became a lifestyle. For example, some graduates served in Vietnam and throughout the world with the Mennonite Central Committee, World Relief Commission, World Vision, and other organizations. In 1972, the Emergency Relief Fund invited David LeShana to a fact-finding mission in Bangladesh, where over three million people had died from war-induced killing and starvation. A speaking tour followed.

Some postwar GFC students and faculty published articles reflecting the era's heightened concern for Christian social activism. Classes, chapels, and other public forums sometimes considered related questions. In the early 1980s, the College established a committee to assist any students denied federal financial aid because of conscientious

refusal to register for the draft. To a great extent, the College fell into step with other Christian campuses of the postwar period.

GEORGE FOX COLLEGE experienced a decrease in foreign students during the late 1970s (from 16 in 1973 to four in 1980), but an increase in American minorities (from four in 1973 to 34 in 1980). The College in 1977 hired Ernest and Katrina Cathcart, both black Americans, as head residents of Pennington Hall; he doubled as part-time instructor in sociology and adviser to minority students.

Two years later, the trustees commended Cathcart's excellent work and studied a paper he had written on race relations at George Fox College. Cathcart decried "institutional racism," the result of failure to maintain a significant minority presence in the faculty and administration.

Cathcart recommended faculty exchanges, visiting professorships, minority personnel, minority curricular content, and training grants for GFC personnel. "As Christians, both black and white, we must not tolerate racism in any form at this college. To not speak out, pray, and work to counteract this present trend at GFC is to be part of the problem."

Cathcart later refused a full-time faculty position. However, in subsequent years two black Americans—Aaron Hamlin and Ralph Greenidge—served on the GFC board. Minority student enrollment declined in the 1980s, and the College hired no full-time minority professors until 1990.

MINORITY PERSONS were not alone in expressing frustration. Some students protested the College's continuing *in locus parentis*. Dean of Students Harold Ankeny suggested in 1970 that a growing, increasingly diverse student body forced the institution to face two particular problems: what to do about the behavior of students who came from churches that held different standards from the Friends (especially regarding social dancing), and whether the College should continue to control student conduct during vacations.

Administrators referred the matter to Northwest Yearly Meeting's Board of Moral Action. Although it declined to recommend altering existing college policy, a gradual relaxation of off-campus controls occurred.

Ron Crecelius, a GFC graduate and former Four Flats quartet member, came to the College as director of church relations in 1968; the next year, he became director of religious activities (generally called chaplain). Crecelius told the trustees in 1972 that increased awareness of the regulations, and assurance that the rules would be enforced, had improved student morale.

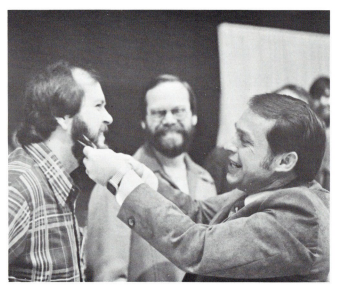

Board Chairman Bob Monroe Buzzing a Bruin's Beard for the Book Budget. Professor Paul Chamberlain is the victim, as Professor Bruce Longstroth observes.

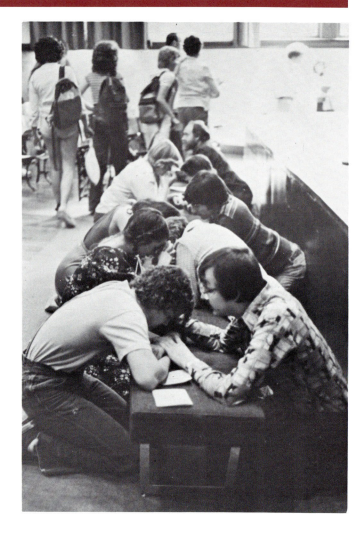

Crecelius's popular approach as chaplain reflected the era's flamboyant Youth For Christ style. He developed highly successful Bible studies and prayer groups, and sent strong deputation teams to churches throughout the Northwest. Under Crecelius's influence, the student ministry flourished.

Some students and faculty complained, however, that the chapels and general campus atmosphere lacked depth. While many applauded the school's conservative pietism, others extolled the reform-oriented, evangelical activism of an increasingly prominent portion of the Christian community.

Some students used the student newspaper, *The Crescent*, to recommend more substantive, evocative chapels that spoke to issues such as drug problems, student activism, and racism. Such articles called students, faculty, and administrators to deeper spiritual lives and to greater involvement in the world.

In 1975-76, a student group published an alternative paper called *Orcrist*, from J. R. R. Tolkien's allusion to weapons of good, to be used for positive purposes. The students offered the sometimes critical publication to fight "misinformation, indecision, and that most horrible, gruesome monster, apathy."

Although students' concerns often related to world issues, some complained about campus problems. Yet one is impressed with the mildness of these protests. Students seemed aware that their criticism could be heard. Almost without exception, they complained within the context of appreciation and loyalty to the institution and its purposes.

Sometimes the students acted on their convictions. Out of a 1977 conversation among student body president Ron Mock and his roommates, chief justice Phil Smith and former *L'Ami* editor Steve Eichenberger, a new idea developed. The Associated Student Community voted 10 percent of its student fees for a service fund, to be administered by the Christian Service Committee.

Although slightly modified in later years, the program originally restricted its grants to off-campus ministries. Among others, the students assisted the mixed-race Piedmont Friends Church, John Perkins' Voice of Calvary Ministries in Mississippi, and the Haiti Christian Development Fund.

In the "Burnside Project," participants related one-to-one with persons in Portland's skid row area. Others ministered in Newberg's Chehalem House, Newberg Human Resources, Albina Resources Center, Give Us This Day, MacLaren School for Boys, and many other locations. On one occasion, when Northwest Yearly Meeting's Friends

Action Board sponsored a house-building project for recently returned missionaries Quentin and Florene Nordyke, many students and some faculty participated.

Sometimes students directly helped the College. Although all-school prune picking and cleanup days had long passed, a group in 1981 became concerned about the need for library books. Several GFC students, among them Jim LeShana, Susan Macy, and Ed Lehman, organized a project called "Beards for Books," or "Buzz a Bruin's Beard for the Book Budget." Thirty students, faculty, and staff offered their facial hair for the cause. When the first $500 had been raised, librarian Genette McNichols artistically shaved sophomore Larry Rodgers during chapel.

Twenty-six more beards eventually littered the chapel floor in priority order, short stubble to old growth; faculty members Mel Schroeder, Bruce Longstroth, Richard Engnell and Paul Chamberlain provided the grand finale as the total moved from $22,000 to $25,000. Board chairman Robert Monroe wielded the blade for the final trimming.

The students also sponsored a "slave auction" that raised $500 for books. One group contributed $100 for two hours of Dave LeShana's services.

ALTHOUGH SOME students reflected the somewhat radical mood of many campuses, most continued to vote conservatively. In 1976, 57 percent registered Republican, 24 Democrat, 19 independent. In that year freshmen overwhelmingly favored President Ford, while seniors narrowly preferred Jimmy Carter.

During the 1970s, the College developed a professional approach to student services. With Eugene Habecker's arrival as dean of student life in 1974, it officially adopted a "whole student" philosophy. Student Life committed

---

"We want to know God's place in the ghetto, in race relations, in the drug problem, and in the student revolts."
—from a student's letter to The Crescent

---

itself to "walking alongside" the student, promoting spiritual, emotional, physical, and intellectual growth. The College later adopted the "confrontation model," encouraging young people to assist in policing their own behavior and that of their peers. Following Habecker, deans of students Julie Hawley and Lee Gerig continued the same emphasis. At the decade's end, the accrediting committee commended the student affairs personnel for "excellent leadership."

The trustees approved a "Biblical Rationale for George Fox College Rules" in 1978, which emphasized redemptive love and understanding, but continued to prohibit gambling, tobacco, alcohol, and other nonmedical drugs.

The statement added: "Our college community has found its best interests served by not sponsoring dances or permitting social dancing on campus or at college-related activities or events."

Through the 1970s, college officials reported a strong interest in missions, biblical studies, and spiritual growth. Although a few students violated school rules, the vast majority apparently maintained a satisfactory level of personal behavior. Administrative personnel dismissed very few for conduct violations.

GFC students typically applauded the sense of Christian community engendered at the small, friendly college. One put it concisely, warmly recalling the "interactive spirit, the dorm life, the Bible studies, and the intramural sports between dorm floors." He added that "even the authorized dorm raids suggested an administration interested in allowing fun without letting it get out of hand."

DURING THE COLLEGE'S second half-century, the spoken word lost primacy to music and drama. Gone were the Agoreton and Helianthus literary societies, the state oratorical and Old Pulpit contests, lyceum, the forensics club, and Actorators. Gone also was the orator president, Chautauqua champion Levi Pennington (although President LeShana could have given him superb oratorical competition).

Music, long a GFC strength, became central to deputation and entertainment. Drama reached a new plateau as a medium for expression.

Music theater combined music and drama, with Professor Joe Gilmore providing the expertise. The major musicals included *Fiddler on the Roof*, starring Tim Minikel as Tevye; *Music Man*, with Steve Cadd playing Harold Hill; *My Fair Lady*, with Bonnie (Johnson) Hampton and Kurt Johnson starring; *The King and I*, with Laurie (Adams) Martin as Anna; Gilbert and Sullivan's *The Pirates of Penzance*, featuring Leah (Pope) Bellamy, Charles Hernandez, Deolinda (Morrow) Willson, Richard Zeller, and Jon Fodge; *Carousel*, starring Pamela Gilmore; *Godspell*, with Jesse Pennoyer and Debbie (Dominy) Seibert; *I Pagliacci*, sung by Joseph Gilmore, Sharon (Fodge) Brown, Ron Mulkey, Burt Rosevear, and Tim Hathaway; and *The Sound of Music*, with Leah (Pope) Bellamy as Maria.

In addition, *A Night on Broadway* in 1980 saw students Leah (Pope) Bellamy, Jerry Murphy, Deolinda (Morrow)

Ankeny (marathon), Eb Buck (decathlon), Steve Blikstad (steeplechase three times), and Chad Neeley (intermediate hurdles). The NAIA selected Rich Allen district coach of the year for all sports in 1978. He was inducted into the NAIA District 2 coaches' Hall of Fame in 1981—the only GFC coach to have made that honor in any sport.

After Dale Orkney initiated cross country in 1966, Burton Lamb, Don Lakin, Gayle Buckley, and Curt Ankeny each coached before Rich Allen took over for 12 years beginning in 1975. Curt Ankeny won the NAIA district championship in 1972 and 1973, and Steve Blikstad took it in 1976. Rich Allen's 1977 team won the district championship with Steve Blikstad, Chris Mwaura, Dave Molstad, Tim Rochholz, and Steve Stuart setting the pace.

In 1972-73 Coach Lorin Miller's basketball team won the NAIA District II championship and went to the nationals in Kansas City before losing to Defiance, Ohio. Miller coached six years, winning 99 and losing 72.

Sam Willard followed for another six seasons. Willard's 1976-77 quintet went 20 and 8, setting 20 team and individual records. Paul Cozens made district all-star for the third year and won NAIA All-American honors—the first in GFC basketball history.

This marked the 31st and last season for "Hester Dome." The next year, 1977-78, the Bruins played in the magnificent new Coleman Wheeler Sports Center, with 2,700 spectators viewing the season-opening Tip-Off Tournament. That year the Bruins went 15 and 14 in a schedule that included Portland State University and the University of Portland. Paul Cozens made his fourth district all-star team and finished his career with 2,187 points, topping Bill Hopper's 1954-58 record of 1,731. Following the season, GFC officials retired Cozens' number 44 jersey—the first retired number in the school's history.

Guard Gary Chenault highlighted the 1978-79 season by making a record-setting 56 consecutive free throws. In

112

The 1976-77 women's basketball team. Front row: Joni (Snyder) O'Halloran, Kelly Davidson, Dena Kaye Holloran, Pam (Sturzinger) Medzegian, Mona (Barnett) Shepherd, Nancy (Kile) Thompson. Back row: Coach Bob Wright, Diane DeWitt, Cheryl Lawrence, Lavonne Kolmar, Diane (Beebe) Eichenberger, Coach Dee Bright.

1980 Hille Vanderkooy tied Bill Hopper's single-game, 42-point scoring record.

Women participated in field hockey, basketball, volleyball, and tennis before initiating track as a full sport in 1976. Marge Weesner, Nadine Brood, Dee Bright, Randy Winston, and Bob Wright all coached.

The 1969-70 basketball squad took the league championship—the fifth in six years—behind Nancy Phillips' stellar play. Sue Knapp in 1976 set a probable all-time GFC scoring record of 40 points in a 63-61 win over nationally ranked Gonzaga. The Women's Conference of Independent Colleges selected Pam (Sturzinger) Medzegian as an all-star eight times in all sports, making her perhaps the most decorated athlete since Carl Sandoz won 17 letters in the 1930s.

Other students won honors outside the College. For example, Crisanne (Pike) Roberts represented Oregon in the 1977 national Homecoming Queen contest at the Orange Bowl in Miami, Florida. Johnson Wax awarded the College a $500 scholarship.

Begun in 1967 from a donation by Lowell Edwards, the student radio station KGFC developed by 1975 into a non-profit enterprise for campus education and entertainment. The low-power station, headquartered in the Student Union Building, transmitted to all campus residence halls.

Student Gary Lewis and Professor Evan Remple, both experienced ham operators, developed the project. Roy Gathercoal served as station manager. Renamed KFOX, the station continued to broadcast Christian music and public service announcements to the campus.

ALTHOUGH GFC had traditionally wanted a strong Friends presence in the student community, it failed to maintain the board's 1964 goal of a constant 50 percent Quaker student body. As dean, Arthur Roberts recommended targeted recruiting and appropriate scholarships to sustain the ratio. The board reiterated the goal in 1971 and approved an intensified recruiting effort among Quakers.

However, the College's growth came primarily from the Evangelical Church of North America and various Baptist bodies. When in 1954 Milo Ross became president, 81 percent of the students were Quakers (a total of 79 students); by LeShana's inaugural in 1969, the percentage had shrunk to 42 (172 Quakers); 12 years later only 22 percent were Friends (163 students). That year the school enrolled 152 students from Wesleyan (Free Methodist, Nazarene, Evangelical Church of North America, etc.) and 124 from Baptist churches.

As a body with only about 7,000 members, Northwest Yearly Meeting provided a relatively small potential for its college's growth. Although the Yearly Meeting grew gradually, the school grew much faster. According to the 45 churches reporting in 1979, a total of 51 percent of Northwest Yearly Meeting's undergraduate students attended GFC. Another 36 percent were in public schools, with 13 percent in other church-related colleges.

Between 1969 and 1981, tuition rose from $1,400 to $4,150 (which still left about $5,000 per student to be paid by other sources). Although some students and parents considered these costs high, by comparison, the College remained quite inexpensive. It generally ranked below the 25th percentile when compared with both Northwest independent colleges and Christian College Consortium schools.

In 1977-78, GFC's board, room, and tuition cost of $3,850 stood about $2,000 below Reed, $500 to $1,000 less than Lewis & Clark College, Pacific University, Willamette University, and Linfield College, and $100 under Seattle Pacific University.

Recent studies of the 1979 and 1982 graduating classes measured the influence of various college programs. "Developing the ability to work well with other people" headed both studies. Other descriptive phrases ranking high included "Understanding the Bible and basic Christian

May Day court, 1980. Front row: Sue (Hart) Thompson, Charlene (Harris) Cox, Sherie (Winslow) Smith, Kathy (Bodin) Holt, Lori (Beebe) Tuning. Back row: Dave Forney, Phil Aronson, Don Kunkle, Randy Haugen, Ron Tuning.

doctrines," "Developing a nurturing faith in Jesus Christ," and "Cultivating the practice of life-long learning." The bottom three of 28 items included: "Developing appreciation for the visual arts," "Developing appreciation for drama," and "Recognizing your rights, responsibilities, and privileges as a citizen."

DAVID LeSHANA RESIGNED in 1982. During his presidency, the College became a larger, more efficient, more professional institution. The success, LeShana noted, required three steps: (1) a clear definition of the objective; (2) careful development of a plan; and (3) courageous implementation of the strategy.

Like Levi Pennington and Milo Ross, LeShana will long be acclaimed by George Fox College constituents. His

"God has been blessing through the great strengths of the administrative team and faculty, their hard work and a lot of effort."
—President David LeShana

motto: "God's work done in God's way will not lack God's supply." George Fox College certainly endeavored to do God's work, and in God's way. As a result, God supplied.

David LeShana credited the Lord. "God has been blessing through the great strengths of the administrative team and faculty, their hard work and a lot of effort. The Lord

114

Herbert Hoover Academic Building

Weesner Village

Shambaugh Library

Edwards Residence Hall

works through strong men and women. But we dare not lose the sense of God's hand in all of this."

Retiring from 34 years as a trustee, former board president Walter P. Lee offered similar sentiments. A veteran of the turbulent 1940s, Lee expressed appreciation for the school's deep Christian commitment and concluded his plea to the trustees: "Oh, Timothy, keep that which is committed to thy trust."

George Fox College did keep the trust. However, the next administration would face hard times unknown during the LeShana years, as a variety of problems tested the institution almost beyond its capacity to endure.

Hobson-Macy-Sutton Residence Hall Complex

115

Wood-Mar Hall

Weesner House

Student Union Building

Brougher Hall

Calder Center

DAVID LeSHANA left George Fox College in 1982 to become Seattle Pacific University's sixth president. Fortunately, Dean William Green was available to serve as interim president while the trustees sought a permanent replacement.

Bill Green's strong academic background and administrative experience prepared him well. He had been at George Fox since 1972 following 23 years as faculty member and administrator at Bryan, Taylor, and Malone colleges, including ten years as Malone's academic dean. Having already predicted declining enrollments and darker days ahead, Green wisely prepared the College for a period of retrenchment.

The difficult years began with two 1982 tragedies. The deaths of young Northwest Yearly Meeting leaders Cyril Carr, 32, and Don Green, 33, wrenched the constituency. Carr taught Old Testament and had earned respect from the faculty and students. William Green's son, Don, pastored Reedwood Friends Church in Portland and had already become an outstanding leader in the Yearly Meeting and Quakerism internationally. He died just four months into his father's interim presidential year.

As Northwest Yearly Meeting and its College mourned these personal losses, an economic recession impacted enrollment and finances. Unemployment approached 10 percent nationwide. The Reagan administration and Congress reduced federal aid to colleges. GFC's enrollment declined, the George Fox College Foundation crumbled, severe indebtedness on the chapel-auditorium threatened, and the Purchase of Educational Services from Independent Colleges (PESIC) funds evaporated. Never had so many negatives plagued the College in so short a time.

The federal aid that had contributed significantly a decade earlier fell sharply in the 1980s. George Fox's allotment of the U.S. Government's Pell Grant dropped from $351,000 to $271,000 in four years. College officials replaced the lost student aid with institutional funds.

As educational costs increased, the College provided additional student aid, offering incentives for academic merit, matching funds to churches, additional athletic awards, and assistance to some international students. As a result, unrestricted institutional grants grew from $25,000 to $322,000 between the 1979-80 and 1983-84 school years. The federal government paid 40 percent of the College's total student aid package in 1979-80 but only 12 percent four years later.

As overhead mounted, the administration and trustees raised tuition prices from $1,824 in 1975-76 to $3,465 in 1980-81, and then up to $5,950 in 1986-87. Although enrollment peaked at 746 students in 1980, it plummeted in successive years to 743, 683, 657, 624, 580, and 549 in 1986—a 26.4 percent loss. Declining new student admissions (from 307 to 197, a 35 percent decrease in six years) accounted for most of the loss, which more than doubled the decrease in high school graduates in Oregon and nationally.

A sharp reduction in Quaker students alarmed some constituents. Friends attendance peaked at 225 (41 percent of the student body) in 1975-76. During the next five years, while total enrollment grew rapidly in spite of increasing costs, Friends matriculants dropped to 160 (22 percent of the student body).

Then, as overall student numbers declined, Quaker enrollment dropped even more sharply. By 1986-87 it had plunged to only 89 students (16 percent). In raw numbers, this was the lowest since the 1950s; the percentage was the least in the College's history until 1990-91, when it fell to 14.4 percent (113 students).

Problems in the George Fox College Foundation dealt another blow. Established by friends of the College in 1969, the Foundation anticipated significant profits after a few deficit years. Not until a decade later did these hopes begin to be fulfilled. Shortly thereafter, the 1982 recession devastated many investors. The organization suffered so many problems that, by late 1982, its assets totaled only $3,600,000 against liabilities of $4,470,000. One year later, the recession-riddled Foundation closed its doors and moved all records to the College's development and business offices.

Although GFC had no legal liability or control over the Foundation, the organization carried the College's name and its anticipated profits had been intended for the school. Agreeing that a moral responsibility existed, the administration and trustees attempted to rectify the matter.

Business Manager Don Millage and Director of Development Maurice Chandler each spent many hours working patiently with those who had been hurt by the debacle. They achieved generally positive results for investors, although some lost money anyway. Annuities issued

Fall Regular Student Enrollment, 1982-1990

1982—683	1985—580	1988—819
1983—657	1986—549	1989—942
1984—624	1987—705	1990—1,072

Powder puff football
game on a typical Fall day,
1983.

Nighttime in Pennington
Hall, 1984.

1983-84 cheerleaders. Women in ascending order: Marcia
Snow, Tina Sparks, Julie-Anne (Edmundson) Mueller, Karon
Walker, Carmen (Pinkerton) Ralls. Men: Marlon Teeters,
Jaime Scott Morgan, Larry Wilkins.

to individuals cost the college up to $65,000 a year for the
lifetimes of those paid.

The loss of PESIC funds presented an even stronger
moral challenge. Begun in 1969, the program reimbursed
private schools for educating Oregon residents (paying
only for nonreligion classes). After a decade, George Fox
College realized over $225,000 annually from this source.

When the American Civil Liberties Union charged that
this use of taxpayers' money violated the constitutional
separation of church and state, GFC joined other private
colleges in contesting the suit. However, in 1982 it became
evident that the court's decision would turn on the defen-
dants' ability to prove their schools were not "pervasively
religious." Recognizing its clearly spiritual mission, George
Fox College withdrew from the case and from the PESIC
program. Although the state had already sharply reduced
PESIC payments, the sacrificed income cost the College
over $130,000 annually.

In building the William and Mary Bauman Chapel/Aud-
itorium, the board temporarily suspended its longstanding
policy prohibiting construction until all funds were in
hand. Facing high inflation, the trustees decided in 1982 to
borrow $1 million against pledges and to begin construc-
tion immediately. The decision seemed wise until the
devastating recession prevented some major donors from
meeting their pledges. As a result, GFC faced about
$100,000 average annual interest payments until it cleared
the debt in 1988.

In total, these financial liabilities—reduction of federal
aid, decreased enrollment, payments to Foundation creditors, loss of PESIC funds, and interest on the chapel/audito-
rium indebtedness—cost the 1982-83 general fund budget
approximately $1 million. This figure increased annually
through the mid-1980s.

Against these adversities, the school's continued strength, perhaps even its survival, resulted from
four major factors: (1) it retained its central mission and
constituency, (2) it balanced each year's annual budget, (3)
it maintained strong administrative leadership and sound
faculty strength, and (4) it developed several attractive new
academic programs.

The decision regarding PESIC illustrates the first point.
GFC officials believed that it would be better to lose the
income than compromise the purpose; they also took some
steps to halt the decline in Quaker matriculants.

Second, in spite of the significant income reductions, the
College lived within its resources, reducing expenditures

118

THE GEORGE FOX SONG
(Tune: "The Flintstones")

George Fox, we're from George Fox
A Quaker Christian family
From the town of Newberg
Also known as Bruin country.

It's the finest place in all the land
Not far from the surf and sea and sand

George Fox, we're from George Fox
Where Hoover never got his degree
But that will not happen
To you and you and you and me.

We'll all study till our brains fall out
Then when we graduate we'll shout

George Fox, we're from George Fox
A yabba-dabba doo school
A really cool school
When you leave you ain't no foooooool.

Lyrics by: Jim Foster
Deb Horn
Lani Nelson

as necessary to avoid long-term debt. Thanks largely to Don Millage's expertise and stubborn determination, the school ended its first century with a string of balanced budgets dating from his arrival in 1972.

In addition, through these difficult years the College maintained a strong administration and faculty that developed numerous attractive programs. Although some key people moved away, the school secured high-quality replacements. The selection of Edward F. Stevens to succeed David LeShana as president proved particularly significant.

ED STEVENS WAS the first George Fox president to go through a competitive candidating process; whereas the board targeted and recruited all nine predecessors, it chose Stevens from 96 aspirants nationwide.

Stevens was also the school's first non-Quaker president. He may have been the first who was not a recorded Friends minister. Some constituents worried that someone unacquainted with Friends might lack empathy and understanding, and thereby damage the College through insensitivity or lack of loyalty to its traditions. When difficult circumstances threatened, would Quaker distinctives become the scapegoat of the president's frustrations?

However, Stevens' management credentials and commitment to evangelical principles convinced the board and faculty. The GFC constituents entered enthusiastically into the decision.

The new president grew up in Wyoming and won degrees from Nebraska Wesleyan University and the University of Nebraska. In 1983 he completed the Ph.D. in higher education and marketing/management at the University of Minnesota, with a dissertation on "Market Segmentation as a Technique for Improved Student Recruitment at Church Related Colleges."

Stevens married Linda Loewenstein in 1962 and taught and coached in high school, then college, before becoming a business executive. He returned to education in 1974 as chief development officer, executive assistant to the president, and associate professor of business at Sioux Falls College before coming to George Fox in 1983.

AS PRESIDENT, STEVENS was not afraid to take bold, even controversial, action. With income falling and expenses mounting, the administration deemed personnel reductions essential. Near the end of his first year, the new president, reluctant to cut academics first, recommended combining the church relations and chaplain's responsibilities into one position. This meant release of Gene Hockett, a respected, well-known former Friends pastor, and reduction to a part-time retirement position for popular chaplain Ron Crecelius, also a recorded Friends minister.

Some segments of the college constituency criticized this release of two GFC graduates who had served the College a combined total of 33 years. However, after a year's delay, procurement as chaplain of Tim Tsohantaridis, a former Ohio Friends pastor, generally appeased the critics. Tsohantaridis served until his return to pastoral work in 1990, when the College brought Crecelius back for a one-year interim appointment.

The reduction to three-fourths time of four faculty members proved equally controversial. This action hit the Division of Fine and Applied Arts hardest, but the entire school felt the impact. The administration asked some teachers to take early retirement. Morale suffered as the institution cut into the careers of some who had served it faithfully for many years.

WILLIAM GREEN RETURNED from his interim presidency to the deanship in 1983-84. He soon announced his retirement, however, effective July 1984. After a long search, Stevens and the board chose Lee Nash, GFC professor of history and chairman of the Division of Social Science, over a field of highly qualified candidates from throughout the United States.

Lee Nash brought superb credentials, including degrees in literature from Cascade College and the University of Washington, and a University of Oregon history Ph.D. After distinguished service to Cascade College (including five years as academic dean) and Northern Arizona University, Nash became a history professor at George Fox in 1975 and served as associate dean of the College while William Green was interim president. An excellent teacher, writer, and speaker, Nash's candidacy enjoyed the support of faculty, students, and other constituents.

Ed Stevens soon restructured the college leadership into an administrative cabinet with four vice presidents: Nash for academic affairs, Don Millage for financial affairs,

A DAY IN THE LIFE OF A FIRST-YEAR PRESIDENT
By Ed Stevens

I returned from a ten-day trip about midnight on a Wednesday. Lee Gerig picked me up and said, "We have problems."

1. Students had advertised a "GFC student-sponsored" dance. Lee had said "No," and now we were to have a special chapel on Thursday morning—to discuss. I would lead the discussion.

2. A student had made a serious attempt at suicide.

3. Two students were involved in a fight. One ended up in jail—the other in the hospital.

After a FULL day Thursday, I met long into the night with the executive committee of the board discussing the various problems. As I was walking back to my office, the campus seemed covered with "darkness"—physical and spiritual—and I came to a stop on the sidewalk, almost afraid to go on. The Lord seemed to speak to me and said, "Fear not for I am with you always." I had a sense of peace and recognized in a new way that this school belonged to Him—not me.

All the issues were resolved with positive and some eternal results. After our long special chapel, the students accepted my request that they voluntarily forego the dance in the best interests of the community. The young man in jail became a believer in Christ and an outstanding leader on our campus. The young woman who attempted suicide came to realize how much God loved her! She led a 15-year-old to Christ while in the hospital recovering.

Lee Gerig for student life, and Maurice Chandler for development. (Deb Lacey replaced Gerig in 1986; Chandler resigned in 1985 and, after some reorganization and interim appointments, Sam Farmer filled his position in 1989. The College added Dirk Barram as vice president for graduate and continuing studies in 1990.)

THE CABINET AGREED that for the school to survive, income must increase. As a tuition-driven institution with students paying 67 percent of the budget, the College needed a higher enrollment. This meant upgrading the admissions process.

120

**Farewell for Maurice Chandler, Ron Crecelius, Alice Dixon,
Catherine Loewen, and Bill Loewen, 1985. All were given
"Pete's Pots," made by art instructor Pete Snow.**

Admissions Director Jim Settle recruited successfully
after coming in 1973. Even before he left a decade later,
however, the sharp tuition increases, declining student
pool, and economic recession restricted enrollment. Two
admissions directors between 1983 and 1986 failed to halt
the decline. By the spring of 1986, the situation became
critical. Stevens therefore recommended a dramatic
change in admissions philosophy and methodology.

Midway through the 1986 recruiting season, the board
hired an outside firm, D. H. Dagley and Associates, to
administer the admissions program. Dagley specialized in
assisting colleges in meeting enrollment objectives through
better selection of prospects, personal service, and home

visitations. In subsequent years, GFC's recruiters made
over 500 home visits annually, using tested marketing
methods to reach their goals.

The Dagley decision met considerable skepticism, particularly among faculty members determined to maintain
the unique student community at George Fox. Would the
Dagley "headhunters" (as one professor labeled them)
bring in misfits? Would the "bottom line" of increased
revenues, for which Dagley was hired, destroy the College's mission by changing the character of its student
body? Would the profit-seeking private corporation serve
the College or become its master?

Fears receded when Jeff Rickey was hired as director
of admissions. Rickey, a 1976 GFC graduate and former
student body president, employed four other alumni as
admissions counselors. The new admissions team
instituted improved methods of selecting prospective students appropriate to the College's mission and succeeded
in recruiting a top-rate, well-suited student community.

In Rickey's first three years, the College admitted 253,
283 and 336 freshmen, transfers, and readmissions—a 71
percent increase from the 1986 low of 197. The Quaker
percentage, which had fallen to 16 percent (89 students),
improved temporarily but slipped to 14.4 percent in
1990—a total of 113 Friends students. The student community, which in six years had dipped from 746 to 549,
rebounded to 786 traditional students by 1990. Rickey
resigned that year to become Dagley's regional director,
and the College replaced him with Randy Comfort,
another GFC alumnus.

IMPROVED RECRUITING only partially explained the
increase, however. A strengthened faculty and some
noteworthy academic initiatives provided Rickey with a
better product to sell. The College improved its faculty

Faculty/staff campaign dinner, 1986, includes prayer of unity.

Bottom: Graduates turning their tassels in 1987. Shown are Rebecca (Blankenbaker) Iverson, Matthew Blair, and Bruce Bishop.

George Fox College began offering the HRM program in 1986; by the end of that academic year, the school held eight classes in Newberg, Portland, and Salem. It added Eugene as a new site in 1989. Classes met in 15-student cluster (cohort) groups under one continuing GFC professor, supplemented by specialists. Each student thus became part of an academic support group comprised of individuals from varied backgrounds who worked together through the demanding 62-week program.

The HRM major provided a strong individual study and research component, helping students assess their own values, develop interpersonal skills, and enhance professional competencies. It included a library orientation, six Saturday seminars, a senior research project, and nine three-semester-hour evening courses: Dynamics of Group and Organizational Behavior, Effective Writing, Organizational Communication, Systems Management, Principles of Management and Supervision, Human Resources Adminis-

"[The Human Resources Management program] changed my life for the better [because] the loving, supportive staff members continually said, 'You can do it.' I had a great deal of anxiety about reentering school, and it wasn't easy to take the first step, but each step along the way is fulfilling."
—HRM graduate Paula Gentzkow

tration, Research Methods in the Behavioral Sciences, Faith and World Views, and Values and Ethics in the Workplace.

Human Resources Management majors averaged 37 years of age, had typically attended at least two other institutions, and took the GFC program while working full time. In 1990, over half of the majors lived in Portland and about one third in Salem.

Marilyn Morris typified the HRM students. The executive director of United Way for Linn County, she had completed nearly 100 transferable credit hours at Multnomah School of the Bible, Portland State, and Linn-Benton Community College. Insurance agent Cliff Canucci transferred 84 hours from Portland State, Portland Community, and The American College. Janis Keeley, an assistant vice-president and corporate training manager, had attended San Jose State, Northwest Intermediate School of Banking, and Mt. Hood Community College.

HRM graduate Paula Gentzkow reported that the program "changed my life for the better" because "the loving, supportive staff members continually said, 'You can do it.' I had a great deal of anxiety about reentering school, and it wasn't easy to take the first step, but each step along the way is fulfilling." Sylvia MacWilliams commended the "positive learning environment with excellent instructors and a 'caring-guiding' atmosphere."

GFC teachers uniformly expressed pleasure with the HRM students' maturity and dedication. Five hundred entered the major in its first four years; 95 percent graduated. As a result, the well-managed, academically valid program won the acclaim of the entire GFC community.

THROUGH THE FIRST century, many graduates served internationally with mission boards and various relief and service organizations. GFC instituted an international studies major in 1983—a logical culmination of the College's long interest in mission and service.

Several faculty members, among them Dennis Hagen, Julie Hobbs, Jerry Friesen, and John Bowman, had already

taken groups overseas. A 1981 study tour guided by Arthur Roberts resulted three years later in the enrollment of GFC's first student from the Democratic Republic of China. Shu-Guo Diao, from Beijing, significantly impacted the campus before her graduation in 1988.

Juniors Abroad built on these international emphases. Faculty member Patricia Landis brought the idea from Nyack College; Lee Nash immediately championed it for George Fox.

Instituted in 1986-87, the program offered any junior who had attended the College six consecutive semesters a transportation-paid, faculty-sponsored, three-week study experience in another country. Administrators anticipated that increased enrollment and improved retention would reimburse the institution for these costs.

Pat Landis and Andy Wong accompanied seven students to China in 1987. The next year, 30 students partici-

pated in three trips: England and Scotland, with Mike Williams and Mark Weinert; the European continent, with John Bowman; and Bolivia and Peru, with Ron Stansell.

Jim Foster and Mark Weinert took 20 students to the Soviet Union and 14 others accompanied Ralph Beebe to Israel/West Bank in 1989. One of the latter tour's highlights occurred when student Ken Robinson, with Free Methodist baptismal credentials, and Quaker professor Ralph Beebe baptized tour members Jerry Miley and Jim Caruthers in the Jordan River. On Jordan's lovely banks stood 400 Ethiopians, accompanying with a beautiful hymn-chant. All participants experienced the One who baptizes with the Holy Spirit and with fire.

Gary Fawver and Paul Chamberlain accompanied 22 students to Australia in 1990, while Pat Landis and Rebecca Ankeny took 24 to Europe, and Warren Koch led six to Kenya. The faculty selected Professors Gerald Wilson (Israel/West Bank), Tim Tsohantaridis (Greece), and John Bowman (Europe) to lead groups in 1991. The Persian Gulf War's aftermath curtailed the 1991 program, but Paul Chamberlain took a group to Australia, Mark Weinert accompanied one to England, and John Bowman led a group to the European continent.

OFFICIALS INITIATED an "English Language Institute" in 1987 to provide international students an opportunity to do precollege language work in the United States. Bruce Carrick, Judy Henske, Martha Iancu, and Ron Parrish taught in this program in its early years. GFC also developed a "home stay" for international high school and college students. Paul Berry, Everett Hackworth, and Ron Parrish directed this program.

Meanwhile, GFC signed "sister college" arrangements with Soai and Allen colleges in Japan, and Kang Nam College of Social Welfare in Korea. The Christian College Coalition's Latin America Studies Program further augmented the international emphasis by offering a semester's study in Costa Rica.

George Fox contracted Manfred Tschan in 1988 as part-time international student coordinator. By 1989-90, the student community contained 43 internationals from nine countries, including 21 Japanese. That year, the College provided several special emphases, including International Foreign Language Week, with appropriate programs, foods, displays, and music on student radio station KFOX. The next year GFC enrolled 46 international students.

George Fox's membership in the Christian College Consortium, for which Dean William Green deserves primary credit, produced excellent dividends. In 1985, the J. Howard

125

Pew Freedom Trust gave the 13-member organization $1.8 million, one third dedicated to an "Internationalizing the Curriculum" emphasis. George Fox's $50,000 share augmented the College's expanding international emphasis.

A follow-up Pew grant in 1989 provided a program called "International Partnering," through which GFC developed relationships with institutions and faculty in Kenya and Israel/West Bank. Engineering teacher Bob Harder headed the former, while religion professor Gerald Wilson developed the latter program.

George Fox began annual participation in the Northwest Model League of Arab States in 1988, playing the role of Libya. The next three years, Elias Jabbour a Palestinian Christian who manages the House of Hope in Israel, came to Newberg and coached the GFC team in its role as Palestine. Laura Engle, Susan (Spencer) Crisman, Kristy (Bendicksen) Lacey, and Christie Silliman won special recognition the first two years. Elaine Payne and Kit Kroker headed GFC's 1990 delegation, with Jerry Miley and John Hurty leading in 1991.

The international emphasis not only correlated with George Fox College's historic spiritual mission, it also reflected the particular needs of American college students. Bonnie Jerke, director of career services, quoted public opinion analyst Louis Harris, who asserted that future employability would require a "global perspective, an intimate knowledge of what the world outside the U.S. is really like. Cross-cultural comprehension and understanding will be not only the mark of an educated person, but a requisite for tomorrow's economic survival. Today's students must be prepared to think for themselves and to think globally."

THE FIRST PEW GRANT also provided funds for writing and ethics. Ed Higgins and Arthur Roberts chaired these programs, which involved special projects and a national conference. The 1990 accrediting visitation team commended GFC's resultant success in promoting writing campus-wide.

Ethics accomplishments included religion professor Ron Stansell's three 12-minute video presentations based on New Testament ethical dilemmas; physical education professor Craig Taylor's special ethical component for a P.E. course; psychologist Mark McMinn's computer simulation, an ethical case study; and a three-week ethics component for business, sociology, and social work classes by sociology professor Mike Allen.

The 1989 extension of the Pew funds renewed the ethics grant. Religion professor Ron Stansell headed this emphasis, entitled "Teaching of Values."

IN REBOUNDING FROM the early 1980s' downturn, the College added new majors in elementary education, telecommunications, computer information science, engineering, and secondary teaching of home economics, health, and chemistry. The addition to the business/economics department of Professor Rod Strieby gave the College sufficient accounting strength to prepare students for the Certified Public Accountant examination.

Before GFC granted its first elementary education degrees in 1985, certification depended on a joint-degree arrangement with Western Oregon State College. With the program's accreditation, however, the major quickly became the school's largest, attracting nearly 25 percent of all students. The three additional majors provided secondary teacher certification in nine fields (biology, chemistry, health education, home economics, language arts, mathematics, music, physical education, and social studies) and teaching minors in four (basic mathematics, drama, health, and speech).

The home economics education major made George Fox one of only three Oregon schools to offer that degree.

126

The library temporarily
transferred to the
Chehalem Room during
the asbestos problem,
1988.

This program became possible when the College added Teresa Boehr to the home economics department, sharing responsibilities with Flora Allen. Health education offered three variations: health with either biology, home economics, or physical education.

In 1988 George Fox initiated an engineering major in conjunction with the University of Portland's Multnomah School of Engineering. The program required five years' study, the first three in general education and introductory engineering courses, the last two in specialization on the U.P. campus. Students received the bachelor's in engineering from the Portland school, along with another bachelor's degree in applied science from George Fox College.

Some constituents complained that engineering seemed far removed from George Fox's traditional liberal arts academic emphasis. The College added the program for two explicit reasons: (1) high student demand and (2) unique ministry opportunity. In its initial years, engineering fulfilled both promises: It attracted several students who wanted a Christian technical education, and to head the program, the school hired Robert Harder, who had renounced personal material ambitions to teach students a "tentmaking" ministry so they could provide human services to developing countries.

George Fox College expanded its Camp Tilikum program during the 1980s. By the decade's end, Gary Fawver, Arnie Mitchell, and Linda Byrd directed numerous academic courses, elderhostels, retreats, and related experiences.

Between 1984 and 1989, GFC graduated 20 students who worked professionally in camping. In 1990 Fawver resigned the Tilikum directorship to put more emphasis on his classroom teaching. The College chose longtime assistant Arnie Mitchell to replace him.

THROUGH THE 1980s, George Fox College developed an exceptional small-college psychology program, anchored by Ohio State Ph.D. Jim Foster and Vanderbilt Ph.D. Mark McMinn.

When in 1989 Western Conservative Baptist Seminary offered GFC its 12-year-old clinical psychology program, the school had the confidence to move quickly. After administrative and faculty study and approval, the trustees accepted the program for the fall 1990 semester.

Offering master's and doctoral degrees in psychology, the new program promised to enhance GFC's historic concern for healing and reconciliation. The College took this major step anticipating rapid approval by the Northwest Association of Schools and Colleges and immediate movement toward an application for accreditation by the American Psychological Association. Seventy-one students transferred to GFC in 1990 as the first Psy.D. class.

This first venture into graduate education nudged other doors. The administration immediately named Dirk Barram as vice president for graduate and continuing studies. As it ended the first century, GFC was developing master's degree programs in education, business management, and Christian studies.

THROUGHOUT GEORGE FOX COLLEGE'S history, visiting committees and accreditation teams persistently criticized the inadequate library and learning resources. The 1962 Shambaugh Library overcame the deficiency for a time, but the College outgrew it by the 1980s.

The 1980 accreditation evaluation underscored this problem: "The recommendation for urgent action in library development stands apart as the leading indicator of the institution's commitment to academic quality in the future. A college-wide task force should be constituted immediately to review the issue and recommend short- and long-term action." Two years later, the Century II Planning Committee proposed a solution—a learning resource center adequate for 1,000 students.

The College therefore launched the "Century II Campaign" in 1986 to raise money for a wrap-around doubling of the Shambaugh Library. Director of Development Dave Adrian headed a leadership team of Esther Klages (President's Council), Bob and Marcena Monroe (Trustees), Frank and Genevieve Cole (Alumni), and Ralph Beebe (Faculty and Staff). Honorary chairpersons included Ken and Joan Austin, Esther Brougher, James and Lila Miller, John and Marilyn Duke, and Arthur Roberts.

The campaign succeeded remarkably. It climaxed when the M. J. Murdock Charitable Trust gave $1.35 million in 1987 as primary funding for the building named to honor the late cofounder of Tektronix, Inc. (The school retained the Shambaugh name for the book and periodical collections.) Director of Library Services Merrill Johnson chaired the broadly based committee that planned and supervised the major improvement.

Opened in 1988, the three-level M. J. Murdock Learning Resource Center housed stacks, the Instructional Media and Study Skills centers, George Fox College and Northwest Yearly Meeting of Friends Church archives, study carrels, rooms for faculty research, a computer laboratory, curriculum library, multipurpose room, and special Quaker, peace, and Herbert Hoover collections.

Its inviting atmosphere augmented by two large skylights, the new learning center provided the campus a warm, quiet, studious academic heart. In the Murdock building, the College gained a real sense of institutional maturity.

In total, the Century II campaign raised about $6 million, with $2.5 million spent for the Murdock center. Other funds went for learning materials, endowment, and scholarships.

T HE M. J. MURDOCK Learning Resource Center provided an enticing study climate. Yet the cornerstone of the school's strength continued to be faculty/student interaction. As first-year business teacher Raymond Gleason expressed it in 1990, the George Fox faculty uniquely understood that "its mission is to work with students and to make them good ministers."

The life of Elver Voth, scientist at GFC for 25 years before his retirement and death from cancer in 1989, symbolizes that special insight in practice. While their mentor was terminally ill, many former students remembered. For example, Brad Grimstead wrote: "I have learned a lot about science, writing and thinking from you. Much more, . . . I have learned honesty, integrity, and most of all, a serving attitude. With much respect, care and love, I say 'thank you.'"

During the decade's final years, the College added several outstanding professors. Among them were Becky (Thomas) Ankeny, Wes Cook, Paul Anderson, Raymond Gleason, Roy Kruger, Bob Harder, Craig Johnson, Beth LaForce, Don Powers, Karen Swenson, and Gerald Wilson.

In 1990, 61 percent of those faculty teaching full loads had doctorates. The advanced degrees came from 19 schools as diverse as the University of Oregon, Michigan State, Yale, and Southern Baptist Theological University.

Ron Stansell, David Howard, Dirk Barram, Beth LaForce, Dennis Mills, and Paul Anderson all completed

doctorates between 1987 and 1989; some received institutional assistance, mostly in the form of full or partial sabbaticals (full pay for one semester, two thirds for a year). Mark Weinert, John Johnson, Craig Taylor, Ed Higgins, and Tom Head each received some assistance for advanced graduate work in the early 1990s.

The average faculty member had taught about 16 years, half at George Fox. Median salaries for 1988-89 assistant professors were $20,910, for professors, $27,647—approximately 85 percent of the Christian College Consortium median and 70 percent that of the University of Oregon.

In the decade's final five years, GFC salary increases averaged nearly ten percent annually, at or near the best gains in both the Christian College Consortium and Northwest independent colleges. By 1990-91, GFC assistant professors averaged $25,400, with professors at $32,600.

When funding tightened in the 1980s, the College's contribution to faculty development lagged somewhat. For example, travel and professional membership budgets plummeted (but were restored in 1988). The teachers created a small research fund by pooling a portion of the

128

stipends paid to those who taught summer students. The resultant $1,000 to $2,000 projects, administered by the Faculty Development Committee, included such titles as "Macroeconomics Study of Chile" (Tom Head); "Floristic Study of the Pueblo Mountains" (Dale Orkney); "Development of a Computerized Nuclear Magnetic Resonance Simulator" (Paul Chamberlain); and a field study "The Socialization Effects of Imported Mass Media on Kenyan Cultural Values" (Warren Koch).

Grants from the J. Howard Pew Trust, which so positively assisted in international programs, also enhanced professional growth by providing George Fox over $200,000 for targeted research, publication, travel, equipment, and program development. After 1986, the school paid expenses for faculty who presented papers at professional conferences.

During the 1980s, GFC professors produced scores of articles and book reviews. They also wrote several books, including Cyril Carr's posthumously published biblical dictionary entitled *A Reader's Hebrew-English Lexicon of the Old Testament*; Mark McMinn, *Your Hidden Half: Blending Your Private and Public Self*; Gerald Wilson, *The Editing of the Hebrew Psalter*; Karen Swenson, *A Student Resource Handbook*; and Jo (Kennison) Lewis, *What Every Christian Should Know.* In addition, Lee Nash edited *The River of the West: The Oregon Years*, and *Understanding Herbert Hoover: Ten Perspectives.*

In 1990, Jim Foster and Mark McMinn produced *Christians in the Crossfire: Guarding Your Mind Against Manipulation and Self-Deception*, Craig Johnson published *Leadership: A Communication Perspective*, Arthur Roberts wrote *Back to Square One*, Ralph Beebe completed *Blessed Are the Peacemakers: A Palestinian Christian in the Occupied West Bank* (with Rev. Audeh G. Rantisi), and Laurel Lee produced her eleventh volume, *Story from a Diary.* Throughout their careers, the fall 1990 teaching faculty had published 42 books.

DURING THE 1980s, the GFC community remained generally Republican and conservative.

Although Quaker faculty voted narrowly Democratic, the college trustees and all other campus segments supported Presidents Reagan and Bush. All groups opposed the death penalty and the Oregon lottery in 1984.

A Christian concern for justice influenced the school in numerous ways; for example, the trustees carefully maintained a "socially responsible" investment program.

The 1987 statement reiterated the College's policy excluding from its investment portfolio: (1) companies on the Department of Defense's 100 largest contractors list; (2) any companies with more than five percent of gross sales derived from military contracts; and (3) companies in the liquor, tobacco, and gambling industries.

Further, the board endeavored to invest in companies with fair employment and pollution control policies and to give a preference to companies that produced life-supportive goods and services. The College also followed the "Sullivan principles" regarding South Africa, investing only in companies that avoided apartheid.

ALTHOUGH THE EBBS and flows of faculty morale defy measurement, most GFC instructors appeared to receive substantial job satisfaction and to relate well to administrators. True, the mid-1980s' financial problems cast an imposing shadow. Differences sometimes caused defensiveness; the administrators sometimes interpreted disagreement as disloyalty.

According to data collected in 1988 for the accreditation self-study, several faculty members decried administrative reluctance to encourage dissent. Some wanted more input into decision-making, and a significant minority questioned the equity and objectivity of budgetary allocations.

In response to faculty pressure for improved communication, the administration authorized a Faculty Council in 1988. Five elected members (initially Flora Allen, Beth La Force, Hank Helsabeck, Mike Allen, and Faculty Representative Marge Weesner) advised administrators and teachers on campus issues and acted as arbiters of campus misunderstandings. The Council intended to bridge faculty and administration, facilitating communication to prevent serious misunderstandings.

With administrative and faculty encouragement, the Center for Peace Learning's conflict resolution specialist Ron Mock developed a dispute resolution process in 1988. Recognizing the inevitability of occasional conflict, the procedure provided "an alternative that aims for justice in an atmosphere where persons are heard and respected."

Although mid-decade pressures sparked some tensions, most were minor, and by the decade's end, campus morale was highly positive. While the improved financial picture played an important role, administrative attempts to communicate bore significant fruit. The faculty evidenced its appreciation for Ed Stevens with a standing ovation following his 1989 pre-school keynote talk. The trustees had already expressed their confidence by awarding the president a five-year contract.

Karon Bell, director of financial and administrative services, measured staff employee morale in 1989. This group

129

Lavonna Zeller and George Myers starring in *The Sound of Music*, 1985. GFC students playing children include Wendy (Troxler) Bales, Miriam (Clark) Staples, and Karla Pixler. Other children are Aaron Young, Shayne Butterfield Kimball, Angela Raske, and Chanda Walker.

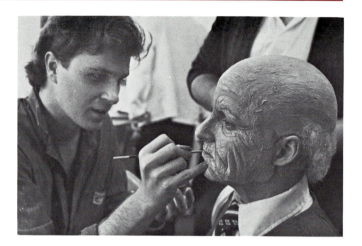

rated the school exceedingly high in reputation and spoke of their pride in telling others where they worked. The majority also considered their work important and interesting and their jobs secure from arbitrary termination. In general, they considered the College well managed and expressed moderate approval of working conditions and relationships with the administration. They considered "Christian environment" as the College's most important attribute relative to their work, followed by "fellow employees" and "recognition of you as an individual." Not surprisingly, the staff employees gave pay and opportunity for advancement the lowest ratings.

Early IN THE College's history, students chose between the arts and sciences, then followed a nearly prescribed course with few electives. A trend toward choice eventually emerged, and when the faculty revised its general education curriculum in 1982-83, it specified only 36.5 percent of total graduation requirements.

In 1985, the faculty approved a return the next year to the semester system (abandoned in 1964) and increased specified general education courses to 43 percent. By the decade's end, on-campus undergraduate students selected from 29 majors in eight divisions of study: Teacher Education, Fine and Applied Arts, Communication and Litera-

ture, Natural Science, Religious Studies, Social Science, Health and Physical Education, and Business and Economics.

Students CONTINUED to be the College's heart, its reason for existence. Sociology/Social Work teachers Mike Allen and Bruce Longstroth countered the national trend toward social conservatism with inducements for community service and an annual Social Awareness Day (the 1990 subject, for example, was "Alcohol and Chemical Dependency: A Community Issue"). Nurse Carolyn Staples sponsored periodic campus blood drives and sometimes drew 100 units. Sixty blood drives in 20 years totaled 5,320 units.

Recognizing exceptional world changes, Paul Anderson's 1990 "Biblical Basis for Peacemaking" class wrote Soviet Secretary General Mikhail Gorbachev, commending his visionary efforts for "increased openness and human rights in the Soviet Union and Eastern Europe." The students ended their message with this paragraph: "Our College was founded by evangelical Christians concerned with social and political justice. We believe that God is working through you, and we will continue praying for you and the people of your country."

As the Middle East war crisis developed in 1990-91, the students formed a peace and justice group that held two campus "teach-ins" and several prayer vigils. Included with prayers for peace were those offered for the endangered relatives of GFC's American and Middle Eastern students, and for Kuwaiti and Iraqi citizens.

As IN PREVIOUS YEARS, the College attracted high-quality student performers and provided numerous opportunities for dramatic and musical involvement. A highlight

occurred in 1981, when Joe Gilmore brought back to campus many former students who had performed in *Fiddler on the Roof*. Tim Minikel again starred as Tevye in the four-night run in Wood-Mar Auditorium.

The William and Mary Bauman Auditorium greatly improved the school's capacity for musical and dramatic performance. Professor Arthur Roberts and student composer David Miller wrote *Children of the Light*, performed in 1983. This musical, which expressed the historical contributions of Quakers, starred Dan Whitcomb as George Fox.

During the decade, the College also performed, among others: *The Sound of Music*, starring Lavonna Zeller and George Myers; *My Fair Lady*, with George Myers and LaManda (Minikel) Dillon; *The Music Man*, featuring Randy Comfort; Gilbert and Sullivan's *H.M.S. Pinafore*, starring Pam Gilmore and Dan Montzengo; *Oklahoma*, with Laurey Williams and Drake Toombs in lead roles; and *Camelot*, featuring Dana Hutcheson as Guenevere, Dave Unis as Arthur, and Tim Eastman as Lancelot.

As part of the centennial celebration, Jo (Hendricks) Kennison Lewis directed *Shake the Country*, a play about George Fox, starring Rich Swingle. Mel Schroeder and Jo Lewis cooperated to produce a student-written centennial pageant, *Our Heritage*, for the 1991 Homecoming. Chris Kilpatrick and Dave Votaw starred.

Through the 1980s, Darlene Graves' Intermission group provided "thinkable theater." This small troupe offered learning experiences throughout the Northwest and sometimes Hawaii. The group became known as the GFC Players when Mel Schroeder replaced Graves in 1987.

Music performance remained central to GFC co-curricular activities. Dennis Hagen's concert band and John Bowman's concert choir each toured the Northwest annually. Chamber singers, jazz band, GFC Singers, and

Joe Gilmore's New Vision Singers continued to perform to appreciative audiences. John Bowman added a handbell choir in 1986. Dayspring represented the College on summer tours until 1985, and again beginning in 1990.

Outstanding instrumentalists included Kathy (Jin) Hagen, David Gilmore, Jim Stickrod, Pam (Hagen) Beebe, Melinda Lee, Kirsten Benson, Shirley Turner, Diann Dodge, and Jeff Peyton. Leah (Pope) Bellamy, Ben Hickenlooper, Dave Frazier, and Richard Zeller were among those who made major vocal contributions. After graduation, Zeller studied with the Metropolitan Opera Association, and Peyton at the Juilliard School of Music. Zeller won first place in the highly prestigious New York City Oratorio Contest. During the centennial year, alumni pianists Kathy (Jin) Hagen, Jim Stickrod, David Gilmore, and Roger Wilhite presented a special community concert.

The Festival Chorus and instrumental groups, combining college and community musicians, performed such major choral works as Handel's *Messiah*, Haydn's *Creation*, and Mendelssohn's *Elijah*. Performance traditions established in the 1980s included "Ye Olde Royale Feast" and the Christmas Candlelight Vespers.

GEORGE FOX COLLEGE inaugurated its sports' support group, the Bruin Club, in 1985. Desiring to improve athletics through scholarships and recruiting assistance, the club attempted to provide moral, spiritual, and financial support. Donors earned membership in four categories: Blue/Gold ($100 annually), Varsity ($250), Lettermen ($500), and Coach's Circle ($1,000). Bill Hopper and Randy Dunn served as presidents during the club's first five years. In 1990 the Bruin Club produced $14,000 for athletic scholarships. In addition, the Miller Trust, established in 1987, provided $40,000 annually for that purpose. (By comparison GFC's endowed nonathletic scholarships totaled $225,000 in 1990.)

GFC fielded five men's and five women's intercollegiate teams through the 1980s. In 1990, the board of trustees inaugurated a sixth women's sport, soccer, to begin the next year.

Mark Vernon took the basketball head coaching responsibilities in 1982 and compiled a 196 and 90 record over the next nine years, making him by far the most successful basketball coach ever to guide the Old Gold and Navy Blue. After starring as a Bruin guard in the 1970s, Vernon produced a 27-7 record in 1984-85 and 27-6 tally two years later. His 1989-90 team won the NAIA regional championship before losing in the first round of the national tournament. That team finished with a 29 and 5 record, the best in Bruin history. The 1990-91 quintet went 24 and 6, losing in the District championship game. In one game that year, forward Jeff Hoffman scored 50 points. The NAIA District 2 twice named Vernon its top coach.

Vernon produced several outstanding players. Among them were Randy Dunn (NAIA regional first team three times and athlete of the year once, All-Northwest first team, National Christian College All-American, NCCAA regional most valuable twice); Kenny Stone (NAIA regional basketball player of the year twice, All-Northwest top NAIA player, NCCAA All-American and regional player of the year three times); Toby Long (NAIA national academic All-American); Larry Jury (NAIA and NCCAA regional first team); Dan Newman (NAIA regional first team three times, NCCAA regional first team twice); Eric Swanson (NAIA and NCCAA regional first teams); Pat Casey (NAIA regional first team); and Dave Wilson (NAIA regional most valuable player).

Melody (Groeneveld) McMaster led successful basketball squads in the early 1980s. She scored 1,629 points in a four-year career, including 37 in a single game. Debby Wiggers set a single season scoring record in 1981-82, with 465 points.

Tammy Lewis and Linda Funderhide starred in the late 1980s. Lewis set rebounding, field goal accuracy, and shots blocked records, including 1,139 career rebounds. Funderhide made 414 assists, a 4.9 average in her first three years (through the 1989-90 season). Coach Craig Taylor's 1987-88 Lady Bruin basketball squad won 20 and lost 9. His 1989-90 quintet went 16 and 13 behind NAIA All-Conference center Tracy Nelson.

Tim Tsohantaridis and Manfred Tschan coached the 1988 men's soccer team to the National Christian College Athletic Association championship. Andy LeVeine, Dan LeVeine, and Jason Koop all won NCCAA All-American

The Madrigal Singers at "Ye Olde Royale Feast," 1989. Brad Clark, Shelley Hawkins, Mark Douglas, Becky (Nauman) Steele, Jonathan Wilson, Lavonna Zeller, Gary Adams, and Pam Troyer.

honors. The NAIA named Andy LeVeine regional co-player of the year; his brother Dan LaVeine joined him on the All-District team. In 1990, Dan LaVeine established a career record of 130 goals, making him the most prolific scorer in collegiate history at any level, including NCAA.

Coach Steve Grant produced some outstanding women's volleyball teams, taking the NCCAA national championship in 1984 and 1987. Grant won NAIA regional and NCCAA national coach of the year honors both seasons. Denise (Iverson) Vernon and Melody (Groeneveld) McMaster starred on the 1984 team, each winning NCCAA All-American honors. Becky Cate, Katie Lange, and Andrea Marthaller made the NCCAA national championship all-tournament team in 1987. Stacy Wright won NCCAA All-American honors in 1989, when the Lady Bruins took second place. Melody (Groeneveld) McMaster, Diane (Walter) Davis, Becky Cate, and Stacy Wright each made NAIA all-district teams during the 1980s.

Scott Ball attained NAIA cross country academic All-American in 1984 and 1985. He won the same honor in track in 1984, as did Dwight Larabee the following year. Jerred Gildehaus took the NAIA regional cross country championship in 1985.

The NAIA named former GFC stars Bob Hadlock, Curt Ankeny, Dave McDonald, Eb Buck, and Steve Blikstad to its regional Players Hall of Fame during the 1980s (requires 10-year waiting period). Paula Wittenberg finished second

1984 ceremony retiring Randy Dunn's No. 42. From left:
President Ed Stevens, Leroy Dunn, Donna Dunn, Randy,
Director of Athletics Rich Allen, Coach Mark Vernon.

Retiring Kenny Stone's No. 34 in 1987. From left: Coach
Mark Vernon, Terry Stone, Kristi Stone, Jeri Stone, Kenny,
President Ed Stevens, Athletic Director Paul Berry. Virginia
and Don Millage are at the scorer's table.

in the national NAIA discus in 1984 and 1985, winning All-
American honors both years. Jill (Jamison) Beals won the
1989 NAIA national 10,000-meter championship and All-
American honors.

Coach Wes Cook joined the Bruin faculty in 1987 and
produced highly successful cross country and track teams.
His 1988 women's cross country squad won the NAIA Dis-
trict II championship and the NCCAA national title. Jill
(Jamison) Beals starred, winning the NCCAA national and
NAIA regional championships, and finishing second in the
NAIA national meet. She made both the NAIA and NCCAA
All-American teams and was named NAIA District II athlete
of the year. The NAIA Region 2 named Cook its 1988
women's cross country coach of the year. The team took
eighth in the NAIA finals, the best ever to that time for a
George Fox athletic team.

Tim Hagen won Academic All-American in 1989, then
made indoor All-American the next year. Later the same
spring, he set the District 2 high jump record with a leap
of seven feet. Hagen bettered his own lifetime mark with
a seven-foot, one-fourth-inch jump in an independent meet
that summer.

Both the men's and women's 1989 cross country squads
were District 2 NAIA champions, a feat never before
accomplished at GFC. Both made the top ten nationally,
also a new George Fox record. The NAIA named Kristin
Potts and Melanie Springer Academic All-Americans, and
Wes Cook regional coach of the year for each squad.

Yet the 1990 cross country teams did even better, again
winning NAIA regional titles and finishing fifth (men) and
sixth (women) in the national championships. Thus, Coach
Wes Cook's teams attained the greatest success in the College's 100-year history.

Pat Casey became baseball coach in 1988 and quickly
developed outstanding diamond nines, compiling winning

133

The Morse family at the dedication of the Curtis and Margaret Morse Athletic Fields. Eight are GFC alumni. Front row: Doug ('83), Sheri, Margaret ('35), Curtis ('33), Monna, Howard ('61). Back row: Paul ('59), Meredith, Dean ('85), Geraldine ('61), Sam ('67).

The College developed its own counseling center in 1986, adding to the service already offered by the dean of students, chaplain, and student life staff. Professor Mark McMinn, a licensed psychologist, served as the first director, followed by Valerie Tsohantaridis and David Arnold.

By fall 1990, enrollment stood at 1,072, including 786 regular, 213 degree-completion (HRM major) students, and 73 Psy.D. candidates. Traditional matriculants (omitting HRM) averaged 446 on the SAT verbal score—slightly above the national and Oregon averages—and 464 on the SAT mathematics score—slightly below both averages. Each score had improved marginally during the 1980s.

BY THE END OF its first century, George Fox College was becoming a high-quality educational institution. The Northwest Association of Schools and Colleges confirmed this following its March 1990 visit.

Among other factors, the accreditors commended GFC for its strong sense of mission, academic freedom, faculty dedication and scholarship, close student-faculty relationships, strong cocurricular program, positive writing emphasis, HRM program, and remarkable financial management. Specifically, the accreditation committee noted:

"The team found a rare degree of consistency throughout the institution in understanding and enthusiastic acceptance of the College's stated mission and objectives. The College's steadfast adherence to Quaker and evangelical Christian traditions throughout its varied liberal arts and professional programs clearly lends distinction to a George Fox education. Given the extraordinary spirit of common purpose and dedication evident among the George Fox faculty, staff and students, the team believes that the College can . . . move into its second century with a confident, clear sense of direction."

The accrediting team recommended a long-range planning program, additional learning resources, a new science facility, improvement in internal communication, and improved faculty and institutional evaluation. It also cautioned against overworking college personnel.

The final board meeting of the 1980s set in motion a master plan for academic and physical growth, including a student services center and a major endowment campaign. It also approved a centennial bell tower, to be designed by Pietro Belluschi, architect of the Coleman Wheeler Sports Center. Belluschi fashioned the 64-foot carillon structure to occupy a central campus location, housing the original college victory bell almost exactly in the place it occupied for more than 60 years in the Hoover Hall tower. A gift from long-time supporter Esther Klages made this possible.

AT AGE 100, the vision of George Fox College's early fathers and mothers remained alive and benefited evangelicals of many denominations. The 1989-90 student population could be roughly classified into several major

136

The parent body and its College came together remarkably in the last half of the 20th century. In 1990, 58 percent of Northwest Yearly Meeting's pastors, 66 percent of its missionaries, 85 percent of its staff, and nearly half the presiding clerks of NWYM Friends churches were GFC alumni.

Two of the Yearly Meeting's outstanding leaders, Jack Willcuts and Dick Beebe, died in September of 1989. Each attended the College in the 1940s and married a fellow student; five of their seven children and five spouses of those children attended the College. Each served for many years on the college board. Willcuts retired from the Northwest Yearly Meeting superintendency two years before his death; Beebe resigned as presiding clerk two months before his. The college alumni association named Willcuts Alumnus of the Year in 1970; it gave Beebe the same honor 15 years later. The board named a residence hall for Willcuts in 1990; it named one for Beebe in 1991.

The Yearly Meeting chose Howard Harmon, a George Fox graduate, as Willcuts' replacement; it chose Mark Ankeny, also a GFC alumnus, as Beebe's. Each had married a graduate. Two of Harmon's three children attended the College; Ankeny's children were not born until the 1980s, but his wife, Becky (Thomas), became a GFC professor in 1988.

Quakers started the school, sustained it through difficult years, and rescued it in two major debt liquidation campaigns between 1957 and 1972. Their support continued through the school's first century.

Although the Yearly Meeting's longstanding policy of minimal giving through its central budget continued, many individuals provided significant support. For example, Northwest Yearly Meeting members gave $1,625,000 between 1986 and 1989—about 43 percent of the College's gift income. Major donors included, among others, Frank and Genevieve Cole, Esther Klages, Esther Brougher, Bill and Judie Wilson, and Phil and Esther Harmon. In 1990-91 the Yearly Meeting moved toward a major campaign that would add significantly to the College's scholarship program.

However, the College's ninth and tenth decades brought significant progress toward integration with the larger evangelical church. The school was supported by a growing body of non-Friends, who in the final years of the first century contributed about 57 percent of its individual gifts. Among the many important financial contributors were John and Marilyn Duke, Bill and Mary Bauman, Jim and Lila Miller, Sam Wheeler, Ken and Joan Austin, Margaret Edwards, and Bob and Darlene Church.

By the 1990s, George Fox College had developed a strong relationship with evangelicals generally. It seemed

groupings: Friends and Anabaptists, 18.3 percent; Wesleyans, 17.6; Baptists, 16.2; nondenominational or community churches, 13.6; charismatics, 9.8; those who reported "none" (some of whom may have been nondenominational Christians), 9.3; Church of God, Christian Church, Church of Christ, 5.8; traditional mainline Protestant churches, 5.1; Catholics, 3.0; Seventh-Day Adventists, 0.6; and Latter Day Saints, 0.3.

About half the full-time faculty and administrators were Quakers, divided about equally between longtime Friends and those who became Quakers after joining the GFC community. As the 1990s began, more Friends students and faculty may have congregated on the Newberg campus than any other U.S. college (followed closely in both categories by Earlham and Malone).

likely that several denominations might soon see high percentages of the school's graduates in leadership positions.

At age 100, GFC provided a significant service to and received major support from a broad spectrum of evangelical Christians.

FROM ITS INCEPTION, Pacific/George Fox College forthrightly declared its intention to "give a thorough training in the Arts and Sciences," to "strive in every possible manner to spread Christian culture," to "offer young men and women the benefits of a liberal Christian education," and to present "decidedly Christian" classrooms. "It is the fond hope of the management that Pacific College shall send forth many Christian teachers, ministers, and missionaries," the first catalog declared.

Anyone analyzing the College's history must be impressed by the tenacity with which the school maintained that mission. Hard times came and went—and undoubtedly would come again—but the College honoring the founder of the Friends church clung obstinately to the Prince of Peace. That fact summarizes the secret of the school's success.

By 1991, more than 10,000 students had enrolled in Pacific/George Fox College classes. Nearly 3,500 had graduated.

The Academy and College had not only satisfied the desires of the early trustees by inspiring Christian teachers, ministers, and missionaries; it also educated many men and women who served varied ministries, from parenting children to providing relief for starving humanity.

Near age 100, the school began to be independently acclaimed as a first-rate educational institution. The Templeton Foundation recognized George Fox in 1989 and 1990 as one of 92 colleges nationwide—the only one in Oregon—"which best exemplify campuses that encourage the development of strong moral character among students." Officially designated "The Templeton Foundation Honor Roll of Character Building Colleges," the listing was a recommendation its sponsor hoped would "be of help to future college students and their parents, as well as to those whose generosity supports higher education."

U.S. News & World Report also applauded GFC, naming it three times before 1991 as one of "America's Best Colleges." In the 1989-90 western regional liberal arts colleges category, George Fox ranked fifth overall and, in academic reputation, an astounding third, behind only Washington's Evergreen College and Southwestern University of Texas. In its centennial year, GFC did even better in academic reputation, ranking second in its category.

SUSTAINED BY a faith-invigorated mission, guided by competent, enterprising leaders, buoyed by creative, scholarly teachers, and supported by dedicated alumni and evangelical constituents, George Fox College entered its second century cautious but hopeful. The best seemed yet to come.

However, fulfilling the hope required maintaining the mission. Life reduced to the frenetic marketplace misses its most beautiful significance, its most fundamental essence, as 20th century Quaker Thomas Kelly understood: "Life is meant to be lived from a Center, a divine Center. Each of us can live such a life of amazing power and peace and serenity, of integration and confidence and simplified multiplicity, on one condition—that is, *if we really want to.* There is a divine Abyss within us all, a holy Infinite Center, a Heart, a Life who speaks in us and through us to the world. We have all heard this holy Whisper at times. At times we have followed the Whisper, and amazing equilibrium of life, amazing effectiveness of living set in . . . ."

If George Fox College is different, that difference lies in its integration with the Divine Center. In 1989, Lee Nash depicted the George Fox spirit at its best:

A QUAKER HERITAGE WEEK MEDITATION

Community . . .

A social group, sharing space and commitments, each honoring the other, building respect and support. Sought all our lives.

Christian community . . .

Knit by a common faith—in the upper room, in the catacombs, confirmed in a million circles over two millennia from Galatia to Glasgow, Boston to Bombay, Cambodia to the Congo.

In Quaker meetings, too. Like here. Where Friends don't dominate (t'would be un-Quakerly). Where the first two faculty clerks (charged to preside over a consensus-seeking business) are a Baptist and a Free Methodist, both superb in the Quaker role!

Where all of us from whatever origins may have our concept of community enriched by three centuries of Spirit-honoring experience. Such as:

- Sensitivity to those hurting—a serving community.
- Inclusion of women—a whole community.
- Concern for peace—a loving community.
- Worship in business—a Spirit-led community.
- Servants as leaders—a democratic community.
- Symbols of simplicity—a stewardly community.

Mary Green receives the prestigious TOTOM for her work with Teacher of Teachers of Mathematics.

Graduate number 3,000, Lori Willeman, 1989. It took the College 78 years to graduate 1,000 students (1969), 12 more to graduate another 1,000 (1981), and eight to graduate the third thousand.

GEORGE FOX, the Christian leader, listened to the Lord three centuries ago: "There is one, even Christ Jesus, that can speak to thy condition." George Fox, the college, hears the message today. The school still represents an ever-living Jesus who inspires and teaches His people, and speaks to whatever their condition.

From Jesus they learn that all truth is God's truth. They learn that He imparts his truth through many sources. The evangelical Christian college has a unique opportunity to challenge people with the truth, through the arts, the sciences, and the professional studies. With the early Friends, they understand that He empowers them to speak truth to power, in whatever principalities power may reside.

George Fox College's founders resolved that their school would "be a strong support not only to the Friends Church, but to Christianity wherever its influence may reach." Happily, the institution fulfilled that pledge for 100 years. It entered the second century determined to keep the faith.

- Directness in communication—a plain-speaking community.
- Openness in worship—a participatory community.
- Encouragement of individuality—a creative community!

Our strengths, tempted some, become our weaknesses. The wonderful Friends encouragement of Spirit-filled prophets may lead any of us to injure community by a self-seeking crusade, a nurtured resentment, a refusal to forgive. Deliver us from temptation, Lord!

And do sustain our community, which blesses us all!

139

M. J. Murdock Learning Resource Center

Video Communication Center

William and Mary Bauman Chapel/Auditorium

Gervas Carey Residence Hall with Hobson Residence Hall in background

Coleman Wheeler Sports Center

140

Appendix

THE RELIGIOUS ANTECEDENTS
OF GEORGE FOX COLLEGE

QUAKERISM BEGAN IN THE religious and civil turmoil of seventeenth-century England, when the quality of spiritual life ebbed low. A deeply sensitive, greatly troubled young man named George Fox abhorred the spiritual coldness that characterized the church. He agonized for months, seeking truth, laboring mightily, wrestling like Jacob with the angel.

Then one day Light dawned in his soul: "And when all my hopes... in all men were gone, so that I had nothing outwardly to help me, nor could [I] tell what to do, then, Oh then, I heard a voice which said, 'There is one, even Christ Jesus, that can speak to thy condition,' and when I heard it my heart did leap for joy."

This spiritual experience profoundly changed his life. No longer just a seeker, he had become a finder. "Now was I come up in spirit through the flaming sword into the paradise of God. All things were new, and all the creation gave another smell unto me than before, beyond what words can utter. I knew nothing but pureness, and innocency, and righteousness, being renewed up into the image of God by Christ Jesus, so that I... was come up to the state of Adam which he was in before he fell."

Fox and those who joined him taught that the risen Jesus is alive, teaching His people today. Truth was not restricted to the Mass to be dispensed solely by the priest, nor to the written Word to be interpreted exclusively by the minister. The Word of Truth was available to all who called on His name. Any believer could hear the voice of God and bear His message to others.

Therefore, in worship Friends waited silently, centering down into communion with God. Presently, His Spirit—the living Jesus—might prompt one or more worshipers to deliver a message or concern. Friends considered a hired pastor superfluous, even counterproductive. Christ, they believed, was the only intermediary between humanity and God. He called all His followers to ministry.

Spiritually hungry England responded to the Quaker imperative. In less than a generation, 50,000 converts accepted the egalitarian message, centered in the life-changing power of Christ Jesus Himself.

Yet as expressed by Quakers, Christ's nonviolent, justice-oriented truth threatened all entrenched power structures, provoking a vicious response from hostile governments. During the first 25 years, authorities jailed about 15,000 Friends—nearly one third of the total. Four hundred fifty died from the brutal treatment. George Fox went to prison eight times for a combined total of about six years. Authorities whipped, fined, and placed recalcitrants in stocks. Many they deported to the American colonies, where some suffered the same fate.

British officialdom attempted to buy George Fox, offering him a lucrative position as an army officer. He scorned the inducement, proclaiming that he lived "... in the virtue of that life and power that took away the occasion of all wars...." Again he avowed: "I was set of God to stand a witness against all violence, and the works of darkness; and to turn people from darkness to light, and to bring them from the causes of war and fighting to the peaceable Gospel."

In the end, suffering won and persecution lost. The bloodless revolution of 1688 gave Friends and other religious dissenters the right to worship as they believed God taught them. They had stood the twin test: They spoke truth to power, and they spoke it in loving nonviolence. Power finally listened and acquiesced.

In England and the American colonies, Friends quickly earned a reputation for self-sacrifice on behalf of the oppressed. Their agenda included slaves, women, prisoners, the insane, and all victims of an impersonal, materialistic world run by self-seeking power structures.

Long before it became fashionable, the eighteenth-century American John Woolman gently but forcefully persuaded his Quaker compatriots to emancipate their slaves. He personally refused even to use commodities produced or served by slaves, or to pay taxes that would finance war. In America as in England, Quakers—perhaps more than any other religious group—gained a respect and influence far beyond their numbers.

Quakers constantly enunciated their central message, that the Divine Light has, in Jesus, been manifest in history. Christ Jesus is "the true Light, which lighteth every [person] that cometh into the world." (John 1:9 *KJV*) In this, Quakers countered the exclusivity of the Calvinistic Puritans, who taught that God is so sovereign and humans so insignificant that mere persons have no control over their own spiritual destinies. Centuries ahead of their time, Quakers argued that Christ Jesus lights all human beings, including even Indians, slaves, and women.

Friends meant that Christ enlightens all and is available for anyone's salvation. As the years went by and Quakerism became more institutionalized, however, some began to subordinate the Light—Christ Jesus himself—to its human recipient. Finally, over the years, a minority completely abandoned the historical Jesus and scriptural authority. A few even adopted a doctrine of universal salvation.

These Friends had departed significantly from the early Quaker experience of an explicit, personal conversion through Christ's direct intervention in one's life. Early in nineteenth-century America, Quakerism split apart amid bitterness that mocked the group's original testimony. Polarization resulted, dealing the movement a series of blows that altered its historic character.

Meanwhile, John Wesley preached a message that strongly impacted England and the United States. Wesley implored eighteenth-century Englishmen to turn unequivocally to Jesus Christ, explicitly renounce personal sin, and accept the holiness available to any believer who sought purification from evil. Thoroughly sanctified souls would express love and concern for one's fellow human beings—with a special emphasis on those victimized by slavery or alcohol.

This highly personal message appealed uniquely to the individualistic Americans. It enticed those Quakers who lamented their body's receding emphasis on biblical truth and individual responsibility for sin and salvation. These Friends, officially called "Orthodox" but often termed "Gurneyite," embraced the nineteenth-century revivalism that exploded on the American frontier (the "second great awakening"). They welcomed the new life and action it breathed into their spiritual and social concern. Soul-winning became a high priority.

Yet most Quakers still treasured silent attention to the divine Teacher's voice. Some aspects of revivalism seemed unQuakerly, emotionally contrived, and smacking more of sales promotion than godly spirituality. Although they loved the renewed emphasis on the scriptural Jesus and applauded revivalism's results, many felt uncomfortable with the method.

Nevertheless, most Friends who were greatly influenced by revivalism eventually accepted its methodology. Gradually it influenced their meetings for worship. Worshipers no longer sat in lengthy silence listening to the Teacher's inward voice, awaiting outward expressions from human message-bearers. As conversions mounted, they hired resident pastors to conduct worship services and provide pastoral care. The resulting emphasis on prepared sermons induced passivity and inhibited message-bearing by worshipers.

In addition, an increasing other-worldly emphasis decreased their concern for people in this life. Conse-

quently, Quaker influence on political and corporate power structures diminished.

When in the early twentieth century "Modernist" and "Fundamentalist" religious groups polarized, many Friends inched toward the latter. The former they associated with "liberal Quakers," from whom their forebears separated in bitterness a century earlier. Considerable ill will reappeared.

The post-World War II period brought influences from both sides of a resurgent evangelical movement. On the right, the neo-evangelical movement produced Christians with conservative political leanings, following leaders such as *Christianity Today* originator Carl F. H. Henry, Campus Crusade founder Bill Bright, Bible scholar Harold Lindsell, and lawyer John Warwick Montgomery. Their counterparts are seen in individuals like Mennonite theologian John Howard Yoder, Baptist theologian Ron Sider, *Sojourner* editor Jim Wallis, and Quaker writer Richard Foster, a George Fox College graduate. The latter group's dynamic, progressive Christian vision recalls the historic Quaker conviction that "there is one, even Christ Jesus," who can speak to the world's condition—one with the power to "turn people from darkness to light, and to bring them from the causes of war and fighting to the peaceable Gospel."

The Quakers who migrated to Oregon beginning in the 1880s were among those influenced by revivalism. Their spiritual descendents, today's "evangelical Friends," package the old Quaker truths in the pastoral system. While generally remaining sensitive to the Friends distinctives, many find it possible to accomodate with much of modern evangelical Protestantism. This produces some ambivalence and at times creates extreme tension between those who lean toward the poles of the religious spectrum.

Some of Pacific/George Fox College's darkest hours trace to theological disharmony. Nevertheless, anyone who examines the school's history must marvel that the discord produced no fatal blows. Especially in recent years, tensions have often proven creative, encouraging a dynamic regard for God's truth. Abhorring divisive dogmatism, the Quaker leaders have successfully ameliorated most disagreements.

Remarkably, in spite of some tension, these diversities coexist amicably on the GFC campus. The College today is an attractive amalgam of Christ-centered historic Quakers, Wesleyans, and Baptists, spiced with a sprinkling from other persuasions and many from nondenominational Bible churches. Most applaud the diversity within a well-understood evangelical Christian consensus.

CHRONOLOGY

1885 Friends Pacific Academy opens with 19 students; two-story, 36- by 48-foot "Academy Building" (later named Hoover Hall) erected

1886 Boarding hall and four cottages built to house girls

1887 Two-story, 40- by 60-foot "Dormitory Building" (later named Kanyon, then Minthorn Hall) erected to house boys

1891 Pacific College opens September 9 with 15 students; Thomas Newlin first president

1892 College and Academy moved from Third and College to present location; "Academy Building" called "College Building," enlarged by a 36- by 58-foot addition

1893 Amos C. Stanbrough wins state oratorical contest

1894 First football game in Newberg—Pacific College loses to Willamette University, 16-0

1895 College students join two barns to create 36- by 48-foot gymnasium

1900 Thomas Newlin resigns; H. Edwin McGrew becomes president

1901 Elwood S. Minchin wins state oratorical contest

1902 Victory bell peals, mortgage burns in bonfire as college community celebrates payment of $12,000 indebtedness; college enrollment peaks at 57

1904 Walter R. Miles wins national speaking contest of Prohibition Association of Colleges

1905 Walter R. Miles wins state oratorical contest

1907 H. Edwin McGrew resigns presidency, replaced by W. Irving Kelsey; Katherine (Romig) Otis wins state oratorical contest; debaters Paul Maris, Ralph W. Rees, and Clarence M. Brown win state championship

1910 Kelsey resigns presidency; William Reagan serves one year as acting president; victory bell and bonfire celebrate success in $30,000 campaign for Wood-Mar Hall; debaters Claude Newlin, Kathryn Bryan, and Roy Fitch win state championship

1911 Levi T. Pennington inaugurated as president

1912 College begins drive for endowment and standardization (accreditation); switches from three terms to two semesters

1915 Bell and bonfire celebrate $119,000 endowment

1917 Basketball and baseball teams win league championships; basketball squad defeats Oregon State College 34-25; Old Pulpit Extemporaneous Speaking Contest begun

1918 World War I cuts enrollment to 27; 25 men provide humanitarian service overseas as conscientious objectors

1919 Pennington takes two-year leave to direct Friends Forward Movement; Professor John Mills serves as acting president

1920 College launches campaign for additional $175,000 endowment and standardization

1922 Small chemistry laboratory building erected, used until 1947

1924 Royal Gettman wins state oratorical contest

1925 Endowment surpasses $200,000; Pacific College recognized as standard college by U.S. Bureau of Education; College celebrates with bell and bonfire

1929 Board decides to close Friends Pacific Academy; students and faculty raise money for College by picking 1,822 boxes of prunes; College completes three-year soccer dynasty with only one loss, yielding but one goal in 1929 season

1932 Faculty requests ten percent salary reduction to create scholarship fund

1934 Enrollment peaks at 126

1941 Pennington resigns presidency; Emmett W. Gulley becomes president

1947 Gulley resigns; Gervas Carey becomes president; Hester Memorial Gymnasium built; war surplus buildings moved to campus for dining hall, fine arts building, and housing; Science Hall constructed; Norval Hadley wins state after-dinner speaking contest; Four Flats win Original All Northwest Barber Shop Ballad Contest

1949 Pacific College renamed George Fox College; Priscilla (Doble) Jeffery wins state after-dinner speaking contest

1950 Carey resigns presidency; Paul E. Parker becomes president

1952 Parker resigns presidency; administrative committee composed of Donald McNichols, Paul Mills, and Harlow Ankeny administer school

1954 Milo C. Ross named president; Hoover Hall, one of two buildings moved from original campus, razed

1956 Rolly Hartley sets career basketball scoring record with 1,027 points in three seasons

1958 Bill Hopper sets career basketball scoring record with 1,731 points

1959 Debt liquidated; Northwest Association of Secondary and Higher Schools grants accreditation

1960 Gilbert and Olive Shambaugh give approximately $275,000 in property for library; Colcord Memorial Field dedicated

1961 Science Hall with new addition renamed Brougher Hall

1962 Shambaugh Library dedicated; Pennington Residence Hall and Weesner Village erected; Kanyon Hall renamed Minthorn Hall

1964 College returns to term scheduling; Edwards Residence Hall constructed

1965 Calder Center and Heacock Commons built; women's volleyball, basketball, softball, and track teams win conference championships

1967 Maintenance Building constructed

1968 Hobson Residence Hall dedicated; Student Union addition constructed

1969 College approved for secondary teacher education; Milo Ross resigns presidency; David LeShana becomes president; George Fox finishes last year in football; Colcord Memorial Field upgraded

1973 James and Lila Miller give more than $600,000, mostly for a new athletic complex; Coach Lorin Miller's basketball team wins NAIA District 2 championship

1974 GFC joins the Christian College Consortium

1975 Camp Tilikum becomes part of College

1977 GFC dedicates four new buildings on October 20: Coleman Wheeler Sports Center, Herbert Hoover Academic Building, Mary Sutton Residence Hall, and Charlotte Macy Residence Hall; biennial Herbert Hoover Symposium begun

1978 Milo C. Ross Center built; Steve Blikstad and Chad Neeley named NAIA track All-Americans for second year; Paul Cozens' No. 44 first ever retired after he sets career basketball scoring record with 2,187 points and is named NAIA All-American

1979 Video Communication Center constructed; Heacock Commons enlarged

1980 College enrollment peaks at 746; Gervas Carey Residence Hall constructed, Weesner House acquired

1981 National Association of Schools of Music accredits GFC music program

1982 William and Mary Bauman Chapel/Auditorium completed; David LeShana resigns presidency; William Green serves as interim president

1983 Edward F. Stevens becomes George Fox College's tenth president

1984 Teacher Standards and Practices Commission approves Elementary Teacher Education program; women's volleyball team wins National Christian College Athletic Association national championship

1985 Center for Peace Learning begun

1986 College enrollment at 549—a 26.4 percent decline in six years; Century II campaign launched; Human Resources Management degree approved and classes begun in Newberg, Portland, and Salem; return to semester scheduling

1987 Juniors Abroad overseas study program begun; women's volleyball team wins NCCAA national championship

1988 M. J. Murdock Learning Resource Center opens, partially as a result of $1.35 million gift from M. J. Murdock Charitable Trust; women's cross country team wins National Christian College Athletic Association championship

1989 Coach Wes Cook's men's and women's cross country teams each win NAIA district championship; Coach Mark Vernon's 1989-90 basketball team goes 29-5, wins NAIA district championship

1990 Largest enrollment in College's first century with 1,072 students: 786 regular undergraduate, 213 in degree completion program, 73 in graduate psychology program; College celebrates beginning of its centennial year on September 9; Centennial Tower constructed; Jack L. Willcuts Residence Hall constructed; College initiates graduate study with master's and doctorate in clinical psychology

1991 Graduate programs in teacher education, business management, and Christian studies approved; Richard H. Beebe Residence Hall constructed

Jake Lautenbach, 1987—
George Layman, 1976-76
David Leach, 1968-79
Walter P. Lee, 1945-79
    Chairman 1947-50
John Lemmons, 1989—
Margaret Lemmons, 1980—
Claude A. Lewis, 1965-85
Verle Lindley, 1964-70
Marla Ludolph-Heikkala, 1984—
Charlotte Macy, 1968-71, 1972-77
Dwight Macy, 1960-75, 1977—
Paul Macy, 1891-94
Roger Martell, 1984—
Evangeline Martin, 1891-95, 1902-27
Philip Martin, 1960-78
Thelma Martin, 1965-73, 1974-86
Joseph McCracken, 1931-1950
Donald McNichols, 1965-88
Jack E. Meadows, 1978-84, 1988—
H. Paul Michener, 1939-47
Herald Mickelson, 1952-53
Anna B. Miles, 1918-37
B. C. Miles, 1894-1912
    Chairman 1901-08
George Millen, 1978-87
James Miller, 1974-86
Ward A. Miller, 1965-71
A. R. Mills, 1894-1933
    Chairman 1923-33
Roger Minthorne, 1973—
    Chairman 1989—
George Mitchell, 1891-1908
Robert Monroe, 1973—
    Chairman 1979-84

Robert Morrill, 1957-61
Paul Morse, 1968-71
Stanley Morse, 1986—
Victor Morse, 1949-55
Horace Mott, 1957-59
Charles Mylander, 1987—
David V. Myton, 1979-89
Fred G. Neumann, Sr., 1986-90
Bernard Newby, 1965-68
Jackson H. Newell, 1978—
Frank D. Nicodem, 1969-75
Robert Nordyke, 1948-59
A. P. Oliver, 1895-1902
Loyde W. Osburn, 1943-49
Arnold Owen, 1957-78
Curtis Parker, 1929-41
J. Ray Pemberton, 1925-48
John Pemberton, 1908-15
    Chairman 1908-10
C. W. Perry, 1978—
Victor Peterson, 1989—
Joseph G. Reece, 1936-52
J. H. Rees, 1894-1931
William Rees, 1921-30
Glen Rinard, 1957-71
Ardys Roberts, 1989—
Dorothy Roberts, 1988—
Wayne Roberts, 1954-84
Edmund Robinson, 1894-97,
    1898-1902
Keith Sarver, 1971-77
John Schmeltzer, 1939-48
Lorene Severson, 1978-84
Olive Shambaugh, 1963-70
Oliver J. Sherman, 1907-08, 1912-26

Bill Sims, 1989—
Dorwin Smith, 1957-76
J. Harlan Smith, 1927-31, 1942-45
J. T. Smith, 1894-98
Kendall Smitherman, 1980-84
William Springer, 1965-65
Amos C. Stanbrough, 1913-21
Asa F. Sutton, 1921-27
Emel Swanson, 1948-69
J. Frank Taylor, 1907-08
Clifford N. Terrell, 1924-33
Kent L. Thornburg, 1983—
J. H. Townsend, 1891-94
Earl Tycksen, 1980-86
Moses Votaw, 1891-94
Robert M. Waggoner, 1946-47
Floyd Watson, 1966—
Lindley A. Wells, 1909-13
Charles O. Whitely, 1912-17
Nancy Wilhite, 1990—
Walter Wilhite, 1957-78, 1979-85
Clare Willcuts, 1958-68
Jack L. Willcuts, 1971-79
Ronald Willcuts, 1979-80
Kenneth M. Williams, 1953-56,
    1965-69
William B. Wilson, 1985—
Arthur Winters, 1948-54
Norman Winters, 1968-86, 1989—
Richard Withnell, 1986-89
Jan Wood, 1977-80
Amanda M. Woodward, 1923-44
E. H. Woodward, 1891-1923
    Chairman 1891-93, 1910-23

HONORARY DEGREES GRANTED

1941   Herbert Hoover, *Doctor of Humanitarian Services*
1956   Lloyd Cressman, *Doctor of Divinity*
1961   Mary C. Sutton, *Doctor of Letters*
1963   Wayne Burt, *Doctor of Science*
1963   John Astleford, *Doctor of Divinity*
1964   M. Lowell Edwards, *Doctor of Science*
1966   Sidney M. Collier, *Doctor of Laws*
1968   Ralph Choate, *Doctor of Letters*
1969   Howard Kershner, *Doctor of Divinity*
1970   Mark O. Hatfield, *Doctor of Letters*
1972   Everett Cattell, *Doctor of Letters*

1973   Dr. John Brougher, *Doctor of Letters*
1975   George Layman, *Doctor of Letters*
1975   Jack L. Willcuts, *Doctor of Divinity*
1976   Charles A. Beals, *Doctor of Divinity*
1980   G. Alvin Roberts, *Doctor of Laws*
1982   David LeShana, *Doctor of Humane Letters*
1984   William D. Green, *Doctor of Humane Letters*
1986   Robin Johnston, *Doctor of Divinity*
1987   Richard J. Foster, *Doctor of Letters*
1987   Kwan Kyu Kim, *Doctor of Divinity*

146

ALUMNUS OF THE YEAR

1962	Olive Shambaugh	1973	Four Flats Quartet—	1981	Lloyd O. Schaad
1963	Lowell Edwards		Ron Crecelius	1982	Roger M. Minthorne
1964	Arthur Roberts		Harlow Ankeny	1983	Loyde and Della Osburn
1965	Edwin Burgess		Dick Cadd	1984	M. Gene Hockett
1966	Claude Lewis		Norval Hadley	1985	Richard H. Beebe
1967	Emmett Gulley	1974	Frank and Genevieve Cole	1986	Glenn O. Koch
1968	Charles Beals	1975	Marion Winslow	1987	Charles E. Mylander
1969	Homer Hester	1976	Elmore Jackson	1988	Wayne V. Burt
1970	T. Eugene Coffin	1977	Elizabeth Edwards	1989	Richard Foster
1971	Jack L. Willcuts	1978	Carl Sandoz	1990	Dorothy Barratt
1972	Delbert Replogle	1979	Lewis M. Hoskins	1991	Wayne Roberts
		1980	Richard S. Taylor		

ASSOCIATED STUDENT BODY PRESIDENTS

1911-12	Ray S. Langworthy	1937-38	Victor Morse	1964-65	Ron Stansell
1912-13	Ray S. Langworthy	1938-39	Verle Emry	1965-66	Fred Gregory
1913-14	Olin C. Hadley	1939-40	Ervin Atrops	1966-67	Charles Smith
1914-15	Paul Lewis	1940-41	Dean Tate	1967-68	Stan Thornburg
1915-16	Robert Dann	1941-42	William Rarick	1968-69	Dorlan Bales
1916-17	Emmett W. Gulley	1942-43	Jim Spirup	1969-70	Marshall Sperling
1917-18	Ross C. Miles	1943-44	David Thomas	1970-71	Cyril Carr
1918-19	Harold E. Hinshaw	1944-45	Orrin Ogier	1971-72	Stan Morse
1919-20	Mary E. (Pennington) Pearson	1945-46	Roger Minthorne	1972-73	John Macy
1920-21	Ellis Beals	1946-47	Glenn Koch	1973-74	Charlie Friesen
1921-22	Cecil Pearson	1947-48	Norval Hadley	1974-75	Tim Bletscher
1922-23	Clara V. (Calkins) Breckel	1948-49	Loren D. Mills	1975-76	Jeff Rickey
1923-24	Davis Woodward	1949-50	David Fendall	1976-77	Ron Mock
1924-25	Hubert Armstrong	1950-51	Wayne Piersall	1977-78	Jon Chandler
1925-26	Harlan Rinard	1951-52	Frank Starkey	1978-79	Fred Van Gorkam
1926-27	Paul Brown	1952-53	Ralph Beebe	1979-80	Mike LaBounty
1927-28	Wendell Hutchens	1953-54	Verne Martin	1980-81	Jim LeShana
1928-29	Sanford Brown	1954-55	Orville Winters	1981-82	Scott Celley
1929-30	Ben Huntington	1955-56	Rolly Hartley	1982-83	Bryce Fendall
1930-31	Ralph Choate	1956-57	Fred Newkirk	1983-84	Brett Barbre
1931-32	Dennis McGuire	1957-58	Dick Mott	1984-85	Allen Hilton
1932-33	Marion DeVine	1958-59	Paul Morse	1985-86	Dan Price
1933-34	Eugene Coffin	1959-60	Dan Nolta	1986-87	Bruce Bishop
1934-35	Elwood Egelston	1960-61	Howard Crow	1987-88	Kristen Diefenbaugh
1935-36	Clayton Hicks	1961-62	Roy Crow	1988-89	Kristen Diefenbaugh
1936-37	John Dimond	1962-63	David Cammack	1989-90	Steve Fawver
		1963-64	Lonny Fendall	1990-91	Scott Winter

THE CRESCENT EDITORS

1891-92	C. J. Edwards	1928-29	Frank L. Cole	1959-60	Loren Hinkle
1892-93	A. C. Stanbrough	1929-30	Ralph Choate	1960-61	Dave Cammack
1893-94	Lida Hanson	1930-31	Lincoln Wirt	1961-62	Lucia Midgley
1894-95	Daisy (Stanley) Lewis	1931-32	Veldon J. Diment		Joyce (LeBaron) Lindbeck
1895-96	Jesse R. Johnson	1932-33	Arthur Sugars	1962-63	Joyce (LeBaron) Lindbeck
1896-97	Oscar Cox	1933-34	Elwood Egelston	1963-64	Ron Stansell
1897-98	Walter C. Woodward	1934-35	Virgil Hiatt	1964-65	Gae (Martin) Reck
1898-99	Clara Vaughn	1935-36	Richard Wilcox		Barbara Baker
1899-00	Mark Wolf	1936-37	Lewis Hoskins	1965-66	Carolyn (Harmon)
1900-01	Robert Jones	1937-38	Maisie (Burt) Webb		McDonald
1901-02	Owen Maris	1938-39	Ervin Atrops	1966-67	Mike Britton
1902-03	Calvin Blair	1939-40	Ervin Atrops	1967-68	Juanita (Roberts) Eoff
1903-04	Orville Johnson	1940-41	Douglas Cowley	1968-69	Darwin Burns
1904-05	Lewis Saunders		Melvin Ashwill	1969-70	Lynette Pasak
1905-06	Lewis Saunders	1941-42	Dale Miller	1970-71	Betty (Ball) Howard
1906-07	Cecil Hoskins	1942-43	Arthur Roberts	1971-72	Charlie Howard
1907-08	H. P. Vickrey	1943-44	Doris (Manning) Six	1972-73	Mike Lowe
1908-09	Russell V. Lewis	1944-45	Mildred (Haworth)		Louise (Minthorne)
1909-10	Harvey A. Wright		Minthorne		Sargent
1910-11	Chris Smith	1945-46	Imogene Degner	1973-74	Daniel Smith
1911-12	Olin W. Hadley	1946-47	Donna (Heacock)	1974-75	Michelle (Underwood)
1912-13	Ellis Pickett		Broderick		Smith
1913-14	Ray Langworthy	1947-48	Mary (McClintick) Hadley	1975-76	Dan Berggren
1914-15	Emmett W. Gulley	1948-49	Harlow Ankeny	1976-77	Robert Claiborne
	Gladys (Hannon) Keyes		Gertrude (Haworth)	1977-78	Robert Claiborne
1915-16	Meade G. Elliott		Ankeny	1978-79	Jean (Peters) Costin
	Marjory Gregory	1949-50	Margaret (Shattuck)	1979-80	Cris (Pike) Roberts
1916-17	Lloyd Edwards		Lemmons	1980-81	Rachel Hampton
1917-18	Norma Harvey	1950-51	Betty May (Street) Hockett	1981-82	Scott Young
1918-19	Irene (Hodgin) Nichols	1951-52	Larry Wyman	1982-83	Scott Young
1919-20	Harold Lee	1952-53	Betty (Brown) Comfort	1983-84	Ed Kidd
1920-21	Anna (Mills) Moore	1953-54	Ralph Beebe	1984-85	Ed Kidd
1921-22	Flora (Campbell) Illinski	1954-55	Florene (Price) Nordyke	1985-86	Ed Kidd
1922-23	Horace Terrell		Ardeth (Beals) Brown	1986-87	Bruce Bishop
1923-24	Benjamin A. Darling	1955-56	Charlotte (Passolt)	1987-88	Jennifer Cooke
1924-25	Florence (Lee) Lienard		Cammack	1988-89	Laura Engle
1925-26	Ivor Jones	1956-57	Bill Hopper	1989-90	Rob Felton
1926-27	Ivor Jones	1957-58	Phyllis George	1990-91	Stacy Wright
1927-28	Philip Gatch	1958-59	Willis Green		

L'AMI EDITORS

1934-35	Delmar Putman	1954-55	Kara (Newell) Wilkin	1973-74	Mike Hermanson
1935-36	no record	1955-56	Quentin Nordyke	1974-75	Janita (Jennings) Caldwell
1936-37	Arney Houser	1956-57	Fay (Hanson) Corlett		Glenna (Grover) Isaacs
1937-38	no record	1957-58	Carol (Riggs) Lohrenz	1975-76	Steve Eichenberger
1938-39	Leroy Pierson	1958-59	Lyle Wilson		Warren Koch
1939-40	Helen Robertson	1959-60	Lyla (Bury) Hadley	1976-77	Cindy (Whitaker) Friesen
1940-41	no record		Barbara Morse	1977-78	Kim (Schmidt) Forbes
1941-42	Betty (Vasey) Ashwill	1960-61	Barbara Morse	1978-79	Juli Phillips
1942-43	Douglas Cowley	1961-62	Barry Hubbell		Priscilla Roberts
1943-44	Geraldine (Tharrington) Willcuts	1962-63	Barry Hubbell	1979-80	Chuck Hernandez
		1963-64	Alice (Hampton) Maurer	1980-81	Mary (Morter) Freeman
1944-45	Herschel Thornburg	1964-65	Howard Macy	1981-82	Pam Gilmore
1945-46	Mildred (Haworth) Minthorne	1965-66	Nancy (Forsythe) Thomas	1982-83	Lani Nelson
		1966-67	Rick Raml		Rick Drury
1946-47	Eleanor (Swanson) Antrim	1967-68	Chris (Shipman) Cranmore	1983-84	Not Published
1947-48	Divonna (Schweitzer) Crecelius	1968-69	Gary Macy	1984-85	Ralph Sprout
		1969-70	Gary Macy	1985-86	Kasey Crocker
1948-49	Helen (Antrim) Cadd	1970-71	Andrea (Roberts) Herling	1986-87	Stephanie Peters
1949-50	Louise (Fivecoat) Ralphs		Marilyn (May) Jackson	1987-88	Susan Davis
1950-51	Norma (Dillon) Beebe	1971-72	Roxie (Calvert) Black	1988-89	Dixie Cochran
1951-52	DeForrest Fletcher		Colleen (Rohde) Pankratz	1989-90	Darci Nolta
1952-53	Margaret (Weber) Winters	1972-73	Charlie Howard	1990-91	Darci Nolta
1953-54	Robert Byrd				

BUILDING NAMES

WILLIAM AND MARY BAUMAN CHAPEL/AUDITORIUM
Honoring William Bauman, an Oregon lumberman and member of the GFC Board of Trustees for 20 years, and his wife, Mary, whose major gift in 1974 began a drive for construction of the building.

RICHARD H. BEEBE RESIDENCE HALL
Honoring Richard Beebe, a 1951 GFC graduate and school superintendent, who for 15 years was a member of the GFC Board of Trustees and was chairman of the Student Life Committee at his death in 1989. He served as presiding clerk of Northwest Yearly Meeting for 16 years.

BROUGHER HALL
Honoring medical doctor John Brougher and his wife, Esther. He served for 30 years on the GFC Board of Trustees, until 1976. Their support of the College included funding for the building, scholarships, establishment of the College museum, and an estate gift.

CALDER CENTER
Honoring Louis Calder, 1897-1963, whose interest in the education of youth in America was carried out through the Calder Foundation, which awarded to GFC funds for building construction.

GERVAS CAREY RESIDENCE HALL
Honoring Gervas Carey, sixth president of the College, serving from 1947 until his retirement in 1950, during which time the College was renamed.

CENTENNIAL TOWER
Commemorating the 100th year of George Fox College, September 9, 1990, to September 9, 1991, and funded by Esther Klages.

EDWARDS RESIDENCE HALL
Honoring Jesse Edwards and his wife, Mary, among the five Newberg pioneer families who founded the College. A member of the College's first board, he served for 39 years until his death in 1924.

HEACOCK COMMONS
Honoring Everett and Bertha Heacock. They established the first underwritten scholarship at George Fox in 1955 and provided funding for the construction of the dining commons in 1966. *(Continued on page 152)*

CAMPUS MAPS

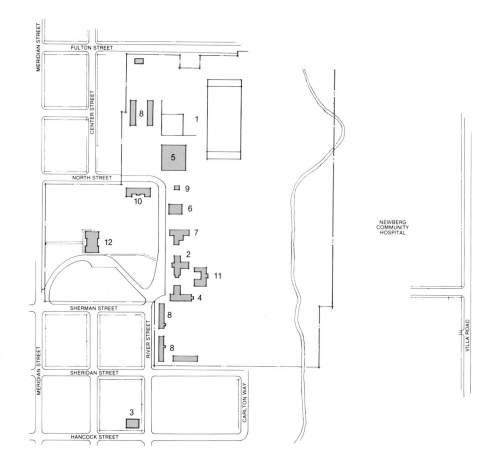

1960

1 Athletic Field
2 Dining Hall
3 Edwards Hall
4 Fine Arts
5 Thomas Hester Memorial Gymnasium
6 Kanyon Hall
7 Library
8 Living Units
9 Maintenance
10 Science Hall
11 Student Union
12 Wood-Mar Hall

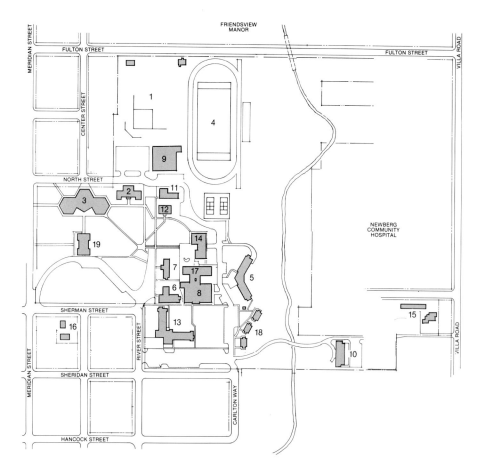

1970

1 Athletic Field
2 Brougher Hall
3 Calder Center
4 Colcord Memorial Field
5 Edwards Residence Hall
6 Fine Arts I
7 Fine Arts II
8 Heacock Commons
9 Hester Memorial Gymnasium
10 Hobson Residence Hall
11 Maintenance
12 Minthorn Hall
13 Pennington Residence Hall
14 Shambaugh Library
15 Sherman Arms Apartments
16 Smith Apartments
17 Student Union
18 Weesner Village
19 Wood-Mar Hall